the Credit Merchants

A History of Spiegel, Inc.

BY ORANGE A. SMALLEY AND FREDERICK D. STURDIVANT

INTRODUCTION BY HAROLD F. WILLIAMSON

Southern Illinois University Press *Carbondale and Edwardsville*

Feffer & Simons, Inc. *London and Amsterdam*

LIBRARY OF CONGRESS CATALOGUING IN PUBLICATION DATA

Smalley, Orange A
    The credit merchants.

    (Southern Illinois University centennial publications)
    Includes bibliographical references.
    1. Spiegel, inc.   I. Sturdivant, Frederick D.,
joint author.   II. Title.   III. Series.
√HF5467.S63S6   338.7'61'38140973   72–75336
  ISBN 0–8093–0589–5

50845

Southern Illinois University Centennial Publications

Contents

Tables

Exhibits

List of Illustrations

(between pages 144–145)

Preface

Professor Williamson in his Introduction to this book explains the circumstances which resulted in my coauthorship of *The Credit Merchants*. The experience of bringing the manuscript to publication was one of both frustration and tremendous satisfaction. The frustrations centered around the state of the original manuscript and the numerous distractions which delayed its completion. The original Smalley manuscript was in rough draft form and exceeded four thousand pages in length. It was an important and exciting account of an innovative marketing enterprise, but it was clear that much work had to be done to prepare it for publication. Several unexpected events delayed the completion of the task. I was residing in Southern California at the time my work on the project began. The events in Watts in August of 1965 caused me to shift my focus from historical to contemporary questions of the role of marketing in society. This change of focus led to a continuing series of studies of marketing as it relates to the poor and minorities. Thus, the Spiegel project received attention on a much less consistent basis than otherwise would have been the case.

The satisfaction is associated not only with the completion of the project, but the freedom with which it was done. The Spiegel management should be commended for its trust in and commitment to academic freedom. The company sponsored the research and yet, it did not require that the manuscript be reviewed by its managers and legal council to correct "factual errors." No one associated with the Spiegel Company has reviewed this manuscript.

This freedom is in vivid contrast to most business histories about which I have personal knowledge. One class, of course, is pure, public relations puffery. However, even many so-called scholarly treatments suffer from implicit or explicit censorship: a few wording changes, a few added superlatives to describe the founder or current chairman of the board, or the playing down of some unhappy acquisition or unprofitable division. Whatever the weaknesses of *The Credit Merchants* may be, lack of candor is not one of them.

Given the length of time which has elapsed since this project began, it is understandable that I have become indebted to many people. Harold F. Williamson has been an exceptionally patient and helpful friend during these years. As a close personal friend of Orange A. Smalley, he was especially interested in its completion. As a leading business historian he was a valued advisor.

I am also indebted to Richard M. Reese, a doctoral candidate at the University of Texas who did the research on the Spiegel experience since 1954. He did a thorough job of reviewing and analyzing the available secondary sources. Of course, I would be remiss not to acknowledge the patience and helpfulness of my wife, Pat. The Spiegel project interfered with more than one vacation and family outing. Support from the Division of Research at the Graduate School of Business Administration, Harvard University, greatly facilitated the completion of the project.

Two others remain who deserve special mention. To my mentor and friend, Howard F. Bennett, Professor of Business History at Northwestern University, is extended my profound appreciation for his wisdom and counsel during the formative years of my professional life. In more recent years, I have come to admire him even more for his tenacious struggle for life and the courage which he has exhibited. And finally, in memory of the man who gave birth to *The Credit Merchants*, the royalties from the sale of this book will become part of the Orange A. Smalley Memorial Fund at the Loyola University Library.

Goose Pond Road   F.D.S.
Lincoln, Massachusetts
January 1972

Introduction

While historians have given considerable attention to changes in technology and methods of production, they have tended to neglect the role that distribution has played in the social and economic development of the United States. This is unfortunate since marketing without a doubt ranks high among the dynamic elements that have operated within the American economy. Indeed, even a slight familiarity with the evolution of our marketing and distributive institutions suggests the extent to which they have contributed to the country's growth and expansion. The itinerant peddlers of early America, the country stores, the city specialty shops and department stores, chains, mail-order companies, supermarkets, and discount houses, along with various types of wholesalers, jobbers, manufacturers' representatives, and advertising agencies have all contributed to making the products of the farms and factories ever more accessible to a growing number of consumers.

The history of Spiegel is an account of the triumphs and disappointments of an organization that was an active participant in this evolution. The story began in 1865 when Joseph Spiegel, recently released from a Confederate prisoner-of-war camp, returned to Chicago and took a job in his brother-in-law's retail furniture and household furnishings store. It ended, as far as the family ownership and control of the organization were concerned, a century later when in 1965 Spiegel, Inc., was merged with a subsidiary of Beneficial Finance Company.

Several important developments in the field of retail marketing between 1865 and 1965 in the United States were reflected in the Spiegel experience. Initially a cash sale, low-pressure retail distributor of high-quality household furnishings, the organization was forced into bankruptcy in 1892. Reorganized in 1893, the emphasis was shifted to high-pressure, credit sales of merchandise designed for the less discriminating members of an expanding group of working-class Chicagoans. In 1904, a somewhat fortuitous experiment with mail-order sales proved so successful that the catalogue business soon outshadowed the company's retail store operations and by the mid-1920s Spiegel had emerged among the leaders in the field. In 1945, Spiegel began adding retail chain stores to its mail-order operations. A decade later, when it became apparent that this decision had been a mistake, the management moved to liquidate the company's recently acquired retail properties and to "rededicate" Spiegel, Inc. to the catalogue business.

On the whole the members of the family, who had dominated Spiegel management from 1865 to 1965, tended to be followers rather than leaders as far as any major marketing innovations were concerned. For example, a number of Chicago retail stores had for some time been selling low-grade household furnishings on credit before Spiegel decided to follow suit in 1893. Montgomery Ward and Sears, Roebuck had been in the mail-order business since 1872 and 1886 respectively when Spiegel in 1904 decided to expand into this type of marketing. It was also the success of Montgomery Ward and Sears, Roebuck with retail chains that prompted Spiegel to move into this area of marketing after World War II.

This is not to suggest that there was any lack of challenging decisions that had to be made by Spiegel management. This was particularly true of the organization's entry into the mail-order business where the risks and uncertainties were substantial. At the time, the company had had no experience with direct mail methods of merchandising, no knowledge of catalogue promotion, no mailing lists, and little basis for estimating the capital requirements of such a venture. It was through an imaginative use of credit and a careful selection of merchandise that Spiegel was able to establish a market niche distinct from those served by Montgomery Ward and Sears, Roebuck.

Obviously, the judgment of the Spiegel management was not infallible. Yet for any organization to remain in business for over one hundred years is in itself an achievement. This, plus the fact that during the greater part of this period the organization was highly profitable to its owners, makes the Spiegel record a noteworthy one.

The overall objectives of the authors of this account of the Spiegel history were to reconstruct, as far as possible, the circumstances under which the company's major policy decisions were made and to account both for the management's successes and its failures. Their success in achieving these objectives makes the volume a valuable case study of entrepreneurs in action, a welcome addition to the history of marketing, and a contribution to a better understanding of how one segment of the business community operated during the years covered.

The preparation of the Spiegel history was carried out under an agreement between the company and the Northwestern University Committee on Business History. Under this agreement Spiegel made a grant to the university to be used to cover the cost of the research and writing involved in completing the history. The Business History Committee in turn agreed to appoint a qualified scholar to undertake the project. It was further understood that the author was to be given full access to the company's records up to an agreed-upon terminal date and was to have complete freedom in conducting his research and preparing the manuscript. These terms were fully met by the company; indeed, without the enthusiastic support and cooperation of various key members of the Spiegel management, the project could never have been completed.

The Business History Committee selected Orange A. Smalley, Professor of Marketing and Chairman of the Marketing Department at Loyola University, Chicago, to prepare the history. Professor Smalley, who held a doctorate degree in economics from Northwestern University, was not only well-grounded in the field of marketing, but had already demonstrated his ability as a researcher and writer. His doctoral dissertation on the investment policies of the Northwestern Mutual Life Insurance Company of Milwaukee, Wisconsin, later incorporated in the published history of the company, created new standards of scholarship in the field.

The tentative target date for finishing the Spiegel history was set for 1965, the organization's centennial. Starting in 1956 and working part time in addition to carrying on his teaching and administrative duties at Loyola University, Professor Smalley had completed the bulk of his research on the history by the end of 1963. His plans to prepare a finished manuscript during 1964–65, however, were cut short by his sudden and wholly unexpected death early in 1964.

To find an immediate replacement for Professor Smalley proved to be an impossible task. Under the circumstances, the company decided to engage a free-lance author, James Cornell, Jr., to prepare a popular history. Published in 1965, on the occasion of Spiegel's 100th anniversary, *The People Get the Credit* was, to quote from the book's acknowledgment, "based, for the most part, on *The Credit Merchants*, an analytical history of Spiegel, Inc. [being] prepared . . . by Professor Orange A. Smalley."

Meanwhile, to insure the completion of the "analytical" history of Spiegel, Inc., the Northwestern Business History Committee, late in 1965, arranged with Frederick D. Sturdivant, at that time a member of the Marketing Department at the University of Southern California, to take over the project. This was an excellent choice. Professor Sturdivant had also been awarded a doctoral degree from Northwestern University and was the author of the history of the American Hospital Supply Company.

In agreeing to complete the Spiegel history project, Professor Sturdivant assumed a major responsibility. At the time of his death, Professor Smalley had put together a massive collection of research notes, plus, in most instances, several rough drafts of various aspects in the Spiegel history. But while the broad outline of the history, as visualized by Professor Smalley, was reasonably clear, there remained the formidable task of organizing the material and of editing or rewriting several thousand pages of original manuscript.

Despite a number of unanticipated interruptions, Professor Sturdivant was able to complete the job of revising and rewriting the Spiegel history by the end of 1969. And following his move to the Harvard Business School in 1970, an arrangement was made with the Southern Illinois University Press to publish the history.

As chairman of the Northwestern University Committee on Business History at the time the Spiegel project was initiated, and as a close friend and colleague of Professor Smalley, I wish to thank Professor Sturdivant for his part in completing the Spiegel history and the Southern Illinois University Press for agreeing to publish it in connection with the celebration of the university's centennial year. The volume is both a credit to the scholarship of Professor Sturdivant and a fitting tribute to the memory of Orange A. Smalley.

Harold F. Williamson

Greenville, Delaware
January 1972

The Credit Merchants

The Roots
of an Enterprise

Chapter 1

As is the case with the history of many American businesses, the origins of Spiegel, Inc. may be traced to the turmoil and discontent of nineteenth-century Europe. The oppression of that era, which contributed so mightily to the influx of immigrants to the shores of the United States, brought to America a family which eventually was to create one of the world's largest mail-order firms. The evolution of this enterprise was to be gradual and marked by a combination of success and failure. In many respects, therefore, the growth of Spiegel, Inc. was almost as uncertain as the future faced by its German forebears.

As the winter of 1847/48 settled across Germany there was a mixture of pessimism and optimism, of despair and elation, depending upon the individual and his background. Among those who were torn in both directions were the German Jews, whose condition of life was generally as desperate and unhappy as that of any serf on any Junker estate in East Prussia or Poland. Following the brief interlude of Napoleon, who to some extent had carried the social concepts of the Revolution on the bayonets of his soldiers, the Congress of Vienna had harshly reimposed the pattern of the Middle Ages upon the Jews. The full or partial emancipation and bestowal of civic rights which occurred between 1806 and 1814 were abruptly reversed. The conditions of the ghetto once

1

again existed, pogroms occurred in Weurzburg in 1819, incited by the same students who but short years before had gallantly taken up arms in the struggle to liberate Germany from the French. In Frankfort, Mannheim, Hamburg, Heidelberg, and Bamberg forcible expulsion and confiscation of property took place.

Jews lived in a state of continuous fear and despair; those who could fled to the west; others accepted conversion to Christianity, particularly the cultured and wealthy. For the rest there existed only the harsh reality of bare subsistence living—of electing between the alternatives of following the ancient orthodoxy or accepting the new religious reform, of submitting hopelessly to the new subjugation or putting their faith in the possible triumph of the German middle classes, who, more liberal and skeptical, were believed to be more favorable to Jewish emancipation than the landowners, princes, and clergy. Thus many Jews who were bourgeois and capitalist in outlook—as in Revolutionary France—were supporters of German liberals and intellectuals; others, both more idealistic and more cynical, made common cause with the younger German radicals. Like their coreligionists in Italy, France, and England, there Jews were nationalists in the same sense that many other Germans were, that is, they desired a united, liberal, constitutional Germany which would guarantee individual freedom and opportunity.[1]

One among the better educated Jews in the town of Abendheim, near the ancient city of Worms in Hesse, viewed the world around him with troubled concern. This was Moses Spiegel, teacher and rabbi to his community. The surname had been adopted during the period of the French occupation, and according to legend it had been inspired by a large mirror that stood before their house. The maiden name of Moses's wife Regina was Greenebaum, apparently because of a green tree painted on the shield posted before the inn owned by her people.[2] Sporadically, both families had enjoyed the uncertain protection of electors and petty princes, but had endured pogroms and expulsion too frequently to consider any particular town or canton a permanent home.

If Moses Spiegel held any hopes for a united and liberal Germany in that winter of 1847/48, these were diluted by doubts and fears; if the push to topple absolutism failed, there was the almost virtual certainty that the reaction that would follow would be more ferocious than that which came in the wake of the French defeat. In addition to the concern he felt for the members of his congregation, there was the safety of his family to consider. Of his five children only Marcus, an intense and rebellious nineteen-year-old, could be depended upon to help; the rest, Joseph, aged eight years, and the daughters Sara, Minna, and Theresa, and his wife, would be only too vulnerable.

When the storm of revolution first broke over Europe, however, it is probable that Moses Spiegel's optimism outran his fears. In February 1848 riots and barricades arose in Paris followed by the flight of Louis Philippe. On March 13 Vienna was racked by revolution and Metternich was also on his way to an English refuge. Within a few days of this Milanese and Venetians attacked Austrian troops, while in the Rhineland the feeble rulers began hastily to grant constitutions and offer reforms to their subjects.[3] On March 18 what began as a demonstration of the unemployed got out of hand and flared into the Berlin uprising when soldiers fired on demonstrators. In the ensuing street fighting, when participants were hastily formed into a loose *Volksturm*, two hundred people were killed, an estimated 10 percent of them being Jews.[4] The confused withdrawal of troops from Berlin on March 19 placed the party of constitutional reform in effective control of events, and when the revolutionaries surrounded the royal residence, the king donned the traditional cockade of liberty, insisted on the army's complete withdrawal, promised a liberal constitution—a promise to be dishonored—and appointed a liberal ministry for Prussia.[5]

Impotent without the support of the army, the new government proved incapable of organizing the country. Thus, when Frederick William IV had rallied his forces and ordered the Prussian army to reoccupy Berlin, the liberal revolution in Prussia and the other German states for all practical purposes came to an end. Revolutionists, radicals, and the liberals who had sided with them when all else was lost were seized and executed or imprisoned wherever the police and soldiers could lay hands upon them.

Some of these "forty-eighters" like Karl Schurz escaped the gallows or prison or were delivered by the desperate efforts of their followers and later became prominent in the United States. Among the younger revolutionists who saw service in the revolutionary *Landsturm* were Franz Sigel, Peter Osterhaus, and, in a

3

minor way, Marcus Spiegel, all of whom were subsequently to command Federal troops during the American Civil War.

Thousands of others became refugees, joining those whose optimism concerning the success of a liberal, democratic state embracing all Germany had been dampened in the summer of 1848. Among the earlier departees was Moses Spiegel and his family who, in August 1848, crossed the French frontier and in September embarked from Havre on the packet *Española* for New York. Marcus Spiegel remained in Germany into 1849, then, a hunted refugee, managed to get to England from where he departed to the United States. The Spiegels were a part of the German migration that after 1848 averaged over two hundred and fifty thousand persons per year, mostly bound for the United States. They were lost to Germany forever, and they represented, according to one authority "the best of their race—the adventurous, the independent, the men who might have made Germany a free and civilized country."[6] To the United States they brought a contribution of inestimable value as well as influences which would reshape a significant proportion of American characteristics and institutions.

The Spiegels were thoroughly bewildered, desperately homesick, even physically impaired upon their arrival in the United States. Weeks in the lodging houses of Havre had been succeeded by the long voyage in the hot, crowded steerage of the *Española;* they lived on brackish water and unappetizing food, with dysentery and fever constant companions. While the entire family survived the voyage, Regina Spiegel contracted an illness which she was unable to overcome and which probably hastened her death. Scarcely anyone, however, was prepared for the jostling turbulence that was the New York of the 1840s. The Jews, regardless of country of origin, were principally town and village dwellers who had earned their bread in trade and handicrafts. They were probably better conditioned for life in that city than were the peasants, whose traditional skills were of little immediate avail. Nevertheless there were handicaps more than sufficient to offset these somewhat dubious advantages. Without money or property, hampered by unfamiliarity with English, they were even without the comfort of being welcomed by coreligionists in the community in which they had arrived.

The Jewish immigrants of the 1840s were overwhelmingly Ash-

kenazim, importing with them the doctrine and ritual of the Reformed fraternities of Berlin, Frankfort, and the Hamburg tem-
ple.[7] As such they were aliens and doubly suspect by the Sephardic
Jews who had preceded them, whose American roots, in fact,
predated the American Revolution. Migrating to America from
England, the Netherlands, Portugal, and Spain, the background of
the latter was diametrically different from that of the newly arriving Ashkenazim, in education, culture, occupations, and philosophy. The Sephardic Jews were orthodox; socially and politically they were essentially aristocratic; fundamentally they remained
aloof from the new immigrants, offering little physical or moral
comfort.

Accustomed to enmity and indifference, inured to insecurity
and hardship, fiercely determined to survive, the new Jewish immigrants were plunged into the life that boiled around them. And
New York, still contesting with Boston and Baltimore for commercial dominance, provided a variety of economic opportunities. In-
fant railroads were pushing out West, North, and South, rapidly
overcoming the initial advantages held by canal and road systems
in the communications network east of the Alleghenies. Over these
roads flowed products of, and for, the West—grains, livestock, tim-
ber, hides, cotton, and whisky, and varieties of manufactured goods
produced both domestically and abroad to meet the expanding
needs of the western settlements.

The services of the new immigrants were thus a more-or-less
welcome increment to the body of labor available to perform the
necessary tasks of construction, manufacturing, distribution, and
transportation. Moses Spiegel, like many of his fellow Jews became a peddler, putting most of his scant resources into the purchase of needles, cloth, thread, and such items which were in demand in the area surrounding the city. The family occupied a few
rooms at what was then 52 Avenue C in Manhattan, and he resumed his functions as rabbi and teacher of the children of his
neighbors. Moses was also forced to assume the double duties of
father and mother, since the incomplete records of the city make
no mention of his wife after 1850, the same year in which his eldest
daughter, Sarah, became the wife of Michael Greenebaum, a second cousin.

In late 1850 or early 1851, young Marcus Spiegel decided to

leave New York for the West.[8] His destination was Chicago and he had good reason for this choice. A bustling town of thirty thousand, rising on the edges of Lake Michigan's southwestern shore, it was a thriving transshipment point for immigrants making their way West, and had developed a position of growing importance in grain and lumber as well as in wholesaling. Further, Marcus's sister Sarah now lived in Chicago with her husband who operated a hardware and tinsmith shop. Michael Greenebaum's brothers, Elias and Henry, worked as clerks in the private banking firm of Richard K. Swift, preparing for careers which would place them among Chicago's leading private bankers. They were part of a small colony of German Jews who struggled to earn livings, build a synagogue, and educate themselves and their children into the mysteries of American life and language. They also found the time and scraped together the resources to help other, less fortunate coreligionists get a start, and among those so aided was Marcus Spiegel. Equipped with a stock of the usual needles, thread, and other merchandise necessary in the farm homestead, he made his way to Cleveland and began peddling in the area surrounding that town.

The life of a peddler in the early 1850s provided both opportunity and stimulation. Marcus Spiegel could familiarize himself with the people with whom he mingled and with the new language. If the letters he wrote during the next several years were any criterion, he learned the language well. But living in boarding houses in Ohio villages or sleeping in farmers' barns or lofts, without close friends or relatives, was lonely and depressing. All this, however, came to an end in Stark County which, whatever its other attractions, provided Marcus Spiegel with a wife and his first permanent roots in America. Caroline Hamlin, with whom he fell in love, was the daughter of one of the original settlers of Uniontown, located some forty-five miles from Cleveland. John Hamlin, her father, had come to Ohio with two brothers from Virginia in the first decade of the nineteenth century and settled in Limaville for several years before moving to Uniontown.[9]

Caroline Hamlin was described in later years as a woman of striking pose and strong convictions; by the standards of the day the Hamlins were relatively well off and Caroline possessed an education comparable to that of small-town women of her class. Marcus Spiegel was a strikingly handsome man with the added advantage of possessing the romantic background of a defeated revolutionary. They were faced with many difficulties both in terms of differences in religion and background, but these were surmounted. And on August 7, 1853, the couple was married by a justice of the peace. The civil ceremonies duly observed, Marcus and Caroline Spiegel journeyed to Chicago where several days later, in a ceremony described as the first of its kind in the history of the city, she was converted to Judaism.

With his new wife Marcus Spiegel found the life of a peddler less enchanting than ever; he rented quarters in Chicago and obtained a job at Frances Clark's Dry Goods Emporium.[10] After the birth of her first child, however, it was difficult for the little family to survive on what Marcus could earn as a dry goods clerk, so Caroline Spiegel returned to Uniontown, Ohio. The two years which elapsed before they were able to resume a life together were apparently agonizing for them. Marcus Spiegel's letters described his life in a Chicago boarding house, the long hours working at his job, his plans to purchase a cottage near the lakeshore, and his desperate intentions to quit Chicago and join her in Ohio.[11] In some of these he wrote in fury of actions which would "make them keep their damned mouths shut"—apparently a reference to people they knew in common who were scornful of his lack of commercial success.

The circumstances which permitted him to return to Ohio are not known, but in 1856 this was accomplished. The Spiegels tarried in Uniontown only long enough to dispose of certain of Caroline's property, then moved to East Liberty where Marcus set up in a modest way as a produce and commission merchant. Within a few years he again moved, this time to Summit, where he continued his commission business and appeared to gain the acceptance of his neighbors. Records show, for example, that in June 1860 Marcus was listed as an officer in the Summit lodge of the Independent Order of Oddfellows, in addition to belonging to the local Masonic lodge.[12]

Later in 1860, in search of opportunities of improving his fortunes, Marcus Spiegel tried to purchase the produce and commission firm of E. Steinbacker in Millersburg, Holmes County, Ohio. Lacking sufficient capital to swing the acquisition independently, he formed a partnership with another German immigrant whom he met in a Millersburg boarding house. In May 1861 they bought out Steinbacker, and Herzer and Spiegel opened for business, dealing in flour, grain, mill stuffs, salt, fish, lime, wool, wood, dried fruit, seeds, butter, and eggs.[13] Moving his family—he now had three children, Clara, Moses, and Hamlin—to Millersburg, Marcus Spiegel threw himself energetically into the life of his new community. He was soon a member of the Royal Arch Masonic lodge and subsequently was elected an officer in the Sons of Malta lodge.

During the years of Marcus Spiegel's struggles the rest of the Spiegel family was making comparable progress in adjusting to American life. Moses Spiegel continued to live in New York, developing a solid reputation as rabbi and teacher, raising his children and providing them with a good education. Joseph Spiegel, the youngest son, began working at an early age, serving an apprenticeship in a variety of retail stores until 1862.[14] Theresa Spiegel, during a visit to Chicago, met and married a recent immigrant from Germany, Henry Liebenstein, in September 1856. Liebenstein had set up as a furniture merchant, was well educated, thoughtful, and gentle. Apparently, he was also a better than ordinary furniture dealer since his enterprises survived until the Chicago Fire, and he provided young Joseph Spiegel with the opportunity of entering the business in 1865.

All of this was played out on the stage of American development which was leading directly to sectional civil war. The actual declaration of war, following the surrender of Fort Sumter in April 1861, presented Marcus Spiegel with a difficult choice. His business was beginning to grow, and there was a wife and three young children to provide for. On the other hand he was one of a limited number of men of field-service age who had an actual experience in warfare. Spiegel was politically a Democrat who had supported Douglas in 1860, proof, ironically observed the *Holmes County Farmer*, a Democrat paper, that he was a "rank secessionist."[15] He therefore shared with other northern Democrats the desire to demonstrate his loyalty to the Union. But the optimism which pervaded the north argued for a short war and there seemed more than sufficient young recruits to man the volunteer regiments. Reverses by the Union forces in military engagements during the summer and fall of 1861, however, changed the early optimism concerning a short war and provided the stimulus which would place Marcus Spiegel in the army and in a hero's grave.

Spiegel elected to join the 67th Volunteer Infantry Regiment which was among the forces General McClellan was assembling near Washington, D.C. during the late fall and winter of 1861. Originally commissioned a second lieutenant in November 1861,[16] Marcus Spiegel had already completed arrangements with his partner for the conduct of his business and provided as best he could for his family before undertaking his initial military duties. These, as the *Cleveland Plain Dealer* reported, were demanding.

We also learn that M. M. Spiegel, Esq., a well-known and influential merchant of Millersburg, Holmes County, has enlisted for the war. He is now vigorously at work raising a company for the same regiment. Mr. Spiegel was an officer under General Seigel [*sic*] in the German Revolution in 1848. He makes personal sacrifices by going into the service but feels as if duty required that men in his circumstances should set an example of devotion to the cause of the country that is not limited by pecuniary or social sacrifices.[17]

When he had completed the enrollment of troops he embarked with them to Camp Chase near Columbus to undergo the induction process typical of the day. On December 18, 1861, he was promoted to the rank of captain and received command of Company C.[18]

Early in January 1862 the 67th Ohio was moved to northwestern Virginia to join the army being mobilized to invade the Shenandoah Valley as a part of a multipronged offensive to be launched in the spring against the South.[19] The grand offensive got off on schedule, with the army to which the 67th Ohio was attached moving south from Harper's Ferry. On March 18, the Union forces were engaged in a fierce battle with the Confederates near Kernstown, Virginia. Stationed at the center of the line that received the brunt of the Southern attack, Captain Spiegel and Company C ably acquitted themselves in their first battle.[20] The 67th Ohio was not again involved in combat during 1862, being transferred in May to General McClellan's forces at Harrison's Landing, Virginia, and subsequently shifted to Norfolk in August. It was here that Captain Spiegel learned that he would not receive a promotion to the rank of major which he believed his campaign record entitled him. In September 1862 he was put on detached service and sent to Ohio for recruiting duty.[21]

In addition to the opportunity of visiting his family, his assignment at Camp Mansfield enabled him to make contact with Daniel French, who had been appointed colonel of the newly authorized 120th Ohio Volunteer Infantry regiment, and who was seeking the services of an experienced combat officer to fill the post of executive officer. On September 20, Governor David Tod of Ohio officially informed Captain Spiegel that the post of major in the 67th Ohio had been given to another officer, observing, however, that this "reflects no want of confidence in you."[22] After he had communicated with brother officers in the 67th, Marcus Spiegel received from them a letter recommending his appointment to the rank of lieutenant-colonel in the 120th Ohio Infantry, and warmly praising his bravery and personal gallantry at Kernstown and subsequent skirmishes.[23] A few days after this, a group of officers of the 120th Ohio signed a similar petition addressed to the governor and the adjutant general of the state forces. Since in that era powerful friends were probably more important in influencing the selection of an officer for an advance in rank than a good combat record, it is likely that Marcus Spiegel had pulled what wires he could in Summit and Holmes Counties. However obtained, the commission of lieutenant-colonel was issued to him and he was posted to the 120th Ohio Infantry on October 2. Colonel Spiegel plunged into the training and organizing responsibilities with characteristic energy.

Before the departure of the regiment to join the Army of the Tennessee which U. S. Grant was then maneuvering against the Confederate stronghold at Vicksburg, it was necessary to appoint a sutler to accompany the troops. The appointment went to Joseph Spiegel, the twenty-two-year-old brother of Marcus, with the permission of Colonel French and the approval of the regimental officers, officially confirmed by the Secretary of War of the United States.[24]

By official regulations, only a single sutler could be appointed by a regiment and subleasing was prohibited. Sutlers could, however, employ assistants and more than one wagon in large units. Sutlers were prohibited from handling intoxicating liquors; their wares included almost anything which did not interfere with the mobility of the army or strain the escort which the military usually provided. With field paydays as uncertain as life or death, sutlers were authorized to offer credit to soldiers, typically being permitted a lien on soldier and officer pay not to exceed one-sixth of the monthly amount due; by presenting soldiers' chits to the regimental paymaster, these amounts were deducted directly from the individual's wage and given to the sutler.[25] Prices which sutlers could charge were fixed by an administrative council of officers of the regiment or brigade, and could be changed not more than once each month. To prevent abuses which could arise from conflicts of interest by officers administering sutler's operations, the regulations prohibited them from having any financial interest in sutling, dereliction punishable by courts martial. Included in such prohibition was the receipt of gifts, favors, rebates, or other services. As businessmen and citizens, sutlers were subject to all the risks which undertaking a retail business in the face of the enemy entailed. Thus, as the sutler for the 120th Ohio Joseph Spiegel faced both military and commercial hazards.

As a part of General Grant's army, members of the 120th Ohio served with distinction in the campaign which culminated in the surrender of Vicksburg on July 4, 1863. It was during this campaign that Colonel French was forced to resign because of illness and Marcus Spiegel was put in command of the 120th Ohio with the rank of full colonel.

Following the capture of Vicksburg, the 120th Ohio was transferred to the Department of the Gulf. In the spring of 1864 the regiment was assigned to the forces that were to invade Texas by way of the Red River, take Shreveport, and curve back to the Gulf.[26] The campaign came to a halt when the attempt to capture Shreveport failed, and the army was ordered to return to New Orleans. As the troop transports moved down the Red River they were subject to heavy artillery fire from Confederate forces along the banks, particularly in the areas above and below Alexandria.

On May 3 the transport *City Belle*, carrying the 120th Ohio complete with sutler's transport, came under heavy fire near Snaggy Point. Near panic resulted when the missiles began exploding on

11

the ship. One shell destroyed the pilot house, killing helmsman and pilot, and the vessel drifted into shore, closer to the Confederate guns.

With more than a score of men already dead or wounded, and facing total destruction, Colonel Spiegel ordered a white flag to be raised. Soldiers on other decks, however, began returning the fire, and the Confederates, who had halted shooting at the sight of the surrender flag, resumed firing. One shell exploded almost over Colonel Spiegel, who was rushing below to halt the action of his soldiers; and by the time Joseph Spiegel reached him, Marcus Spiegel was dead. Hundreds of soldiers jumped into the water and succeeded in gaining the opposite shore, but the rest were captured by Confederate cavalry when the vessel went aground.[27] The captives, numbering 275, included all the regimental field officers and Sutler Joseph Spiegel, who assisted in the burial of his brother the next day. Ironically, the recommendation for the promotion of Marcus Spiegel to brevet brigadier general had already received favorable endorsement and his name had been forwarded to Congress for promotion.

So for Marcus Spiegel the war had ended on a muddy river in Louisiana. For Joseph Spiegel, too, the war was over, except for suffering the heat, cold, dirt, sickness, and hunger which was the lot of prisoners of war. With the sullen officers and men of the 120th Ohio, he was marched overland to Shreveport, and then again marched into Texas and their final destination, the POW pen at Fort Camp. Here they remained until turned over to the exchange agents of the Union army at the mouth of the Red River on May 27, 1865.

Whether Joseph Spiegel remained for a time in New Orleans after his liberation engaging, as family legend insists, in cotton speculation, is not known. To have done so would have required a quick settlement of his claim for compensation to the Federal government. He did, however, accept the invitation of his sister Theresa to make his home with her family in Chicago, and there he resided for five years. His reasons for choosing Chicago were obvious. In addition to having two married sisters there, plus some assorted cousins, Chicago had grown rapidly during the war years in population and economic activity, and Theresa's husband, Henry

Liebenstein, offered him a position in the prosperous furniture business Liebenstein had founded in 1855.

The years spent with the Liebensteins were apparently fruitful for Joseph Spiegel, providing him with his first sense of settling down. Fortunately too, the personality and character of his brother-in-law offered him ample opportunity to acquire experience and exercise considerable authority in the direction of the business. Liebenstein, after emigrating to America in 1849, had for some time been engaged in both furniture manufacturing and wholesaling, independently and in partnership with other men.[28] In 1865 he had decided to concentrate principally on retailing; his shop at 160 Randolph Street became one of the most prosperous of its type in the city.

Joseph Spiegel learned how to be a good furniture man under Liebenstein's direction, as did other men who became prominent in Chicago.* But Henry Liebenstein did not possess a single-minded devotion to commerce, and was apparently pleased that Joseph Spiegel was so eager to take on many of the onerous responsibilities of the furniture business. By 1870 their relationship had changed from employer-employee to that of equals as they reorganized the shop into a formal partnership.[29]

With a partnership in hand and a future bright with promise, Joseph Spiegel married and set up his own home at 833 Prairie Avenue, a comfortable but unpretentious house located in one of Chicago's better residential neighborhoods. His wife, Matilda, was the daughter of Joseph Liebenstein, Henry's brother. Like Henry, Joseph Liebenstein was also in the furniture business, having operated with a third brother, Jacob, the J. and A. Liebenstein Company at 175 Lake Street, dealing in cabinets, upholstery, and hardware. Matilda Spiegel was a woman much like Joseph's sister Theresa, capable, energetic, and warmhearted, intensely interested in her family and its welfare.

The years which preceded their marriage on June 22, 1870, had been marked by the uncertainties which fluctuations in the na-

* Joseph Schaffner, for example, who later was identified with the firm of Hart, Schaffner & Marx, learned about fabrics, workmanship, and sound business practice from Liebenstein; while Simon Mandel, of Mandel Brothers, a large Chicago department store, served a five-year apprenticeship in the upholstery trade under him.

tional and local economies determined, but were exciting and promising nevertheless. For within the small but vigorous Jewish community of Chicago there was an active religious and cultural life. Shortly after returning from the South Joseph Spiegel joined the newly organized Sinai Congregation, set up as a reformed body which sought to have Jews regarded as members of a religion rather than as a nation in exile, and thus opposed to the idea of an eventual return to Israel. The congregation included the Greenebaum brothers and Gerhard and Henry Foreman, all of whom were to be important bankers in the city.[30] Joseph Spiegel also became a Mason and eventually a master of the lodge which numbered among its members the Greenebaums; Leon Mandel, founder of the department store; Abraham Hart, one of the founders of the men's clothing manufactory; and Abraham Kohn, clerk of the Common Council of Chicago in 1859–61.[31]

Further, there were various cultural and social diversions to entertain a young couple in the Chicago of 1870. Plays, concerts, and opera were available at McVicker's Theater, Crosby's Opera House, Hooley's Opera House, and the Globe Theater, where the upper and middle social classes could enjoy the traveling companies, musicians, and musical stars who toured the country. The city possessed an orchestral union, and outdoor concerts were held in parks and on the courthouse steps on summer evenings; there were also exhibitions of painting and sculpture sponsored by the city's social elite, the Ogdens, Blairs, Newberrys, and Ryersons. Alternative entertainment was provided by horse racing at Dexter Park, baseball as played by the Chicago White Stockings of the Northwestern Base Association, prize fights, bullbaiting, and dog and cock fights; while books and magazines were provided as popular diversions for the middle class by such publishers as Robert Fergus, Goodman and Donnelley, and S. C. Griggs and Company.

On April 21, 1871, the Spiegel's first child was born and named after Joseph's father, Moses. Much later this name was changed to Modie, again according to family legend, because a small niece, unable to enunciate Moses, insisted upon it. Business demanded more than a full share of Joseph Spiegel's time, for Liebenstein's interests tended to be diverted to other matters, and the combined enterprises were required to produce profits sufficient to support two families. Through the hot summer of 1871 Joseph Spiegel worked hard to improve the partnership operation, and with measurable success. The world was bright and promising as the fall season began, and not even the fire which broke out in Chicago's west division on October 7, destroying lumber yards, mills, and a paper box factory, together with squalid shacks housing the city's poor, prompted too much concern. While the coals from this conflagration still smoldered, another fire began on De Koven Street, jumped the narrow streets, then the west branch of the river, and despite the most heroic efforts of firemen still exhausted from the first fire, swept through the business district. Led by General Philip Sheridan the citizens of Chicago finally halted the blaze to the south by the use of gunpowder, but the settled northern district was destroyed. Everything seemed to have gone; the courthouse, bridges, rail yards, the reaper works, grain elevators, stables, and stores; brick and stone mansions and the little wood houses of the poor were obliterated in what was the greatest catastrophe ever visited on an American city of this size and prominence. Included in the awesome list of casualties was H. Liebenstein and Company and the other small enterprises in which Liebenstein and Joseph Spiegel had interests.

It is probable that Henry Liebenstein was, as his daughter recalled, entirely wiped out by the fire.[32] But he still had his home, as did Joseph Spiegel, and it is possible that they raised money on mortgages on these, for they leased a lot at 320 Michigan Avenue, in the midst of the temporary structures other Chicago merchants were erecting there, and both H. Liebenstein and Company and Phillips and Liebenstein resumed business at this address by the end of the year. Neither of the partners could be considered old men—Joseph Spiegel was only thirty-one years of age—and with some capital and determination the opportunities to recoup were great. Before a truly healthy financial condition had been attained, however, Chicago and the entire country were swept into the long depression which was ushered in by the panic of 1873. With income, output, sales, and production collapsing the resources of H. Liebenstein and Company and Phillips and Liebenstein were exhausted and both firms went to the wall.[33]

Henry Liebenstein was evidently too gentle and unaggressive to fight back against this new manifestation of adversity; he never again attempted to operate another enterprise of his own. But something more than the Chicago fire and the panic of '73 were required to crush the spirited and determined Joseph Spiegel who had survived a Confederate prison pen. He needed capital and someone to back him who had confidence in his experience and ability, and both qualities he found in Jacob L. Cahn. No information is available concerning Cahn, but it is likely that he was older than Spiegel (he retired from business in 1880); it is certain that he possessed the capital to finance the new partnership of Spiegel & Cahn and to persuade the owners of the new building at 222 Wabash Avenue to accept his name on a lease. Whatever the division of labor between the partners may have been, the firm prospered. When Cahn withdrew from the business in 1879, Joseph Liebenstein, Spiegel's father-in-law, joined him as a partner. About the same time the company expanded the space it occupied and the firm name "J. Spiegel & Company" was adopted. This arrangement persisted until 1885 when Liebenstein died and his interest in the business was inherited by his son, Albert.[34] During the entire period the companies with which Joseph Spiegel was associated dealt primarily in fine furniture and provided their own upholstering services. Retailing was the principal operation although there is some indication that the companies did engage in some wholesaling, particularly of upholstered furniture.

Building a successful enterprise during the 1870s required intensive attention to operations, to the selection of good merchandise, and to effective display and merchandising. Joseph Spiegel's success attested to his skill in precisely these areas. During the 1880s, as the economy began to emerge from the deflationary era that had begun over a decade earlier, Spiegel & Company began to enjoy an increased prosperity, and the Spiegel family increased also with the birth of a third son, Arthur, in January 1884.

Whether the addition of a third son and the desire to provide for him in the family business or the changing nature of furniture retailing in the Chicago of the 1880s was the primary cause, J. Spiegel & Company became increasingly aggressive by mid-decade. Beginning in 1885, for example, the company began advertising on a fairly consistent basis in city newspapers, principally the *Tribune*, the *Daily News*, and the *Inter-Ocean*. Nor were other forms of promotion such as furnishing the settings and other equipage for theatrical presentations ignored. The advertisements emphasized purchase terms—cash only—merchandise assortments that included "high art novelties," and associated high quality furniture with special price reductions.[35] Whether brought about by advertising promotion, pricing, or as a function of rising incomes and increasing prosperity in the city, Spiegel & Company became pressed for space. In 1886 a lease was signed for six floors and a basement in a larger building on State Street near Van Buren, and additional warehouse space was leased outside the central district.[36]

By 1888 Joseph Spiegel had brought two of his sons, Modie and Sidney, into the firm, the former as a salesman and the latter as a bookkeeper. Sidney, however, evidently worked only part time, for the City Directory of 1888 listed him as a student in the Bryant and Stratton Business College. Joseph Spiegel also was concerned with integrating the retail furniture business with manufacturing and in producing materials useful in furniture production, for he organized another partnership, Sturm & Spiegel, in 1888. This company manufactured cabinets, chairs, and certain upholstered items; a second new enterprise, Spiegel & Company, was organized to handle glue stocks. His brother-in-law, Albert Liebenstein and Adolph Sturm were his partners in the manufactory which was located at 11 Ann Street, and a manager, I. L. Stern, was hired to operate the glue works.

Furniture retailing during these years was evidently fiercely competitive, with specialized stores facing increasing competition from department stores and from shops emphasizing installment credit terms. Many retailers, it was evident, sought trade from outlying towns by making catalogs available to people who read the advertisements in Chicago newspapers which circulated in such communities. John M. Smyth, Tobey Furniture Company, Wirts & Scholle, and other houses vied with the merchandising and promotion offered by the Fair Store and Schlesinger and Mayer, department stores which catered to middle-class families of modest income. By 1888 J. Spiegel & Company had resorted to the distribution of furniture catalogs, the 103-page books being offered to any reader who responded to a company advertisement and paid fifteen cents to cover postage.[37] This offer was sweetened

during the next several years by eliminating the postage requirement, and offering it to "any out-of-town address."[38] The company's purpose in distributing these catalogs was to stimulate
personal calls from persons living in towns beyond the limits of
Chicago, and was not part of a mail-order program designed to
encourage orders by post. The prospective customers were expected to use the catalog to gain a comprehensive picture of the
merchandise and values offered by the firm; if the prices, values,
and quality proved sufficiently attractive the reader would make
the journey to the store to make his purchase. This practice, apparently, was followed by other furniture dealers, although a few
of the department stores were prepared to receive mail orders and
ship directly by freight.

Adherence to a cash policy corresponded well with the nature
of the clientele which Spiegel served, and was designed to permit
the company to operate with a minimum of outside financing. But
cash terms provided for thirty days of credit, typically, and to
achieve a rapid turnover of working capital and minimum borrowing demanded some vigor in collection practice. Since Spiegel
customers in that era were essentially middle class and interested
in furnishing their homes with taste and in emulation of the upper-
class elite, whose manners and consumption habits they admired
and aspired to, it was understandable why Joseph Spiegel was reluctant to resort to aggressive dunning. Why his customers tended
to hold back in meeting their obligations may have been related
to the propensity to overextend their resources to acquire posses-
sions, but it might just as well have reflected a company policy
which was implicitly understood by seller and buyer alike. Whatever the reason for these practices, their existence placed a serious
strain on the company's financial resources, a greater strain than the
sales volume seemed to warrant. To this strain was added that imposed by Sturm & Spiegel, which branched into wholesaling as
well as manufacture, and which required financing sales to retailers as well as inventories. Resort was made increasingly to
Herman Schaffner & Company and A. G. Becker, private Chicago
bankers.

Until 1891 Joseph Spiegel gave no indication that he was concerned about these conditions as profits were good. In 1891, however, it became apparent that if the firms in which he had interests

were to continue to operate at the scale already reached additional working capital was necessary. Although the firm's credit was good, the money obtainable from bankers was short term and insufficient for the purposes needed. In Joseph Spiegel's experience the accepted method of introducing outside capital was to reorganize the firm and bring in another partner, and in March 1891, Alexander Bergman was admitted to partnership, bringing with him $25,000 in cash.[39] But even this injection of new capital was insufficient to restore the Spiegel companies to a healthy condition and by mid-summer 1892 a serious crisis had developed.

As of 1892, Chicago was experiencing relatively good times, with employment high, the elevated transportation system nearing completion, and business and residential construction at a high level. All of which acted to maintain the demand for furniture and home furnishings, and to intensify the transition from the traditional cabinetmakers' workshops to the more sophisticated merchandising and display facilities which characterized J. A. Colby & Sons, the Tobey Furniture Company, Spiegel & Company, and John M. Smyth. Both Spiegel and Smyth concentrated on the sale of goods produced by others, while Colby and Tobey combined the production of merchandise to customer order with the resale of furnishings purchased from independent manufacturers. Further, Chicago was also anticipating boom conditions as a result of the opening of the Columbian Exposition, the permanent buildings of which were already rising in the area of Jackson Park on the South Side. In view of these conditions, and the solid financial stability of the other big furniture stores in the city, the crisis which faced Spiegel & Company was all the more surprising, as was its ultimate result.

By the summer of 1892, Spiegel & Company had assets of over $140,000 but a considerable proportion of this was in book accounts and inventory. Assets exceeded liabilities but the company's illiquidity prevented it from meeting its current obligations to merchandise suppliers, bankers, and individual creditors. On the advice of counsel, Spiegel & Company arranged loans from individuals who were related to Joseph Spiegel, the borrowed funds, together with whatever receivables could be liquidated, going to pay off some $40,000 in notes held by Schaffner & Company. The rest of the assets, including receivables, inventories, fixtures, and incidental property would be sold for the satisfaction of creditors.[40] On September 16 Joseph Spiegel notified the company's creditors that Spiegel & Company was proceeding to determine the amount of its assets which would be available to creditors and promised "an offer of compromise to *all* our creditors which . . . will meet with your approval."[41] The following week he explained that[42]

we are satisfied that if the sheriff, who is now in possession of our property, sells the same, it will not realize sufficient to pay the judgments against us. Many of our creditors, including some of our largest merchandise creditors, have consulted with us, and have advised us to offer a cash settlement on the basis of twenty-five per cent. Without assistance we have not the means with which to do this. Our friends have kindly undertaken to advance sufficient money for such a purpose, so we are now enabled to offer you that amount (25 percentum) of your claim against us, providing all our creditors promptly accept this proposition.

Whatever attitude was taken by the other merchandise creditors, one, the Oriel Cabinet Company of Michigan, refused to accept this compromise of its claims against Spiegel & Company. Oriel's counsel applied to the Superior Court of Cook County for an injunction against the sheriff's sale, charging that Joseph Spiegel had arranged with his counsel to have the tangible assets of the firm withdrawn[43]

and placed in the hands of the sheriff of the County of Cook to be sold and the proceeds thereof to be divided among the persons in whose favor said judgment notes were executed and in whose favor said judgments were up in such a manner as to enable the defendants to be benefitted by coercing their merchandise creditors into a compromise of their claims on terms suitable to the defendants.

Oriel's attorney further charged that all outstanding accounts receivable owed Spiegel had, as part of the arrangement between Joseph Spiegel and the friends and relatives who had advanced money to pay off the Schaffner notes, been transferred to the latter, all of whom had entered judgments against Spiegel & Company. Which meant, of course, that all of the assets of the company were by this means placed beyond the reach of merchandise creditors; the purpose of this was to force the latter to accept whatever terms of settlement were offered "even to the extent, if settlement failed, of depriving all the merchandise creditors of any participation whatever in the assets of the firm."[44] Furthermore, Oriel's attorney charged, Joseph Spiegel had busied himself September 13 in transferring and conveying to his son, Modie, two lots of Woodlawn Ridge real estate which was really the property of the partnership. These, of course, were merely allegations, but sufficient to arouse the court to issue a writ of injunction on all defendants and the sheriff to stop the scheduled sale.

Upon representation of Spiegel's counsel the injunction was dissolved and a counter suit was initiated charging that Joseph Spiegel and the other defendants had suffered losses of $3,000 as a result of the injunction, two-thirds of which were attorney fees.[45] The court later reduced the amount of such damages to $1,500, but at the hearing on the suggestion for damages Oriel's attorney got some further allegations into the record. He charged that his claims of fraud were well founded, claiming that of the $39,615 of Spiegel judgment notes held by Herman Schaffner & Company, $25,000 were pure fiction, having been added to the actual amount owed so that when payment was finally made the original investment Bergman had made to Spiegel & Company would be repaid to him in full. He further alleged that all the defendants were blood relatives and had entered a conspiracy when it became clear to Joseph Spiegel that he could not remain solvent. Joseph Schaffner, testifying in his own defense, claimed that his firm had lent $39,615 to Spiegel & Company over a period of time, and had brought judgment only when notified that the company could not meet its obligations. Joseph Spiegel indignantly denied the charge that he had set out intentionally to defraud his creditors; he further denied using Bergman's money for his own personal account, insisting it "went into the general assets of Spiegel & Company and was used as firm property."[46]

Oriel, however, was not satisfied. The case was continued for almost five years when the Superior Court of Cook County found for them against the judgment-holding defendants Ella and Leo Fox, Lena, Charles, and Theresa Liebenstein, Moses Greenebaum, A. G. Becker, and Joseph Spiegel. This decision relieved Oriel only of the damages originally assessed against them.[47] But because the allegations made by Oriel's attorney had been so strong, and, in the opinion of the counsel for the original defendants, so serious and prejudicial of individual reputations, this decision was ap-

21

pealed and vindication was eventually won from the appellate branch of the Supreme Court of Illinois in June 1897.[48] Eventually, in 1899, there was a compromise of the small damages worked out between attorneys, but this was insignificant when compared to the assuagement of individual reputations which had been besmirched. This, however, was not won until seven years after the fact, and in October 1892, with winter coming on, Joseph Spiegel was out of business, his business and personal reputation under a cloud, his ordinary credit gone, and a nine-year-old son to provide for. Starting again was something he had been able to face courageously and successfully after the fire of 1871, and the panic of 1873; but that had been twenty years earlier. The prospects for a man fifty-one years old were hardly reassuring, but with the assistance of friends and relatives, and the forceful personality of his oldest son, he began to pick himself up for the third time.

The Spiegel House
Furnishings Company
1893–1903

Chapter 2

The failure of his company affected Joseph Spiegel much more than that of its financial loss, serious though this was. Most painful to bear was the fact of personal failure in something precious to him, in an enterprise he knew intimately. Further, he was despondent over what he considered his responsibility to his partners and for their losses. While he still dominated his household, much of his habitual assurance gave way to a certain vagueness. It was this erosion which alarmed his older sons, particularly Modie, who could not bring himself to regard the bankruptcy as more than a temporary interruption in the family's destined success. More importantly, it was Modie who provided both the idea for a fresh start and the enthusiasm to launch it as an operating plan.

Modie Spiegel's idea was essentially simple: copy the methods successfully used by an increasing number of furniture retailers in Chicago, which was to sell house furnishings on installment terms, with modest down payments and regular collections from customers who would most likely come to the store to make their payments. To Modie Spiegel the times and circumstances for this method of selling seemed ripe. Chicago was full of people working more or less regularly, people who needed furniture and were willing to pay for it if they could do so out of weekly or monthly income. Other companies were giving them a chance to do this, and if the Spiegels provided the same opportunities, why should not these people buy from them?

To the extent that he hoped to rouse his father from depression Modie was successful; and he probably accurately anticipated the reaction. Joseph Spiegel was outraged at the suggestion. He was all too familiar with the junk, the *schlock*, that passed for furniture in such places—with the miserable construction, the poor material, the shoddy workmanship; with the overpricing, the covert sales methods that did not always draw the line at outright fraud. Others could do so, but not Joseph Spiegel, who had learned his trade and honest values from the best in Chicago and who had already successfully run high-grade stores. His furious responses, liberally sprinkled with the vivid vernacular acquired in bivouac and stockade, posed the question that even if he were willing to try such an unthinkable thing, where would the money come from? Perhaps the son had forgotten they no longer had a store or any money.

Modie's brother Sidney, a year younger and closer to his father in temperament and personality, was wedded to Joseph Spiegel's concepts of quality and the old ways of doing business. Simultaneously, he was strongly drawn to the prospects which Modie's ideas seemed to open if the family could get the money to start in business again. Despite his never completely concealed resentment of Modie, Sidney sided with his brother in this matter, and together they won their father's reluctant consent to sound out family friends and relatives as to their opinion of the plan and their willingness to invest in it. This victory over parental resistance was neither easily nor quickly won; nor did Joseph Spiegel ever enthusiastically embrace the venture.

In Modie Spiegel's view his father's reluctance was not as important as his acquiescence, without which it would not have been possible to obtain the support of people able to help found the kind of business he conceived. Armed with this grudging blessing, however, Modie proceeded to play the role for which he was superbly suited. He sold his ideas and the prospects of the proposed venture enthusiastically and dramatically. More importantly, for the businessmen friends and relatives he canvassed, he knew what he was talking about in terms of markets and merchandise. To these men and women, several of whom had been involved in the bankruptcy of Spiegel & Company, the combination of a pair of bright young men with a business background and an experienced father, plus a good idea, appeared attractive.

The combination was, in fact, quite effective. Modie Spiegel wanted to make money, he liked the risk and exhilaration of a gamble, and he possessed a native flair for showmanship and the histrionic. Never profound, Modie Spiegel learned quickly and absorbed characteristics of speech, dress, and manner which gave him an air of apparent ease. In 1893 he was over six feet in height, strong, erect, with a flowing cavalryman's moustache. His desires were straightforward and uncomplicated. If he could have made money by marketing high-quality furniture by conservative methods he would have done so; but apparently the bankruptcy of his father's firm convinced him that the route to riches in conventional quality furniture was too elusive, or at least too remote. If what he wanted was obtainable from high-pressure installment selling of low-quality furniture, termed "borax" in the trade, he had no qualms. What was crucial, of course, was that somebody other than Modie believe in what he was proposing.

Fortunately there existed a bedrock foundation for his plan. Chicago's population had expanded rapidly since 1865 and was approaching one million. The stockyards, packing plants, steel and metal industries, construction, and the scores of heterogeneous trades had drawn foreign and American immigrants to the city in cumulating waves. The new arrivals were typically poor and uneducated, with skills poorly suited to the occupations available to them. They were also confronted with agonizing lingual and social adjustments to their adopted land and city. But Chicago had experienced five years of relatively full employment in 1892, and while the hours were grueling and the pay small, the people who had arrived during the past decade were able to make a living; many even found it possible to improve their surroundings, particularly their furnishings, by patronizing retailers who had geared their merchandise and prices to fit the market. Such retailers as Siegel-Cooper, the Boston Store, Schlesinger & Mayer, and Simon, Straus & Company had found them a profitable patronage—hardworking, generally honest, and prompt in meeting bills.

While the general merchandise houses typically sold for cash, the furniture stores, clothing shops, and others resorted to installment credit. Although expensive, such a selling technique enabled families to acquire necessary goods out of income by making frequent small installments. Certainly many such families would not have been able to exert the necessary self-discipline to accumulate the money for full payment of many goods in the absence of a semiforced savings scheme. Equally certain, moreover, many retailing concerns would not have been able to exist without using installment credit as their principal marketing technique.

In addition to the wholesale influx of immigrants Chicago was experiencing a high birth-and-family-formation rate during these years, and new residential construction was absorbing the great open spaces within the city limits. Such rapid household formation provided a favorable and growing market for low-priced furniture and furnishings.

Modie Spiegel's marketing plan was not complicated. The proposed company would stock low- to medium-quality upholstered and case goods, chairs, cabinets, springs and mattresses, cheap china and crockery, floorcoverings, iceboxes, and decorations; in short, a complete line of house furnishings. All merchandise was to be offered for sale on installment terms with no discount for cash business, at least not as official policy. The length of time given buyers to pay out obligations would vary with the dollar value of purchases, but in general the period of payout was to be within the year of purchase. No direct charge would be made for credit. Instead all customers would bear the credit collection and bad debt costs in the prices they paid.

There was, of course, the risk factor involved in the use of installment credit for the kind of retailing Modie Spiegel proposed. Since it was principally durable or semidurable, repossessed merchandise had some resale value, particularly if less than one year old. But this was relatively small and scarcely absorbable from the planned markups of 100 percent on cost which this kind of selling involved. There was, of course, recourse through the courts, provided the sales contracts included confessions of judgment. But Modie Spiegel counted on two other factors to hold down the bad debt losses: first, the probabilities that most people were relatively honest; second, that individuals interested in buying household furnishings had some pride and sense of responsibility. These factors he believed would cover the majority of buyers; available

26

instruments of harrassment, the courts, and high margins would cover the rest.

There remained, of course, the question of credit investigation and approval. There was no easy answer to this problem, but there were certain bench marks considered useful to the installment seller. During the early 1890s, for example, the typical weekly budget for an unskilled worker in Chicago provided roughly for nine dollars—two for rent, four for food, two for clothing and transportation, the rest for riotous living! For a skilled worker the budget—and income—was a little higher, and fifty cents to a dollar a week allocated to the purchase of furniture was entirely feasible.[1] Thus a retail credit man might set the lower income limit at eleven or twelve dollars, modify this by the number of dependents, and make his decision within these limits on what evidences he had of character—the willingness or intention to pay. With, at this time, a weekly average wage for sixty hours of about twelve dollars in manufacturing industry, eleven in railroading, and under nine for low-skilled work, perhaps 30 percent of Chicago's families came within these credit limits.[2]

Of considerable importance for the Spiegels and those who were prepared to back their installment-house venture financially were economic conditions and expectations. As of late 1892, business conditions were favorable and expectations were high. The financial crises which would grip Europe shortly were not yet apparent in the United States. Business had been good since the mid-1880s and was improving, Chicago was working hard and prospering, and there seemed every reason to believe this prosperity would continue. Further, the city was becoming excited over the preparations for the Columbian Exposition which it would hold in 1893 to celebrate the four-hundredth anniversary of the discovery of America, and which was expected to bring vast crowds of visitors.

By December 1892 Modie Spiegel and his father and brother, had obtained firm commitments from friends and relatives to finance a new store. They had also arranged to lease space in a building at Van Buren and State Streets, at the southeast end of the city's Loop business district. Because of his bankruptcy and the Oriel suit, Joseph Spiegel acquired no equity interest in the business. Instead, in order to provide protection for the new firm and its backers, the business was to be incorporated, a maneuver that enabled Joseph Spiegel and his sons to hold one share each as directors of the company, to issue other shares to the lenders according to the amount of their investment. Apparently an agreement was also reached whereby these stockholder-creditors would receive a fixed annual return of 6 percent on their capital.

The purpose of the financial assistance rendered by these Spiegel relatives and friends was obviously to put Joseph and his sons back in business, to enable them to acquire control and full ownership as quickly as the progress of the business permitted through repurchase of outstanding stock at par value, and to provide the capital which a corporation required through the ostensible purchase of capital stock. One of the lending group was to represent their joint interests on the board of directors and hold rank as vice president, but effective direction of the business was left in the hands of the Spiegels.

Application for a corporate charter in the name of "Spiegel House Furnishings Company of Chicago" was made January 7, 1893, which would permit the firm to manufacture, buy, and sell furniture, heating and cooking stoves, floorcoverings, dishes, crockery, "and other house furnishing goods and other kinds of merchandise." The proposed capitalization was set at $50,000 and permission was requested to issue 500 shares of $100 par value stock.[3] By January 28, 1893, when the charter was approved, subscriptions had been accepted for 325 shares, three directors had been elected, and these, in turn, had appointed the company's first officers.[4] Joseph and Modie Spiegel, of course, became directors and, respectively, president and secretary-treasurer. The representative of the lenders on the board was Leo Fox, whose wife was a sister to Joseph Spiegel. The salary of Joseph Spiegel was set at $3,900 annually and that of Modie Spiegel at $1,800.[5]

All in all, nine families contributed $32,000 to finance the new company, accepting one share of stock for each $100 loaned.* This

* These individuals, with the number of shares subscribed were: fifty shares to Nathan Becker, Joseph Biefeld, Joseph Rosenbaum, Abraham B. Schaffner, and Milton Strauss; twenty-five shares to Charles Haas and Adolph Sturm; and ten shares to Henry Klopfer and Louis Spiegel. Schaffner was a member of the private banking firm, Herman Schaffner & Company which would fail during the financial crisis later that year and was also associated with Hart, Schaffner & Marx. Becker was also a banker, member of A. G. Becker & Company. His firm had served Joseph Spiegel before his bankruptcy

amount, plus the $500 put up by the Spiegels, provided the company with an initial capital of $32,500. Until late 1896 the only long-term capital added to Spiegel House Furnishings would come from what it could earn and retain in the business after paying the 6 percent interest (which was called a "dividend") on borrowed funds. In addition, the Spiegel company was also able to arrange for a line of credit from several commercial banks in the city, and acquired assurance of further financial assistance from Becker & Company.

Many of the manufacturers and jobbers who had supplied the old company were willing to do business with Joseph Spiegel again. Sidney Spiegel, who was put in charge of purchasing, acquired valuable experience in dealing with sources by visiting furniture shows and learning values. Modie assumed responsibility for recruiting a force of personal salesmen, for developing advertising which would pull business into the store, and for managing the problems of display, trading with customers, and customer relations. A professional credit man was added, a small office force, and a crew of stock and delivery men. Still vigorous, Joseph Spiegel provided the general administrative experience for the company and remained for many years the chief executive.

Within a year of its founding the store introduced the practice of remaining open from 9 A.M. to 9 P.M. on weekdays and to 6 P.M. on Saturdays. With half-hour lunch periods the rule, this meant a sixty-three-hour work week for most employees. During the first few years they had no trouble finding salesmen with experience, particularly as the depression deepened after 1893. According to a former employee, from seven to ten men worked the several floors of the store for wages ranging between five and twenty-five dollars weekly and/or commissions.[6]

During the first years of operations when Modie and Sidney were sharpening their skills on the sales floor and in tough bar-

---

and would contribute to the new enterprise similar services. Milton Strauss was already prominent in Chicago's financial community; and Modie Spiegel was destined to marry into his immediate family. Biefeld, whose sons earned an international reputation as fine hotelkeepers, headed his own firm in the financial district. Haas, Klopfer, and Rosenbaum were associated with Rosenbaum Brothers & Company at the Chicago stockyards, while Sturm had been a partner of Joseph Spiegel in upholstery and furniture the previous year. Louis Spiegel, who is a mysterious figure only because nothing can be uncovered about him, operated a tobacco shop in downtown Chicago.

gaining with suppliers, Joseph Spiegel customarily stationed himself at the State Street entrance to provide a personal reception to customers and guide them to take-over men. Of course there was more to operating a business than greeting customers. Joseph Spiegel spent long hours reviewing accounts, in searching for reasons why customers discontinued trading, and in doing what he could to keep his best clientele satisfied. He kept a sharp eye on the flow of collections, the accounts which fell behind in payment, the amounts spent for advertising. He drove his sons and his employees hard; he kept his bills paid, his credit lines clean; he was tough, with a rough tongue and an explosive temper, and he won and held the respect of those who worked for him, friends and businessmen, and his family.

The business policies and merchandising practices which served Spiegel House Furnishings during these formative years were simple, time-tested, and in that era, reliable. The company purchased standard items from manufacturers directly and through wholesalers. For case goods, upholstered products, carpeting, and chairs, buying practice included receiving direct calls from salesmen and going into the field, both to visit the furniture shows and to call on sources directly. Merchandising skills were important in terms of selecting the items from manufacturers' or wholesalers' lines which based on experience would be acceptable to the company's customers.

Since styles and fashion for the heavier furniture and furnishings tended to change slowly, past experience was usually an effective guide; the trick was to be able to select styles and designs with a slightly different appearance than those adopted by competitors, and by persuasive salesmanship to convince customers of the store's superiority. Of equal importance was the skill in buying merchandise at sufficiently low prices to permit the store's markup and still have it appear as an obvious value to customers, or at least a value that could be made obvious by a skilled salesman.

Price policy was a combination of a flat markup of 100 percent on cost, with some give and take as to final selling price permitted salesmen in individual transactions. Such list prices enabled the company to hold frequent clearance and special sales. The sales featured items which failed to sell and which could be cleared from stock only by drastic price cuts.

In some cases dead stock was sold to jobbers. Spiegel utilized both local and out-of-town jobbers for this purpose and in later years set up its own Mercury store on the near South Side.[7] Here, in an outlet unit totally disassociated in the public mind from Spiegel House Furnishings, nonmoving merchandise was sold at cut-rate prices for cash only. The company also made an arrangement of a similar kind with the Murphy (later the New Era) Furniture Store, in which Matilda Spiegel purchased an interest in partnership with one of the company's branch managers. A difference existed, as a result of price reductions such as these, between originally marked-up prices and final selling prices, the eventual gross margins received by the house were, if the experience of later years can be regarded as acceptable criteria, probably around 42 percent of sales.

Sales policy was a more complex phenomenon. Dealing in borax or low-quality merchandise and promoting credit and prices within the reach of quantitatively significant markets, the basic orientation of the store was toward pressure selling. Where survival and profit depended upon rapid turnover of inventory and working capital, and where customers were poorly informed in the marketplace with respect to the factors of quality, workmanship, construction, and materials, it could hardly be otherwise. But within this framework Joseph Spiegel and his past traditions in furniture exerted a temporizing influence. Sidney Spiegel tended to be more his father's son in this respect than did Modie, who in retail reflected an out-and-out *caveat emptor*.[8] Joseph Spiegel laid down a policy that customers were to be treated with respect, that the business would be built on the foundation of satisfied patrons who returned when they were again in the market and who would recommend the store to their friends. But this longer proprietorial view consistently tangled with and was not infrequently lost to the shorter-run interest of salesmen and to Modie Spiegel's irrepressible addiction for the dramatic. Since, despite his youth, Modie Spiegel was the natural leader of the sales force, it tended to follow his lead and adopt his attitudes.

The techniques of floor selling in vogue in the 1890s, and which have changed imperceptibly during the intervening years, lent themselves to high-pressure promotion. The turnover system was extensively employed wherein one salesman, unable to close a sale, signaled to another to whom he "turned over" the customer for new or different treatment. The second man was typically introduced as a buyer, department manager, or intimate of the boss, and would apply that facet of urgency or calm which the situation and the "prestige" conferred by the spur-of-the-moment title indicated as suitable. The house even came eventually to install a wire system with buzzers located below counters by the use of which turnover men could be summoned from another part of the store, as if by accident, with an old price list or dealer's book in hand, thus lending an aura of authenticity to the role he was to act. Spiegel salesmen were an alert and imaginative group, perhaps too cynical, and a bit too tiredly contemptuous of customers who took at face value too much of what was told them.

A proper and stimulating display of merchandise, to enhance its appearance or trade up its appeal, was a cardinal tenet of good merchandising, regardless of product quality. At Spiegel display tended to be a continuum, with practice oscillating between sound layout and outright craftiness. From time to time, for example, the men in the floorcoverings department would set off their wares by erecting something which resembled the desert abode of a sheikh, with a rich pile of throw rugs and hangings to lend authenticity to their implications that those rugs had but lately arrived from the Near East.

Apparently, also, this display formed the arena of action involving the proprietresses of certain establishments which infested the adjacent area and whose appearance brightened the day for the sales employees. While these women were not the usual run of Spiegel clientele they turned up on occasion to inspect Spiegel wares and bask in the obvious interest of the staff. Spurred by the legendary success of the swank and high-priced bordello operated by the Everleigh sisters, any number of madams sought fortune through blind imitation. They equated the appeal of the Everleigh establishment with the richness of its furnishings and proceeded to equip their own houses similarly. With little sense of fine style and even less of taste and restraint they also equated quality with high prices, a failing they shared with others in occupations more respectable. That a cheaper-line house such as Spiegel should have attracted their patronage was not surprising; their tastes were conditioned by the working- and lower-middle-class backgrounds common to most of the store's patrons. Thus some of the merchandise displayed in the Spiegel windows won their interest, but the displayed prices, of course, would as rapidly have lost it had it not been for the perception of the salesmen. A veteran of these years recounts the visit of one madam seeking a "classy" suite for her parlor. The most expensive suite in the store was priced beneath the contempt of the madam, but a salesman confided that a special purchase of imported furniture had not yet been uncrated, but that if she would amuse herself for thirty minutes he would have it displayed for her. While he escorted her to a nearby spirit shop, stockmen quickly applied a fresh coat of wax to the best suite on the floor, put down the best carpet to set it off, and put on a new price tag, double the original charge. It was, he reported, somewhat inelegantly, "a pushover."[9]

The floor crew tried these techniques on all kinds of people, and all kinds of merchandise. Some domestic tapestries, undistinguished products of machine make, were provided a glamour by the application of a small amount of rock salt and water. Hung on a wall they were called "imports, right off the boat." Skeptical customers were invited to stand on chairs and "smell the sea water."[10] There even were salesmen who worked the floor during these years who sold merchandise with the solemn assurance that the pieces were treasured heirlooms "taken right out of the Spiegel home."

These practices were common to a substantial part of retail furniture distribution, both then and later.* They were not unique to Spiegel, although their recount provides a flavor of the hectic and highly competitive era of the formative years. Further, although his father's presence was a strong one, lending a discipline and stability to the organization which was critical for its survival, Spiegel House Furnishings became Modie's store.

Modie Spiegel acquired skills commensurate with his natural interests and talents. He was as constitutionally unable to become a detail executive as he was to resist temptations to dramatize or to restrain his propensity to bellow. He delegated responsibility freely, particularly after the company expanded into a branch-

* In fact, such practices are especially common in low-income urban areas. See David Caplovitz, *The Poor Pay More* (New York: The Free Press, 1967), and Frederick D. Sturdivant, ed., *The Ghetto Marketplace* (New York: The Free Press, 1969).

store operation, but even when it was sufficiently small to lend itself to effective one-man direction. Such tendency, however, was less a recognition of the advantages of a carefully controlled division of responsibility in organization than an indisposition to be bothered with operating details. Furthermore, the roles played by his father and brother were not encouraging to the development of any strong sense of need to gather all reins of authority directly into his own hands. The business, in fact, developed in the direction of a loose partnership, where the respective father-son roles were mitigated by the interpersonal forces of personality and character.

During the first decade of Spiegel House Furnishings Modie Spiegel learned to do well some things which, though vital for the survival and success of the business, were distasteful to him—the matter of credit evaluation was one. In such an enterprise, of course, the role of the credit man was of critical importance. The questions asked of credit applicants then, as now, were asked to provide some guidelines for acceptance or rejection of individual risks. These included questions regarding employment, wages, marital status, dependents, residence, age, and type of work. But then retail credit agencies were not as well-developed sources of information as they became later, and credit men were valuable to the extent that they acquired a sensitivity regarding the character of an applicant—largely how determined he was to meet his obligations. Thus a personal contact with the applicant was vital in credit passing, where the credit man could bring to bear his experience with the way people responded to questions as well as with the information they provided.

During the first few years the firm employed retail credit men hired from other stores, but very quickly Modie Spiegel demonstrated a very reliable capacity in judging credit risks. According to those who knew and worked with him in these and later years, after he had taken over the responsibility for credit passing his overall record was excellent. The store had worked out an evaluation card containing questions and the comments of salesmen and the credit man; this had to be approved by Modie Spiegel before a credit sale could be recorded. On a busy day scores of such cards would be brought to him on the floor, and he was known to ask a few questions of the salesman, a few of the customer, and scrawl

his initials on the presented card. This, however, was not care-
lessness; years of experience provided him with the ability to
appraise an applicant quickly and accurately. The Spiegel record
of moderate bad debt losses during these years attests favorably
to his judgment. For the years 1893–1910, for example, a careful
survey of the records of the Cook County courts revealed less than
a dozen suits entered against defaulting customers by the company. While this could also indicate that collection techniques at
action levels lower than the courts were highly effective, it strongly
argues for the presence of good credit screening.[11]

Vital though credit was at Spiegel House Furnishings during
that epoch, it was but one element in the composite of promotional
elements which current marketing writers rather inelegantly insist
upon calling "the mix." Before a substantial body of customers
could be impressed with Spiegel salesmanship and merchandise,
they had to be attracted to the store, and this necessitated the use
of available mass media. Resort was early made to newspapers,
with the company limiting its advertisements to one or two of the
half-dozen or so journals then published in the city. During the
store's formative years typical advertisements covered no more
than one or two columns on a half-page, featuring credit availability and price, the convenience of evening hours. Before the end
of the century, however, Modie had been able to persuade his
father and brother that "pages pay," and it became standard procedure for the company to insert advertisements of one-half and
full pages in two or more Chicago dailies, and during the first
decade of the new century to use two-page inside spreads and
special inserts in certain Sunday issues.[12] After further experience
with the pulling power of advertisements and with larger promotional budgets, Spiegel even made use of color in newspaper advertisements, crude though such process was in that era.

Whatever deficiencies Modie Spiegel had as a merchant, a keen
awareness of his market and the need to promote it aggressively
were not among them. In terms of merchandise he was interested
only in providing the store with items which had some utility to
the buyers in the defined market, and which were not noticeably
inferior in appearance to those of rival merchants in the same
general price brackets. Getting prospects into the store and pushing the goods onto them was the function of advertising and vig-

orous personal selling. How careful an analysis Modie Spiegel
made of advertising effectiveness for the company is not known.
He used Chicago advertising agencies and apparently paid careful
attention to the volume of patronage which followed the appearance of advertisements in Chicago newspapers. At least veterans
from that period recall placards which Modie had plastered on the
walls of employee's rest rooms calling their attention to the business done as a result of a given day's advertising.[13]

Sidney Spiegel was, by externally judged criteria, the complete
antithesis of his brother. With none of Modie's predisposition for
externalization, he tended to be withdrawn socially, limiting his
contacts to a few persons. In personality as in physical appearance
he more closely resembled his father than did either of his brothers;
he was relatively small, he read, he was very serious, and as he
grew older tended to be imperious. Having attended business
school he knew something of the bookkeeping procedure and office
organization common to the day. He learned from his father about
the physical properties of furniture, about its manufacture and construction, about materials, and about workmanship. During the
early years when the Spiegels' energies were harnessed to the
store for more than sixty hours a week, Sidney performed a broad
variety of tasks; clerical, supervisory, accounting, warehouse, and
even selling. Undistinquished as a salesman in that environment
he demonstrated his greatest capacity as a buyer. What constituted merchandise planning at that time was apparently a loose
council of the three Spiegels, in which different points of view
were worked into a manageable compromise as to what to offer
and at what prices. But it was Sidney who came to be the company's merchandising manager in fact.

The merchandise offered by the company throughout its first decade of operation provides an interesting commentary on American
consumption behavior and tastes, particularly the lower-income
segments of the population. Comparisons of Spiegel advertisements in Chicago newspapers with those of other home furnishings retailers of that era indicate that with the exception of stores
obviously catering to upper-income people, the merchandise was
substantially uniform in style and design. The Spiegel inventory
included furniture which showed the earlier influence of Elsie

de Wolfe and William Morris, for the factories of Grand Rapids and High Point were capable of turning out reproductions that at least superficially resembled the styles and designs featured in the upper-middle-class homes of America.[14] In the hands of good craftsmen and designed with a disciplined taste such pieces were graceful and gracious; but too frequently the cheap reproductions were neither. The same was true for the reproductions of period furniture, whether French, English, or American.

But the style which apparently was most popular and which comprised the backbone of the Spiegel furniture line was Mission. This design appeared in the line almost from the first, for some of the advertisements appearing in the summer of 1893 featured library suites consisting of a table, brass lamp, magazine rack, two chairs—one a rocker—and a framed picture. All this, with a throw rug included, was priced at $33. Mission is difficult to describe since it is frustrating to sort out the original elements of the design from the mass-produced monstrosities which came to be identified with the name. For most Americans, however, taste was dead centered at a rather low common denominator. Mission and the other styles in mass-produced furniture were made available to them at prices they could afford by retailers who offered credit terms they could meet, and this was what they bought and apparently believed it beautiful.

It was not beautiful to Joseph Spiegel, of course, who had as frank an admiration for "sincere craftsmanship" as any furniture man, and he knew that the manufacturers of Grand Rapids Functional used screws and nails, not dowels; and could no more have afforded not to use veneers at the prices they charged than he could. But then it was not necessary for him to admire it. He and Sidney bought it, Modie and his sales force and advertising sold it. And in this mutual effort they were quite successful.

On the whole, the Spiegel management team had good reason to be proud of its accomplishments during the first eleven years of its operations. Spiegel House Furnishings Company in fact had an astonishingly favorable first year, with 1893 profits reported at $16,517.[15] The impact of the depression was reflected a year later when profits fell to $1,389.[16] With economic recovery, profits rose to $12,313 in 1895, a return, incidentally, sufficiently large to warrant salary increases to Joseph and Modie Spiegel which were voted at the beginning of the year. In 1896 profits again moved up to approximately $16,500.[17]

By the end of 1896 the future of Spiegel House Furnishings Company was indeed roseate. The Spiegels had successfully weathered the difficult task of launching a business and nursing it through a depression. Joseph Spiegel and his sons were in an excellent position to take advantage of the growing prosperity and expansion of the Chicago area. Thus, in a spirit of optimism steps were taken to enlarge the company's role in Chicago retailing. In 1896 the company moved from the corner of Van Buren and State streets to take larger quarters one block south at the corner of State and Congress. In 1898 they established a branch store at 48th Street and Ashland, and in 1900 a second branch was opened on the far South Side at 9133 Commercial Avenue.

Their subsequent success was reflected in the general upward trend of profits, after the dip in 1897, through 1903, shown in table 1. Based upon the assumption of rough comparability between

1. Spiegel House Furnishings Company, reported annual profits, 1897–1903

Year	Amount	Year	Amount
1897	$ 5,894	1901	$ 34,245
1898	18,296	1902	63,707
1899	48,084	1903	106,843
1900	24,531		

Source: Spiegel House Furnishings Company, *Stockholders Minutes.* January meetings, 1898–1904.

modern accounting systems and that used at Spiegel, aggregate profits for the 1897–1903 period were $301,600. Estimated dividends amounted to $33,467, with approximately $7,226 being distributed to nonfamily shareholders, the balance to the Spiegels. The remaining 89 percent of earnings remained invested in the company. It is likely that in a strict, corporate accounting sense profits would have been increased by $53,800, the amount which the stockholders permitted Joseph Spiegel and his sons during this period to draw out as "extra compensation."[18]

How profitable this performance was in terms of sales turnover

cannot be estimated in the absence of sales data, but measured
by the criterion of return on long-term capital employed in the
business, it was a most creditable showing. As shown in table 2,

**2. Spiegel House Furnishings Company, return on
net working capital, 1897–1903**

Year	Net Working Capital	Current Ratio	Average Net Worth	Return on Average Net Worth
1897	$ 94,900	5.5	$ 92,900	6.3%
1898	76,900	3.1	86,800	21.1
1899	122,000	3.6	101,300	47.5
1900	132,400	4.0	129,100	19.0
1901	165,900	2.8	151,100	22.6
1902	270,900	3.4	220,600	28.9
1903	480,600	5.1	379,800	28.1

Source: Spiegel House Furnishings Company, corporate records, 1897–1903.

using average long-term funds available annually as base, the
rate of profit fell below 19 percent only once between 1897 and
1903, while the average annual rate of return for the period was
26 percent.

A payback period of under four years is, of course, excellent by
most standards. The rates of interest generally charged by commercial banks and other lending institutions for funds to be used
in a consumer credit business do not indicate that the risks were
considered abnormal, and reinforces the presumption that the
Spiegels made excellent use of capital. This conclusion tends to
be borne out by the steady rise in the company's net working
capital during these years, and by the fact that the firm's capital
was kept in a highly liquid form, principally customer receivables
and inventory. And while inventory levels were increased by approximately 12 percent between 1896 and 1904, inventories never
exceeded one-third the company's current assets. During this
period the Spiegels also paid off all the remaining men who had
originally financed the company in 1893, and by 1904 all five hundred authorized shares had been issued and were jointly held by
Joseph Spiegel and his sons.

In short, the Spiegels had clearly vindicated the faith which
family friends had shown in them eleven years before and in the
process had developed one of the most prosperous furniture firms

in Chicago. While there was no ready market value for Spiegel stock, the book valuation, based on an estimated net worth in 1903 of $486,400, was $972.80 per share. Furthermore, the company was, as a result of an arrangement then being worked out, in a position to continue its expansion in the Chicago market, and to reap further advantages from the excellent credit position it had achieved. Although Joseph Spiegel was then sixty-three years old, Modie and Sidney had but recently turned thirty, and were experienced, demonstrably able, and ready to assume all but titular responsibility for the company. In addition, there was a nineteen-year-old brother, Arthur, who had been brought into the business, and from whom the family expected much if he could curb a streak of wildness and find something to absorb his tremendous energies.

The Spiegel House
Furnishings Company
1903–1922

Chapter 3

The year 1903 marked the beginning of an era of important change for the Spiegel House Furnishings Company. This new period was inaugurated by a seemingly routine transfer of the company's headquarters; however, the negotiations for this move resulted in the establishment of what would prove to be a significant business relationship with May, Stern and Company, another furniture firm. This change in the company's headquarters was followed in 1904 by Spiegel's first experiment in mail-order selling, and this innovation, as will be seen in detail later, was to spawn an enterprise which would dwarf the Spiegel family's earlier business operations.

The initial stimulus for the chain of events which was to bring about such dramatic changes in Spiegel was the need for a new headquarters in downtown Chicago. The company's move to State and Congress had provided both good location and space sufficient to handle the increased volume of sales which materialized after 1895, but because of the nature of household furnishings and the buying practices of householders the Spiegels were interested in obtaining a new downtown headquarters. The completion of the elevated railroad system around the Loop provided improved transportation for customers to all points in the city's main shopping and business district, and the center of the retail furniture trade had been concentrated in the southeast corner of the Loop, particularly along Wabash Avenue. This was specifically where the Spiegels desired to locate, but until 1903 no opportunity could be found to establish the company in space sufficient to accommodate retail and storage facilities, with adequate loading docks, on terms which would permit maintenance of the desired profit levels.

The circumstances which enabled the movement to Wabash Avenue were accidental. During the late 1890s May, Stern and Company, which had established a chain of furniture, home furnishings, and jewelry stores in such midwestern cities as Indianapolis, St. Louis, Kansas City, and Milwaukee, leased property at 182 Wabash Avenue for a Chicago outlet which the firm expected to become one of its most profitable producers. In addition to the selling and office space at the corner of Monroe Street, warehouse space was obtained in a building directly back of that location, facing on Michigan Avenue. May, Stern invested heavily in the Chicago facility, in leasehold improvements, fixtures, and delivery stock and equipment. Its merchandising policies were apparently applied in Chicago without modification; the firm sold on installment credit, offering substantially the same goods in the same way that had proved effective in their other outlets. Whether this was the principal cause or not, before 1902 the May, Stern management had apparently given up on the venture and was seeking some means of unloading the lease, receivables, and inventory.

During the period when May, Stern was searching for relief, Aaron Waldheim, one of the founders of the firm and its president, was in Chicago and by chance met Modie Spiegel. Waldheim knew of the Spiegel success in the home-furnishings market in Chicago, and was further impressed by his investigation of the company. By late December 1902, an arrangement had been made which satisfied both companies.

According to this contract, Spiegel House Furnishings Company was to acquire from May, Stern and Company all furnishings, fixtures, eight vans, and eleven horses, plus the merchandise inventory up to a total value of $90,000. In addition, Spiegel agreed to sublease the Michigan Avenue facility through April 1905; and the Wabash Avenue location through the end of 1905. The monthly rental of the former was $250; the annual rental of the latter was

$25,000. Into immediate escrow went $20,000 from Spiegel, to be paid May, Stern by December 31, 1902, if the terms were carried out; an additional $20,000 was also to be paid by the year's end. Further, Spiegel also gave May, Stern six $2,000 notes due serially from January through June 1903, and six additional notes for $5,000 each, due serially from July through December 1903.*

It is indicative of Spiegel's growing financial strength that it was not only able to lay out these funds in 1903, but to spend an additional $25,000 in 1904 acquiring Simon, Straus & Company, a small furniture store located on Madison Street. As a matter of fact, while profits declined from their previous peak of over $106,000 in 1903 to $78,837 in 1904, they moved up to a new high of $143,060 in 1905. This new record, however, did not reflect any fundamental change in the company's efficiency in the operation of its retail stores. It was attributable instead to a significant departure from the geographic market upon which the company's success had been founded, namely a move into the mail-order business sparked by Arthur Spiegel, the youngest of the Spiegel brothers.

Born in 1884, when his father was forty-four years old, Arthur Spiegel early exhibited a strong-willed independence, a quick mind, and energies that exhausted his parents. Following his graduation from high school he was brought into the business in 1903. During that year he showed little interest in the various jobs to which he was assigned to give him a sound working knowledge of Spiegel's operations. And he was tried at most of them: the sales floor, the warehouse, and the buying office. But direct selling bored him, and it hardly seemed appropriate to keep him permanently in the warehouse. It was not until he was pulled into the office that he became fascinated with the idea of expanding Spiegel's operation into the mail-order business. His immediate interest in this possibility was stimulated when he was put in charge of answering out-of-town inquiries and orders for Spiegel merchandise.

Spiegel had long advertised in Chicago newspapers, and although principally concerned with readership in the city proper, accepted business from persons living outside Chicago whose in-

* Unfortunately, the notes for this chapter were missing from the original Smalley materials.

terest was stimulated by seeing the company's advertisements in the out-of-town editions. There was no problem when such individuals came to one of the company's stores, performed the routine application for credit, and were qualified as customers. But many out-of-town residents found the low prices and "credit—all you want—on your own terms" appeals irresistible, even though they could not or did not want to come to the city to open an account. The result was a continuous flow of letters to the company, requesting merchandise, and stating the amounts which the writers wanted to pay in installments. The company had received such mail requests for years, and customarily replied with a courteous refusal and the suggestion to apply in person for conventional treatment.

Management's reasons for refusing mail orders was, of course, understandable, particularly if the number of such orders was small and their receipt unpredictable. Shipment out of town required special handling and packing, and the need to become familiar with railroad freight rates. Procedures for investigating credit applicants and making collections could be worked out for out-of-town dwellers, but they were considerably different from the routine set up for Chicago customers. Freight charges would have to be added to list prices, and thus reduce Spiegel's appeal vis-à-vis retail furniture dealers in smaller towns. As long as the business prospered with conventionally solicited business, there seemed no good reason for incurring additional expense, stocking shipping materials, and learning procedures which would produce only a small increment of profitable business. Furthermore, in the regular order of operations, the Spiegel executives were probably convinced that the volume of mail requests was unimportant, and made no attempt at accurate measurement.

Arthur Spiegel's proposal to build up this side of the business met with considerable resistance, but he was persistent and in 1904 was given a chance to try out his ideas. He was assigned office space on the mezzanine floor of the main store, provided with the services of a part-time clerk, a small budget, together with a small salary. While he could copy the company's method for handling customer accounts, he had to develop his own system for approving credit applications and getting information about applicants, and learn enough about crating and packing, about railroad freight rates to be able to deliver on any orders he might get. He found out what he could from the firm's legal counsel about the niceties of chattel mortgages and seller's rights under the law. He studied the questions company credit men asked applicants, and queried them to distraction. And to his immense gratification he began to get orders as a result of his answers to mail inquiries stimulated by regular company newspaper advertising.

The actual volume of business done by Arthur Spiegel's little mail-order department in 1904 is unknown; but it was obviously sufficient to impress his elders for they rewarded him with a bonus of $1,000 for the year. It was also sufficient to absorb most of the mezzanine space with office equipment, to add more than a dozen people to the work force, and to cause Arthur to hire a warehouse superintendent to take charge of physical order-filling and shipping, and to put a boyhood friend, Edward Goldsmith, on his payroll as assistant. Moreover, it gave him considerably greater prestige and a much more commanding presence when, late in 1904, he asked for permission to expand the mail-order department.

What he proposed was expansion through the use of mail-order techniques which had been proven effective by Montgomery Ward and Sears, Roebuck and Company, and scores of smaller sellers, including department stores. Specifically, Arthur Spiegel wanted to solicit business aggressively through the distribution of catalogs and other sales literature direct to prospects. The mail business from outside Chicago had, he could point out, been of sufficient volume to prove profitable and to justify the special organization and handlings which he had been responsible for establishing. If business which practically had to fight its way into the house was this profitable, what were the possibilities if such patronage was directly and aggressively solicited? The risks of selling on installment to people you never saw were reduced by three factors. First, the kind of merchandise which was sold; second, the Spiegel experience and skills in credit analysis and collections; and third, the previous year's experience gained in limited mail-order credit merchandising.

How much resistance the proposal encountered from Joseph Spiegel and Arthur's older brothers is unknown. That there was some is evident from the limitations imposed by management during 1905, when the geographical market was restricted to an area which lay within a radius of one hundred miles from Chicago. A number of serious questions could have been raised concerning the venture. For one thing, nobody at Spiegel, including Arthur, had any experience with direct-mail promotional methods, with catalog production and distribution, with acquiring and culling names of prospects, and with the refinements of merchandising for a mail-order enterprise. There was a question of the size of the market which could be reached from Chicago as a shipping point, as well as uncertainty whether potential customers in such a market would respond to Spiegel's sales and pricing policies. In general the rural areas in which department stores and chains had not yet appeared, offered the best possibility of gaining consumer acceptance. But the reluctance of most farmers toward going into debt for consumer goods and the unpredictability of farm incomes ran counter to Spiegel's emphasis on installment selling.

However, it seems highly unlikely that the Spiegels were fully aware of the uncertainties or risks of expanding into the mail-order field. If they had been, it is quite possible that Joseph Spiegel and Modie and Sidney would have smothered the proposal. Actually, however, their principal concern was to limit the scale of the new venture to manageable proportions in such a way that if it failed it would involve no serious financial loss to the company.

Although his operations were restricted to the territory within a one-hundred-mile radius of Chicago, Arthur Spiegel had plenty to occupy his time and absorb his energy. A catalog had to be prepared and put into the mail for the spring buying season. Merchandise had to be purchased or contracted for with guarantees from suppliers to fill reorders. Of special importance was a list of names of people living within the market area, some of which were purchased and others illegally obtained from United States postmasters or simply taken from town directories.

The first catalog was a modest twenty-four page affair, printed on thin paper with a harder paper cover, and weighed well under eight ounces. It is noteworthy principally because of the terms of sale it provided, and because the merchandise featured was overwhelmingly furniture. Terms ranged from a down payment of 15 percent and ten months to pay the balance for the most expensive unit, a "genuine leather sofa bed," to 13 percent down and the same maturity for the cheapest article offered, a "solid oak library case." The highest price listed was $82.50; the lowest, $5.25. Down payments varied from a low of $0.75 to $12.50, while the range of monthly installments was from $0.50 to $7.00. The furniture featured included individual pieces, and suites for living rooms and parlors, dining rooms, bedrooms, and kitchens. Only one rug was offered—a Wilton velvet—in two sizes, with an Oriental pattern in red, tan, blue, and green. On the other hand, five models of kitchen ranges of different weights and oven sizes were featured, the cheapest being $19.75 (265 pounds and sixteen-inch oven), the costliest, $39.50 (325 pounds and eighteen-inch oven).

Just how this merchandise compared in value with that offered by other mail-order houses is almost impossible to judge. Items comparable in appearance in the catalogs of Montgomery Ward and Sears, Roebuck for the same year carried prices which were from 5 percent to 25 percent lower than Spiegel prices. If quality was comparable these were obviously better values for consumers who paid cash, but Sears had just started to sell a few merchandise items on credit, while Ward's terms were cash only.

The catalog is also of interest in revealing something of the promotional strategy which Arthur Spiegel adopted. The company's slogan, for example, was modified to reflect the broadened market, becoming, "We Trust the People—Everywhere." The selling editorial, prepared by Arthur Spiegel, was keyed to three themes: (1) that Spiegel was a house of distinguished reputation which dealt in good quality furniture; (2) that the company offered a combination of price, quality, and credit greatly superior to local furniture dealers and other mail-order houses, alike; and (3) that the credit accommodation provided a respectable, convenient means of acquiring house-furnishing goods which had hitherto been available only to residents of large cities. While there was a great deal of rhetorical hyperbole in the editorial, considerable wishful thinking, and not a little gross distortion, it was well within the general advertising practice of the day, particularly the mail-order variety. Moreover, it was technically effective in that it made eminently clear what was being offered, what the products could do for users, why they should patronize Spiegel, and how they could get what was offered.

The quality of the seller was made clear by such passages as, "for the first time in the country's history, a high-class furniture house extends instalment credit to the nation," the "one million homes" Spiegel had already furnished, the "thirty-seven year experience" of credit selling in Chicago. Spiegel superiority over mail-order competitors and local small-town merchants was extolled in such passages as: "We do not handle cheap furniture such as that offered by general mail-order houses," and, the credit method "so completely overshadows the cash method of payment exacted by mail-order houses." Further, "your local dealer will charge you higher prices and MAKE YOU PAY CASH for goods that are inferior in design and inferior in quality to ours . . . we sell them to you at the prices we would charge your dealer."

But the pinnacle of the Spiegel sales theme was in furnishing reasons why readers of the catalog should buy for credit, and, at least at Spiegel, had this privilege for the asking. First, buying on time made more comforts possible to people of limited income; it provided for farmers, laborers, young married couples, and the "great army of wage earners" advantages they could secure in no other way, providing them with the chance that would "save them money . . . make happy homes possible within the time it takes for a freight train to bring the goods . . . and will in no sense embarrass them." The justification for credit buying which the company offered was that "two-thirds of the American people work on salary . . . and have been limited in their purchases and . . . possibilities, because of the outlay of cash required to buy the necessaries of life." All the working people of Chicago had the opportunity of using the Spiegel credit plan, which, "because it has proved such a boon to wage earners," the company would extend to "country people and those living in small towns where stocks are limited and prices necessarily high." There was no attempt at this stage to provide a justification for installment credit buying other than its convenience and the absence of cost. The customer must, of course, pay the cost of transporting the merchandise to his home, but the catalog pointed out that he had to do this regardless of from whom or where he bought. The company also guaranteed to reimburse purchasers for freight paid on merchandise which was not acceptable, a necessary condition in mail-order selling.

In spite of the geographical restriction imposed, the mail-order department in early 1905 was selling more merchandise than had been anticipated. With orders flowing in, the physical space originally allotted was quickly exhausted, and additional provision had to be made for the estimated thirty-five persons working in mail order. The company improvised, transferring the department to a newly leased floor in the warehouse which Spiegel had used for several years at Sangamon and 16th streets; by the end of 1905, over seventy employees comprised the mail-order staff.

The spring season results provided Arthur Spiegel with the argument necessary to convince his father and brothers that mail order offered more potential than they had dreamed possible. He was authorized to distribute a fall catalog five times the size of the original book and to a much broader readership, for the geographical limitation came off and mailing lists were acquired for an area which included twenty-three states and portions of southern Canada.

The September book was more systematic and better organized than the first catalog. It also reflected a management decision to promote merchandise credit aggressively by lengthening terms. Instead of specifying the down payments and monthly installments for each item shown, there was a standardized table of terms, and a printed order form was inserted in each book. The new terms established a company policy which would persist for decades. First, no cash-on-delivery orders were acceptable; second, the minimum purchase was set at $5. Cash, express or money orders, and personal checks were acceptable tender, but not postage stamps. The earlier company policy of a 15 percent down payment was maintained, but because of the tabular classification of order amounts into groups actual down payments varied from around 12 percent to over 16 percent. The maximum maturity permitted varied with the size of the order, being below one year for amounts under $20, increasing to sixteen months for the largest permissible orders.

How much mail order contributed to the firm's 1905 profits is unknown, but it must have been impressive. Even so, it paled to insignificance during the following year, particularly during the spring season, when in addition to the regular catalog the company prepared and distributed two special books, a twenty-four page refrigerator promotion, and one of sixty-four pages devoted to

baby carriages and similar merchandise. In September, the fall
general catalog, one hundred and forty pages, and a seventy-two
page duplicate of a special stove catalog of the previous autumn
were mailed.

The volume of business which these efforts poured in was impressive indeed. Total mail-order sales for 1906 were reported as
being in excess of $984,000, or roughly double the estimated vol-
ume of Spiegel's retail sales. And, as would recur in the future, the
capacity to attract business outran the capacity to handle orders
and the operating departments were swamped. Orders were delayed in office and warehouse alike; inventory jams were matched
by out-of-stock conditions in different merchandise categories;
correspondence and ledger-posting, billing, credit check-ups, and
collection follow-ups fell weeks behind schedule. Buyers were
sent back to markets to get what merchandise they could to fill
out stocks, and new clerks and stockmen were hired practically off
the streets, pressed into service to obtain what training they could
as they stumbled through strange and exhausting duties, pressured
by equally harried foremen. At the height of the spring season most
of the mail-order staff were working a ninety-hour week, and one
veteran reported that he began the season weighing 158 pounds
and by June had lost 30 of these.

The principal reasons for the huge leap in mail-order sales were
promotional, reflecting the expansion of the catalog with its greater
merchandising coverage, the increased number of catalogs produced, and—most important—the sheer quantity of circulation.
While the number of catalogs distributed in 1906 is unknown,
company records show that sales were made that year in every
state of the Union, and in Canada.

The emphasis upon installment credit was as heavy in 1906 as
it had been the previous year, and the sole new dimension was
the awareness manifested by the 1906 editorials of the bitter anti-
mail-order campaigns then raging in the country, led by the independent merchants of the villages and towns. Local merchants
in the small towns that lay within effective transportation range
of Chicago had suffered serious loss of patronage from the rigorous competition offered by the mail-order leaders, Sears, Roebuck
and Montgomery Ward. By 1905 the merchants had organized
lobbies in the legislatures of many states. They had what to all

outward appearances seemed to be a solid populist opposition to these "foreign" corporations who "drained off the money" from the agrarian states to the big cities, and they had by almost every means, which did not stop with a form of blackmail, succeeded in enlisting local and state politicians in support of their movement to have mail-order competition restrained by legislation and taxation. The support, while real, was not as massive as the merchants would have liked. In town and village, the anti-mail-order group could organize book burnings; offer free admission to the first, crude, moving pictures to children who would bring the family mail-order catalog to the proprietor; intimidate and ostracize individuals who received packages from mail-order companies. But families learned how to appear to go along with the verbalized and mob pressures while continuing to patronize the mail-order sellers; patronize them they did, for they were apparently more impressed by the lower prices, better selections, and improved service than they were by appeals to parochialism. They would bring catalogs to the book-burning rites, but they were usually of an older vintage; the current issue was safely hidden at home. But this would have been fruitless if they identified—and punitively sanctioned—the goods when it arrived at the railroad stations bearing the name of the seller. The mail-order houses reacted to the actions of their small-town competitors by protecting customers through the use of unmarked crates and packages. Sears made such an offer in 1903, and Arthur Spiegel followed suit in 1905–6, when Spiegel became aware of the inroads which the anti-mail-order campaign could make upon demand. The prospective buyer, urged the editorial, should not

hesitate to send us your order on account of thinking that your home merchant or friends or neighbors will know of your dealings with us. Our business is transacted in the utmost confidence. . . . Our goods are all shipped in plain packages with plain tags, and bear no marking as having come from us . . . unless you choose to tell your friends . . . they will never know of it.

While Spiegel was to face a hostile environment for some years, much of the internal frenzy and disorder of the spring 1906 season had disappeared by fall when better organization, more experienced personnel, and more systematic procedures permitted the mail-order department to take the seasonal business in stride. This stride, however, still included an excessively long work week. It is also probable that the apparently enhanced efficiency resulted from a reduction of volume. The tremendous increase of business during spring undoubtedly absorbed working capital in receivables and inventory more rapidly than it could be replaced. With resources running out, management had either to curtail the scale of catalog distribution or make adjustments in terms or the standards of credit acceptance. Since no changes occurred in terms of sale during the fall of 1906, it appears more likely that the flow of new orders was adjusted by reducing the number of catalogs mailed. Such a step would have curtailed promotional outlays directly, with the strong likelihood of a corresponding reduction in financial outlays for purchasing.

That such steps were necessary at all dramatized for management the problems of commercial success and the need to obtain additional financing if expansion were to continue at anything approaching the current rate. In other words, if they were not to lose the advantage of the momentum already generated the Spiegels had to decide on an acceptable and feasible method of financing the rapidly expanding mail-order business.

For various reasons they were reluctant to increase their short-term loans or to assume the burden of a long-term debt. Even more unattractive was the alternative of diluting the family control of Spiegel House Furnishings Company by selling stock to outsiders. The final decision instead was to organize a new company to take over the assets of the mail-order business in exchange for its stock, a portion of which could be sold for cash.

This proposition proved attractive to Aaron Waldheim, president of May, Stern and Company, whose property the Spiegels had leased in 1903. As finally worked out, Waldheim agreed to invest $225,000 in the proposed new company in return for 40 percent of the stock. Spiegel House Furnishings in turn agreed to turn over to the new company the mail-order assets valued at $560,000 in return for the remaining 60 percent of the stock. Waldheim's stock was to have voting power equal to that held by the Spiegels but was not to have any responsibility for the company's operations. This was to be assumed by Arthur Spiegel. It only remained to complete the formal incorporation of the proposed new company.

This was accomplished late in 1906, when Spiegel, May, Stern and Company was chartered under the corporative code of West Virginia. Spiegel House Furnishings Company was out of the mail-order business and again able to concentrate its resources and the attention of its principal management personnel on conventional retailing.

In general, there were few changes in the policies of Spiegel House Furnishings Company after 1906. One more outlet was added to the Chicago retail chain in 1907, but otherwise operating practices and procedures and the atmosphere of the stores tended to follow the pattern established during the preceding decade.

In the absence of the mail-order income, net sales during 1907–9 ranged apparently well below the approximate $1.4 million reached in 1906. Profits reflected the course of the business cycle, dropping from the $64,446 reported in 1907, to $13,277 in 1908, only to rise again to $64,762 in 1909.

Sales and profit data are not available for 1910, but thereafter, net sales fluctuated between a low of $675,700 in 1914 and a high of nearly $1.87 million in 1920. Profits continued to reflect the influence of the cyclical behavior of the economy. This was especially evident in 1914 when in the face of a sharp contraction in business activity and growing unemployment, the company had a net loss of $23,500, the largest it had yet experienced.

Actually, Spiegel's growth rate for the war years, and indeed for the entire decade, 1909–19, was substantially below that of chain store furniture dealers in the country as a whole. Moreover, the profit rate on net sales for 1916–18 averaged 3.36 percent compared to the 8.77 percent average for the 1911–13 period.

The reasons for this performance are obscure. Apparently, it was in part the result of some deterioration in the company's supervision and control over credit management and collections. In 1916, for example, at the insistence of the auditors, some $36,000 was set aside as a reserve against bad debts. The company during these years had also increased its dependence on short-term bank credit, at least suggesting a modification in the earlier policy of reinvesting a high proportion of earnings in the business.

There was, however, a definite improvement in the operating efficiency of the company by the end of 1918. By this date, several experienced individuals had been added to the staff, including a general manager, Albert S. Baum, who in 1919 received $6,500 "additional compensation for his services."

Increased resort to professional management, tighter controls of credit extension, more vigorous collection activity, and increased credit lines combined to put the company in a position where it could increase its sales volume after the war ended. And there was serious need for such expansion. For although the dollar results in 1918 showed a slight improvement over the previous year, both years had been inferior to 1916. Furthermore, when price changes are accounted for, the 1917–18 results were much less impressive than indicated by changes in the dollar volume of sales. Had the company increased its prices only to the extent of the changes in wholesale furniture prices during 1917–18, it would have had to sell approximately $1.5 million of merchandise in 1918.

This improvement in management was reflected in net sales that rose to nearly $1.6 million in 1919 and close to $1.9 million in 1920, although profits dropped sharply from $158,600 in 1919 to $4,900 the following year. Even more impressive was the company's record during the sharp depression that hit the American economy in 1921 and sent prices tumbling. Spiegel apparently had neither contracted for large orders nor built up its inventory prior to the price decline. Thus, while net sales in 1921 were off about 20 percent compared to 1920, the net loss for the year was a modest $300.

But if Spiegel House Furnishings Company escaped the full impact of an inventory deflation, this was not true of other firms in the trade, including that of Aaron Waldheim. Because of his need for cash, he indicated a willingness to sell his interest in Spiegel, May, Stern, thus paving the way for the Spiegels to reacquire the mail-order business and amalgamate it with retail furniture selling.

Even though Spiegel House Furnishings Company may not have realized its full growth potential after 1907, and despite a considerable variation in net profits, the company did provide the members of the Spiegel family with a growing source of income. This source, as will be noted in more detail later, was supplemented by dividends on the 60 percent stock interest in Spiegel, May, Stern and Company acquired by the family in 1906.

In respect to Spiegel House Furnishings Company, however, which was wholly family owned after 1904, Joseph Spiegel, Modie Spiegel, and, to a lesser extent, Sidney and Arthur chose to receive their income directly as salaries and bonuses rather than by attempting to maximize profits and dividends. This system had the advantage of rewarding the family members of management according to duties and responsibilities with the company. In 1907, for example, Joseph Spiegel, Modie, and Sidney each received an annual salary of $15,000. Joseph's continued at this rate until 1917, when it was raised to $25,000, where it remained until his death the following year.

As the *de facto* head of the company Modie's salary moved up almost every year after 1907 to a figure of $35,000 in 1914. Sidney, who subsequently spent a considerable part of his time with Spiegel, May, Stern and Company, was paid $10,500 annually by Spiegel House Furnishings, beginning in 1908. Arthur Spiegel, who devoted full time to Spiegel, May, Stern after 1907, was not on the payroll of Spiegel House Furnishings.

In addition to their salaries, Joseph Spiegel and his two older sons also drew on the company's resources to finance a variety of personal and business activities. One technique was to draw funds in excess of their salaries which were treated as bonuses and "credited against surplus." By the end of 1916, the total amount of such overdrafts was $185,000. As of the same date, there were outstanding loans of $101,000 to the three men backed by their personal notes. Thus, the Spiegel family and its enterprises were prepared financially for the boom period of the 1920s.

Spiegel, May, Stern and Company Merchandising Activities 1907–1921

Chapter 4

The bases of agreement between Aaron Waldheim and the Spiegels were formalized in Spiegel, May, Stern's charter and in the initial meeting of stockholders which took place January 3, 1907, in Chicago. Because of Waldheim's insistence upon equal voting power, two classes of stock were issued, each share of $100 par value. The 3,000 shares of Class A, equal to 3,000 votes, were surrendered to Modie Spiegel; together with a note for $80,852, they represented the net assets surrendered by Spiegel House Furnishings Company. Class B stock, 2,000 shares having 3,000 votes, went to Waldheim. Four directors were elected: Arthur and Modie Spiegel, Waldheim, and Charles B. Sommers, Waldheim's brother-in-law. Arthur Spiegel was appointed president, Waldheim, vice president, and Modie Spiegel, secretary and treasurer. Waldheim received no salary, while the two Spiegels were voted stipends of $10,000 and $5,000, respectively.[1] Although no audited inventory of assets was made, reconstruction from an introductory notation in the corporation's minute book and from subsequent directors' meetings and a few surviving financial statements suggests that the initial equity amounted to $592,187.[2] Of the initial assets, $491,000 represented trade receivables, $71,000 merchandise and supplies inventory, with nearly $100,000 unspecified.

The resources of the new corporation, however, were consider-

56

ably richer than these few accounting notations indicate. They included a going business, a sound, if limited, knowledge of a specific segment of the home furnishings market, a productive customer list and a basic knowledge of how to replenish it, and three years' experience in customer-accounting and order-handling methods. Of critical importance was the niche in the market which installment credit had provided, a protective base from which a market position could be further expanded while, simultaneously, being sheltered from the full and direct competition of others in the house furnishings market.

There were, in addition, the skills, personalities, and judgments of the principal members of mangement. Arthur Spiegel, as has been shown, combined a shrewd intelligence with unbounded energy and ambition. He possessed a real talent for leadership, had demonstrated skill in putting together a line of promotable merchandise, and had a keen insight into his market. His principal deficiencies included a limited understanding of organization, little knowledge of the use of quantitative information in planning, and no background in the management of capital, deficiencies normally associated with youth and inexperience. They were correctable over time, and in the process of learning he should have been helped by his associates, particularly by Modie Spiegel and Aaron Waldheim, although as already noted, Modie Spiegel had no exceptional talent for organization and his principal interest was in Spiegel House Furnishings Company.

Waldheim, on the other hand, had organization talents. He had put together one of the largest chains of house furnishings stores then in existence and possessed a keen appreciation for the problems of capital management and finance. While he did not participate directly in administration he was available for counsel, and since his approval was necessary in all major decisions, Spiegel, May, Stern policy had to reflect his point of view and conditioned experience. Further, while the name of his own company had been joined with that of Spiegel in the new corporation, the investment involved only Waldheim money. Since he was concerned with both appreciation of his investment and income, it was inevitable that he would insist upon reinvestment of earnings until a sound financial position was achieved, before favoring a distribution of earnings.

To the extent that this goal encouraged growth there would be no conflict of interest with Arthur Spiegel, and Waldheim's contribution to management would be substantial. But he was also in a position to block what he might consider overly ambitious schemes for expansion. Differences of opinion over the course to be followed by the company did, in fact, lead to tensions and conflicts in management.

Perhaps the greatest initial challenge facing Spiegel, May, Stern was the creation of a workable organization. There were some gaping holes in organization and administration, particularly in order-handling and customer accounting, which needed filling; the merchandising-buying functions required strengthening; and a better system of accounting and financial controls was needed. Later, as volume increased and competition became more vigorous, a more professional approach to the selling and circulation control problems would be required, but for the first four years Arthur Spiegel would bear this burden with relatively little assistance.

It was undoubtedly Waldheim who insisted upon immediately adding some professional administrators to deal with the most pressing organizational and control problems. At the time of its organization the company had approximately twenty thousand active customer accounts and was energetically soliciting more. Continuing the practice which it had inherited from the retail company, Spiegel, May, Stern mailed a monthly statement to customers with outstanding balances in addition to performing all the necessary functions of posting remittances to customer accounts, dealing with complaints, returned or refused merchandise, and follow up of delinquent patrons. To this considerable volume of paper work was added the flow of new orders, credit checking, opening new accounts, preparation of sales slips, physical order-handling and assembly, preparation of shipping documents, and the transportation of shipments to common carriers. It was important that the paper work involved be accurate and speedily executed and equally important that it be carried out at low unit cost. The system, however, was prone to breakdown under stress, with resultant confusion, tardy postings and delayed shipment of orders, increased consumer correspondence, and poor collection follow up.

To remedy this situation the company hired Houston E. Landis, who had acquired an excellent background in mail-order choosing able assistants. He demonstrated this talent at the beginning of his career at Spiegel, May, Stern, by bringing with him from Sears, Frederick L. Innis, a young man who had already shown his capacity for developing work-flow procedures, paper-handling systems, internal-control bookkeeping, and improvisation of office equipment to special tasks. For Modie Spiegel, who had no urgent desire to participate directly in day-to-day administration of the mail-order business, the employment of Landis and Innis offered him an opportunity to reduce the time he spent at Spiegel, May, Stern. He continued to serve as treasurer and participated in meetings with bankers and other businessmen.

With the need for more merchandising experience in mail order, it was logical for the third brother, Sidney Spiegel, to shift his activities and he became titular merchandise manager for Spiegel, May, Stern. Operationally, he headed the small staff of buyers, was technically responsible for the operation of the warehouse, and worked with Arthur Spiegel in planning the selling pages of the catalogs and sales books. Sidney Spiegel prided himself on a knowledge of furniture values and an appreciation of quality. Unquestionably he was responsible for whatever quality the house furnishings line possessed, and veterans of that period insist that the merchandise sold by Spiegel, May, Stern was superior to that carried by Spiegel House Furnishings. His ability to judge value, however, was not necessarily appropriate to mail-order merchandising requirements. As long as Arthur Spiegel remained active general manager, his influence generally determined product selection and promotion, but after Arthur's death in 1916 Sidney Spiegel imposed his own tastes on merchandise policy. Scornful of anything but furniture and house furnishings, single-minded with respect to credit policy and pricing, he was nevertheless both intelligent and generous. Unlike his more gregarious brothers, however, he went to unusual pains to conceal from people his generosity and his desire for understanding. He greatly admired his younger brother, and following the deaths of Arthur and his own wife, he tended to become more introspective and lonely, with the edge of antagonism which had existed between himself and Modie Spiegel sharpening as the two were forced to work more intimately in the family businesses.

The final addition to the top management group during this period was made in October 1910, when Edward L. Swikard was hired to direct the advertising and selling functions. During the years when mail order was a branch of Spiegel House Furnishings Company, Arthur Spiegel had taken full responsibility for the preparation of advertising. In addition, he gradually created a small sales department. In spite of his success, it was apparent that Arthur Spiegel was not the instinctive mail-order sales manager that Richard Sears proved to be; he did not possess the flair for copy preparation or the intuitive grasp of rural psychology which contributed to Sears' unique position in the mail-order world. Hence, in 1910, he began an intensive search for a professional mail-order advertiser. This search led to the hiring of Swikard.

Swikard's credentials were impressive. A native Chicagoan, he had entered mail-order advertising through his first job as country circulation manager for the *Chicago Daily News*, then, successively, with Draper Publishing Company, the *Chicago Record Herald*, and A. W. Shaw Company, publishers of *Systems* magazine. Until then his experience had been largely restricted to problems of circulation and its control, but at *Systems* he developed an outstanding capacity for copy and layout, an appreciation for the contributions which able people in the graphic arts could make to mail-order selling, and sharpened his appreciation for effective control of sales literature. From Shaw, Swikard moved on to manage circulation for Businessman's Publishing Company in Detroit, then back to Chicago in 1908 to assume an important position in the American Correspondence School.

This group of executives led Spiegel, May, Stern Company into an expanded role in mail order. With one exception, the initial policies of Spiegel, May, Stern were adopted intact from those which had guided the mail-order department of Spiegel House Furnishings in 1904–6. Briefly reviewed, these included: (1) installment credit as the underlying selling plan; (2) concentration upon relatively small towns lying within a radius of five hundred miles from Chicago; (3) merchandise corresponding to the incomes and tastes of lower-middle- and working-class people living in such communities; (4) a pricing convention based on a general markup of 100 percent on net cost of merchandise; (5) reliance upon catalogs and other mailing efforts as the basic promotional program; (6) product line to be restricted to furniture and house furnishings goods; and (7) long-term capital to be supplied from retained earnings, with banking facilities supplying short-term financing according to the scale of business enjoyed. With the geographical extent of the market determined by transportation costs and technology, all other policies were conditioned by the credit plan, for installment credit not only provided the company with a shelter against vigorous price and product competition from other mail-order institutions, but raised unique problems and placed more rigorous limits on expansion.

The exception alluded to involved merchandise policy, specifically the extent of the product line to be offered. Merchandise policy had evolved from the retail enterprise; household goods, generally durable, were limited in quality and priced to the needs of the market which the company served. Depth of merchandise within any specific product classification was determined by available resources, estimates of market demand, and the desirability of offering a broad variety of products.

As of 1907, Spiegel, May, Stern offered a line of merchandise which was reasonably deep in certain categories, such as chairs, and thin in others, such as household hardware. Sears and Montgomery Ward, in contrast, were generally richer in depth in most categories of merchandise handled by Spiegel, while also offering goods which the latter did not stock.

There were some decided advantages in specialization, not the least being the ability of a seller to compete with large rivals by devoting its resources to servicing skillfully a limited consumer demand. Thus, with incomparably smaller capital, Spiegel, May, Stern could achieve a profitable position. At the same time, specialization tended to restrict the prospects of the organization by limiting it to some absolute size and growth consistent with its products and the availability of substitutes. Further, as a specialist, the company was vulnerable to competition from rivals offering broader and more varied lines of products at any time the latter decided it was necessary or advisable to contend seriously for the limited segment. One reason, obviously, was the ability of larger organizations to finance a low-profit or loss operation in one product category from the earnings of the others; but there were other reasons, some equally potent, and few of which were available to the specialist.

Further, there was the matter of scale economies. To the extent that costs are variable, and in the absence of restricted technical information, specialized equipment, and other barriers, the unit costs of a multiple-line seller might not differ significantly from those of a limited-line specialist. But with any considerable proportion of costs fixed in amount, the multiple-product seller was generally in a better position to spread the fixed charges over a larger number of units. Technically, of course, the same opportunities existed for the specialist who increased his output, but the market appeal of a broad line was usually greater than for a limited line, with a pronounced difference in revenue expectations. That is, *ceteris paribus*, a seller offering a complete line of household furniture can be expected to sell more merchandise than can the specialist in bedroom furniture only. This expectation of greater sales revenue tends to stimulate greater effort (increased total cost), and reduced unit-fixed costs enhance the prospects of profitability.

In mail order, with its dependence upon catalogs and sale books for promotional tools, these elements of revenue expectations and fixed costs are nowhere more cleanly delineated than in the sales cost-circulation control problem. Catalog costs include both variable and fixed elements, such that within some fairly broad range of output the variable unit costs tend to be constant, fixed costs per unit decrease, and total unit costs then decline slowly until the upper limit of the range is reached. Thus, one element of business-getting costs is such that management has some justification for pushing the catalog into more and more hands; or, more accurately, for giving it to more people who are likely to order from it. In view of what has been stated before, catalog costs, per dollar of sales revenue, tend to be lower for the general-line seller than for the limited-line house. Furthermore, the general-line firm, because it is less restrictive, can be less selective in distributing catalogs, that is, its revenue-distributional cost break-even point tends to be lower than for the limited-line concern.

The Spiegel, May, Stern management group was much concerned with these problems in 1907. Arthur Spiegel, in particular, was keenly aware of the need to broaden the merchandise line. For him, the key questions were the products to be added and the effect their addition might have on credit risk. The most desirable products were those for which a brisk demand already existed and whose addition would not require such an investment in working capital as to thin out existing lines of goods. From the standpoint of credit risk, desirable products would be those which could be treated on the same terms of sale that applied to house furnishings. There were several classes of products which suggested themselves, including apparel, hardware, building materials, and tools. Sears enjoyed a particular success with the latter types and National Bellas Hess with the former. After considerable investigation and much soul-searching, Arthur Spiegel decided to expand into apparel.

Some of Arthur Spiegel's associates took issue on the basis of the credit risk involved in selling clothing, plus the problems of credit management in the event the risk of selling apparel proved to be greater than that attached to house furnishings. Other questions were also raised, particularly with respect to the capital needs involved, the necessity of obtaining competent and experienced personnel to merchandise the apparel lines, and the operating and physical-handling apparatus needed. But essentially it was credit which bothered management most. As Frederick W. Spiegel later observed, "They were always scared witless about credit losses in apparel."[3] It was undoubtedly this fear which conditioned the attitude of management for twenty years, causing top executives to rage against what they termed "the dirty rag business."[4] This issue was so central to the final resolution of the problem of adding apparel lines that it warrants critical treatment.

Once the decision to extend credit as a sales policy has been taken by a merchant, he must, to protect himself, screen applicants to determine (1) whether the privilege is sought in good faith with every intention to pay, (2) the present and future ability of the applicant to repay, (3) the likelihood of the debtor to preserve his intention to liquidate the obligation, and (4) the adequacy of collateral or the legal remedies available in the event he is unable or chooses not to pay.[5] He is thus concerned with the character of credit applicants as well as with their total socioeconomic position, or, to what one writer has called "life station."[6]

Logically both the income and the previous commitments of the applicant should be in occupations enjoying reasonable predictability and stability of earnings, and life stations should be such that "the desire and social pressure to repay debts will be an active factor to assure extinguishment of the obligation." [7]

While attempting to provide for the remedies with which to treat delinquency and to obtain satisfactory indications of good character and income stability, the Spiegel House Furnishings Company and the mail-order division had learned to rely heavily on the relationship between house furnishing goods and life station. Home furnishings purchases implied reasonable permanence, marriage, children, and some sense of personal responsibility. While by no means infallible, the relationship was sufficiently strong to provide reasonable security. In addition, of course, the company had a chance to realize some salvage value from a bad debtor through repossession and resale since a high proportion of the merchandise it sold was durable.

But no such relationship existed for apparel, or for cheap jewelry or watches, for that matter, or, if it did, Spiegel management was unaware of it. As credit merchants they were aware that the risk of default varied inversely with the size of the customer's equity and directly with the maturity of the obligation. They recognized the possibility that a customer, deciding that his suit was no longer worth the amount he still owed on it, would default, and force them to repossess. Obviously, a solution which increased the buyer's equity rapidly by increasing the amount of installments and shortening the maturity would diminish management's fears but only at the price of intensifying other problems. House furnishings purchases required reasonably long terms of sale—eight to twelve months—considered by management overly dangerous for apparel. If apparel was added directly to the line there were three alternatives open: (1) two sets of credit terms; (2) adopting the shorter terms that applied to apparel to all merchandise sold; and (3) retaining the current terms for all merchandise, including clothing. The first was incompatible with basic policy, economical operation, and good customer relations. It would complicate an otherwise simple procedure for customers, render chaotic the operation of the customer accounts division, and conceivably discourage the patronage of people who frequently became confused when ordering by the multiple computations of a single set of terms, two sets of transportation-rate schedules, and measurement instructions. The second alternative unquestionably would diminish sales of household goods and could conceivably prove fatal to the company's marketing position. The third, in the existing climate of managerial opinion, was unthinkable.

Refusing to abandon his idea, Arthur Spiegel searched for a compromise solution and found it in a small, ladies' wear enterprise which was then being organized by an acquaintance, Bernard Mayer. Mayer was putting together a company to distribute both ready-to-wear and made-to-order apparel, but had difficulties raising capital and was more than eager to undertake mail-order distribution. He was an experienced ladies' wear merchant, having been with Schlesinger & Mayer, a downtown Chicago department store which was absorbed by Carson, Pirie, Scott & Company. In October 1907, the Bernard Mayer & Company was incorporated with a capital of $50,000 of which Arthur Spiegel committed Spiegel, May, Stern to one-half, obtaining formal authorization from his board the following January.[8]

The advantages of the compromise plan were obvious. Spiegel, May, Stern obtained experienced personnel to direct the merchandising and marketing of ladies' wear, obtained a solution for the credit risk problem without jeopardizing the fundamental position of the company, and reduced the investment which would have been necessary had the firm organized a wholly owned subsidiary. Further, the partners would be motivated by sharing in profits. According to the agreement, Mayer would be general manager, responsible for merchandising and physical operations; Spiegel, May, Stern would provide mailing lists and assume responsibility for the preparation and distribution of sales literature in addition to assisting in the creation of operating organization.

With ladies' wear distribution thus under control, Arthur Spiegel extended the compromise plan to men's wear. Modie Spiegel was personally interested in a mail-order venture in male apparel and persuaded an experienced Chicago merchant tailor, Samuel Regensburg, to join in a partnership with Spiegel, May, Stern. The organization was titled Clement & Company, and the three partners shared equally in the initial $15,000 capitalization.[9] Before the end of 1908, however, the capital was increased to $50,-

ooo, one-half being contributed by Spiegel, May, Stern.[10] Clement Company was organized as a direct counterpart of Bernard Mayer & Company, with Spiegel, May, Stern providing mailing lists, all promotional functions, and guidance in establishing the operating organization. In both affiliates, obviously, the influence of the larger company would be powerful and, to the extent permitted by merchandising apparel, basic Spiegel, May, Stern policies would be applied.

An objective appraisal of the compromise plan for entering the apparel industry is hazardous in the absence of information which would make possible a valid analysis of opportunity cost. For example, the basic capital commitment of the company in both affiliates was $50,000, but to this should be added whatever managerial skills, technical talents, and other property was advanced and not directly compensated. Had this investment been made instead in Spiegel, May, Stern directly, by hiring experienced personnel, initial stockpiling, and adding apparel pages to the catalogs, would it have resulted in a different return than that which the company obtained on one-half the combined net results of Clement and Bernard Mayer? Certainly several potential opportunities for exploiting scale economies were foregone by the decision. Some expansion of existing organizational facilities would have been necessary had apparel been added to the existing lines of goods, but this should have been less onerous than a duplication of operating functions. Further, even with the sharing of advertising and catalog distribution services by the three firms, the total costs of preparing three separate sets of catalogs were greater than would have been the addition of pages to the Spiegel, May, Stern books. In addition, multiple catalogs and multiple identities lost to all three organizations the strength which the Spiegel, May, Stern name might have directly lent; the big house had a reputation, the new affiliates had to pay for the investment in acquiring some public esteem.

These considerations, however, faded in importance relative to the question of credit loss for the Spiegel management. The terms of sale of both affiliates during the first several years after 1907 were at least twice as conservative as those of the bigger company. The importance attached to the credit loss problem, and indeed the cost and efficiency differential itself, were valid if a differential actually existed in the payment behavior of apparel customers and house furnishings patrons. But, curiously, the management of Spiegel, May, Stern apparently never actually knew whether a significant payment behavior differential really existed. During many years, as a matter of fact, the company featured pages of apparel advertising *on the same terms* as for other merchandise, and in direct competition with its affiliates. Thus, although the apparent rationale of the compromise plan was defendable, a more comprehensive *ex post* evaluation strips it of logic. Perhaps it was the earnings of the affiliated companies that clouded the issue for management.

The financial performance of Clement Company is impossible to measure, although its continuous existence for over fifteen years suggests it was profitable. But there are a few other indications. During its first years of operation, Clement retained all earnings for working capital. For 1910 it added $30,000 to surplus, and by 1914 and 1917, respectively, its net worth had grown to $135,000 and $180,000, according to Spiegel, May, Stern records.[11] Thus for the first nine years of its operation, even if no dividend was paid, there was a net capital gain of 260 percent, or an average of almost 29 percent per year. Since Spiegel, May, Stern records indicate no change in Clement's net worth between 1917 and 1922, and since it would have been virtually impossible for them not to have made money during the booming war and postwar years, they obviously adopted a cash dividend policy after 1917.[12] This record of progress was reflected at Spiegel by writing up the book value of Clement stock owned by the company.

A careful comparison of the merchandise illustrated in Clement catalogs with that featured by Sears and Montgomery Ward indicates: (1) a higher general level of Clement prices, (2) an apparent superiority of Clement styling and fashion, year by year. The latter, of course, are tenuous bases for comparison since differences could have resulted purely from differences in page layout and the graphic arts, but it is also undeniable that Sears, although selling vast quantities of apparel, never developed a commanding reputation in such merchandise. The vision of the farmer wearing his "Sears, Roebuck suit" was for long either a fact or cherished fiction for city dwellers in America. But a comparison of Clement advertising with that of Chicago men's furnishing stores for the same period suggests no significant styling and fashion differences, which suggests the basis of the company's success. For the retailing of men's wear in small towns was considerably behind that in Chicago, thus Clement clothes must have enjoyed a differential fashion advantage which overcame whatever price disadvantages they faced. But the basic conservatism of mail-order merchandising was ever present in Clement styling and catalog copy. Representative of this was the theme in its spring 1909 book which, while considerably exaggerating itself as a "style originator" with "a London-trained designer," eschewed "freak clothes" in favor of "those used by the ultra-fashionable merchant tailors of New York and Chicago . . . who charge from $65 to $95 for a suit or overcoat."

In general, Clement prices reflected depth of line as well as variety of customer incomes and tastes. Suits were offered within the range $12.95 to $27.50 in cheviots, serges, tweeds, and worsteds, but certain models always bore a premium, and a differential of about 15 percent was charged for made-to-order suits. Overcoats reflected a broader range of prices, while topcoats typically sold from $11.95 to $13.75, approximately the same as for rainwear. Prices between 1914 and 1920 rose about 100 percent on average, the greatest gains occurring in shoes, suits, overcoats, and hats. In general, the overall range of price changes at Clement closely approximated those of Spiegel, May, Stern throughout the period.[13]

Bernard Mayer & Company was a more complex organization than Clement Company. The composition of its management and sharp personality difference between Mayer and Arthur Spiegel were bound to result in major difficulties between the partners. Initially, the optimism which prompted Arthur Spiegel to undertake women's wear merchandising seemed justified. During 1910 Mayer's net earnings were reported to have been $90,000, with Spiegel promptly writing up the value of its investment from $25,000 to $70,000, and, apparently, settling its notes to the affiliate.[14] But a substantial downward revision was required the following year when it was observed that "the $40,000 dividend and the loss sustained" had reduced the appreciated value of Mayer stock owned by the Spiegels to the extent of $66,293.[15] It would appear that Spiegel's own bookkeeping was somewhat bizarre if it took a capital gain and a dividend on the same $20,000. But on the basis of the company's accounting, its share of Mayer's net worth after 1912 would have been $3,707. Combined with certain other events, Mayer's 1911 performance removed much of Arthur Spiegel's high opinion of his partner.

By 1912 Arthur Spiegel's disenchantment with Mayer had advanced to a point where he was determined to terminate the association. It must be assumed that the feeling was mutual, for despite his personal charm and acumen, Spiegel was obdurate and impatient with interference and restraint. He issued a buy-or-sell ultimatum to Mayer who chose to buy; the agreed upon price was $125,000, one-half being paid in cash and three notes, maturing successively every six months until July 1, 1914.[16]

In light of the profitability of women's wear, it was hardly surprising that Arthur Spiegel insisted that the company remain in the field despite the trouble with Mayer. In the Christmas Sale book, 1912, women's wear commanded much more space than was customary, and during 1913 the general house furnishings catalogs were expanded to promote ladies' wear under its new brand name, "Martha Lane Adams." To protect the name against encroachment and in anticipation of the desirability of reorganizing ladies' wear as a subsidiary firm, a new corporation was set up called Martha Lane Adams.[17] Originally capitalized at $2,500, with the three Spiegel brothers purchasing the twenty-five shares of stock, the company was a paper enterprise until January 1914. Then, with a board composed of Arthur Spiegel, Waldheim, and Walter S. Oberfelder, who had been hired as general manager, and its title modified to include the word "Company," it began active operations as a wholly owned Spiegel subsidiary.[18] Walter Oberfelder was Arthur Spiegel's brother-in-law and an able merchant in his own right, with an extensive experience in the field. His appointment to the board attests to the confidence in which he was held by Arthur Spiegel, and the area of agreement which was reached between them with respect to the policies which should guide the subsidiary.

Although 1914 was a year of economic contraction, the little subsidiary performed sufficiently well to encourage Spiegel, May, Stern to expand its organization and scale of operation. In September, approval was obtained to increase its capital to $250,000, its entire 2,500 shares being subscribed for by Spiegel, May, Stern's president, who proceeded to advance funds, personnel, and functional assistance for the remainder of the year.[19] By November 1917 the amount of financial assistance which had accumulated since the subsidiary had been organized was $200,000. Then, apparently for taxation and future dividend purposes, the parent company "sold" its North Building, which Martha Lane Adams had occupied since 1914, to the subsidiary, and advanced it $400,000 to pay for the property and to "liquidate" its debt.[20] The subsidiary also assumed the remaining installments on the North Building mortgage.

While operating methods for Martha Lane Adams differed in no important way from those which had characterized its predecessor, functional coordination unquestionably was superior, particularly with respect to merchandising-promotion planning and the development of controls over circulation and credit. On the other hand, the subsidiary maintained its own clerical and physical order-handling apparatus and operated its own warehouse. Its buyers were in contact with the parent organization only to the extent that catalog planning demanded their participation. Once past the 1914 hurdle, the subsidiary was evidently prosperous, for their before-tax profits for the years 1915–17 are estimated at $640,000, all of which was retained in the business. Then, commencing July 1918, dividends were liberal, with a total of $465,000 being thus transferred to the parent house in three years.[21]

Although the economic expansion of the years 1916–20 contributed importantly, credit for the success of Martha Lane Adams must be given to Walter Oberfelder and Arthur Spiegel, neither of whom was around when the subsidiary was being milked for dividends. Oberfelder built a sound organization, developed persisting and strong contacts with the New York markets, and, in cooperation with the advertising department headed by Edward L. Swikard, promoted a balanced and salable line of women's wear. During Arthur Spiegel's lifetime the subsidiary offered terms comparable to those of the parent company, carefully conserving earnings and forming the basis for sound mercantile expansion; its net sales had grown to $1.2 million in 1916 and to just under $2 million the following year, or approximately two-thirds of the size of the parent company. At the end of 1917, the company's net working capital is estimated to have been $764,000; three years later it had been reduced to under $450,000. But with Arthur Spiegel's death in 1916 the close identity of interest which had existed between Oberfelder and Spiegel, May, Stern weakened. Policy differences arose over the issues of terms of credit and reinvestment of earnings, and these were magnified by a sheer incompatibility of personalities. In mid-1917, following a particularly vituperative and essentially childish attack upon him by one or both of the Spiegels, Oberfelder terminated his association with Martha Lane Adams.[22]

From the point of view of a professional executive concerned with the development of a healthy organization, capable of sustained growth, Oberfelder's contribution to Martha Lane Adams was substantial. Under his direction—and Arthur Spiegel's protective aegis—the subsidiary steadily expanded its market share, building increased sales and profits upon a foundation of retained earnings. The prosperity it enjoyed during the years prior to the postwar depression emerged from the sound building during his tenure as general manager. This was dissipated by the policies followed from 1918 through 1920, and it is notable that Martha Lane Adams, while continuing as a separate subsidiary until 1927, never recaptured the vitality it had enjoyed during Oberfelder's administration.

To fill the gap caused by Oberfelder's resignation, Spiegel, May, Stern appointed Houston Landis as general manager of the subsidiary. But while able, Landis was not a merchant, and the hole left in women's apparel merchandising remained until early 1919 when William H. Garvey was hired. Garvey, who had left Sears, Roebuck where he had been a successful outerwear buyer, was given the responsibility of merchandise manager for Martha Lane Adams Company and retained that post until the company was disbanded in 1927. He was, however, never in the position which Walter Oberfelder had occupied; policies were set by the parent company and the general manager, and his influence on general policy was never considerable. When ladies' wear was finally transferred into Spiegel, May, Stern proper, Garvey reverted to his former specialty, buyer for women's coats and suits.

The development of Clement Company, Bernard Mayer & Company, and Martha Lane Adams to add apparel to the company's basic house furnishings lines made as much, or as little, sense as organizational techniques as the weight which was assigned to the company's fears about credit losses. As time and experience later demonstrated, it would have been wiser to incorporate apparel directly into the existing product line, but management was not omniscient. This organizational pattern did have the merit of contributing to the solution of mail-order merchandising problems, and of tying rather effectively fairly heterogeneous elements of resources to a common end. But the disposition to organize new companies did not end here, and the other subsidiaries and affiliate firms without exception reflected insufficient purpose for being, insufficient integration with the main company, or both. They were universally unsuccessful.

Proliferation of new organizations was not confined to apparel, as Spiegel, May, Stern did not hesitate to create others to help in the marketing of jewelry and watches, pianos, and even grave monuments. A variety of motivations contended in these enterprises, some of which may have had some foundation in fact. For example, in late 1908 it occurred to management that the line could be profitably enlarged by adding watches and cheap jewelry. Either there was some reluctance by American watch manufacturers to distribute through mail-order houses, or Spiegel believed there was. Certainly watch manufacturers with a developed network of retailers would have been reluctant to undercut their distributors by selling certain brands through mail order, but there were others who found mass distribution under a variety of brands more attractive marketing strategy than the demands upon resources which the slower buildup of a retailer net would have entailed, and firms such as Sears and Ward obviously had little difficulty obtaining supplies of watches sufficient for their large needs. Nevertheless, it was suggested that Spiegel could overcome supply problems by establishing some intermediary organization which would buy watches on its own account, then resell them to distributors. Whether there was ever any plan to have the new companies serve buyers other than Spiegel. May, Stern, is not known. Since the prices which Spiegel charged for watches, despite some amusing nonsense to the contrary, were not particularly low, it is somewhat surprising that management believed such deception necessary. Furthermore, any such artifice was, to say the least, curiously lacking in guile if it was intended to deceive any manufacturer seriously concerned with restricting his channels of distribution.

Thus the Landis Watch & Jewelry Company was born, incorporated in West Virginia with an authorized capital of $50,000, all five hundred shares being duly subscribed by Spiegel.[23] Whether the company did more than subscribe, however, is extremely doubtful; certainly, examination of the surviving balance sheets from the period fail to turn up any investment in Landis, and it was apparently limited to a minor role in supplying letterheads, a checkbook, and some modest right to draw upon Spiegel balances for the purchase of inventory for the parent company. Having failed to accomplish the obscure purposes for which it was founded, Landis Company gave way two years later to a more energetic substitute. For "ten dollars and other good and valuable considerations," Spiegel, May, Stern acquired the stock of the Lincoln Company, another creature of West Virginia incorporation law. It must be supposed that the assets which the "other considerations" procured were priceless—they apparently could not be sufficiently abstracted to find their way into the Spiegel, May, Stern balance sheet—but still could not keep adversity at bay for more than a few years. Both Landis and Lincoln suffered an early demise.

There were other subsidiaries and affiliates organized by Spiegel, May, Stern through these years, none of which was especially important. The S. & K. Tire Company was a brainchild of Modie Spiegel, whose imagination had been fired by the possibility of puncture-proof tires. The E. B. Radford & Company and the U.S. School of Correspondence were unsuccessful attempts in an area of mail-order promotion which was being profitably exploited by others. In 1909, the Beckman Piano Company was formed to tap this rapidly growing market. The remaining companies were credit investigation and collection firms, such as the Merchants' Collection Company, which provided a means of special dunning or were set up actually to undertake some field collection service for Spiegel and other sellers. None of these ventures proved very rewarding and thus the parent company continued to receive the greatest attention.

Throughout the period between 1907 and 1922 Spiegel, May, Stern Company followed a relatively unaggressive, essentially unimaginative, merchandising philosophy.* Except in credit management (and selling) company merchandise policies were ingenuous, cautiously avoiding innovation, eschewing experiment in favor of conservative policies and practices. This was nowhere more apparent than in pricing. In mail order, Sears, Roebuck, to take but one illustration, was highly aggressive in pricing, accepting low margins on certain goods in the anticipation that heavy volume would produce profits whether on low-markup goods or on those which patrons would buy in addition to them. But pricing at Spiegel was done on a formula: take the net cost of purchases and multiply by two. Even merchandise purchased for particular sales events showed no important variation from this convention. "Come-on" pricing, price- and loss-leaders, and other techniques never disturbed the calm surface of Spiegel price philosophy.[24]

Overall pricing patterns at Spiegel, May, Stern reflected the cyclical changes of wholesale prices, and efforts to adjust the company fortunes to economic conditions and to buyer attitudes. After a strenuous effort to boost sales in 1913 ended in rigorous limitations being imposed by the company's bankers and a general business decline in 1914, Spiegel first attempted to improve its position by kicking prices up across the board from 5 to 15 percent in the spring 1914 promotions, but when the facts of depression became obvious, reduced them again in the fall catalog. But with the steady inflation that began after 1914, the average price level for the company generally followed the trend. Not in all items, of course, as management had no hesitancy in jettisoning certain suppliers when they felt that price levels of products important in their customer budgets were going up too fast to permit them to remain competitive. Either new substitute products of the same quality were obtained elsewhere, the items were discontinued entirely, or the

---

* In this study the term *merchandising* includes those activities, functions, and managerial decisions pertaining to the acquisition of merchandise for resale to final consumers, and with the treatment of these goods such that their market appeal stimulates demand and results in positive profits. Merchandising, as such, is thus concerned with the problems of line range and depth, with providing variety in style, design, color, material, and size. It is concerned also with setting prices, with credit standards, and credit management. Technically, the resale of merchandise involves another set of functions and decisions, but merchandising, as here defined, would include promotional activities designed to enhance the desirability of goods to consumers. For analytical and descriptive purposes, however, the selling and promotional functions will be treated separately from merchandising.

price increase was concealed by substituting a lower quality goods at the previous season's price. Adequate evidence of these pricing and product policies is available in a comparison of company catalogs for the years 1915–21, and it was a rare product indeed that remained in the book for all seven years. This practice makes almost impossible any accurate analysis of the real change in prices which occurred, but by the use of twenty items which remained constant in the catalogs, that is, continued to have the same catalog numbers and descriptions, it is possible to estimate that the unweighted price level rose by almost 169 percent between 1915 and 1920, then declined roughly 10 percent between fall 1920 and spring 1921, and continued to drop an additional 20 percent until fall 1922. The real price level, however, weighted by quantities sold of different products, may have declined more after 1920 than this index shows.

One fact, however, was certain. Spiegel, May, Stern did not find its life complicated or its survival threatened by the inventory which nearly ruined Sears, Roebuck during the 1921 depression. This relatively fortunate circumstance can be attributed almost exclusively to the absence of aggressive marketing philosophy. Management was quite content to ride the inflationary wave without exerting any great effort to accelerate it. Edward Swikard remembered that,

In the war years it didn't take much brains to get three million dollars in sales. Our average order in house furnishings, year in and year out, had run around twenty dollars. During the war, prices began to go up and up, and the result was that our average order rose to around thirty-seven, thirty-eight dollars. So we were doing real well, we could get double the earlier business with only a little extra effort and expense in promotion. When the bottom fell out, as it did in 1921, down went our average order again, back to around twenty dollars. Now, to counter this, to try to keep total sales up, we would have had to get out enough new catalogs, enough new sellers to double the number of active customers. But we didn't do this, we couldn't anticipate it.

Furthermore, while management had made some attempts to resist the continuous upward movement in prices, using some of the techniques that were earlier described, it had made no strenuous attempts to buy ahead of rises and sell at bargain prices out of long inventories. While its stocks on hand were about normal with respect to sales volume in 1919–20, and thus caused some loss with the sharp decline in 1921 price levels, these were readily absorbed.

This same simplicity was evident in the merchandise lines carried. Essentially, it must be admitted, conservatism was the soundest basis for a mail-order merchant. A metropolitan department store would be very safe in including cooking stoves which operated on natural gas, or lamps to be powered by electric current; it tended to serve consumers living in an area in which electricity and gas were available. But the mail-order house selling over an incomparably broader geographical market, had no such assurance. Thus it restricted its stove and lamp lines to models which operated on wood, coal, and oil. Further, the local town or city merchant could with relative safety buy a few units of a product which had no market experience. If they failed to create a demand he would probably lose all or part of their purchase price, but he did not have to continue to display them in valuable window or floor space, or deprive himself of the opportunity to exploit more efficiently this space with alternative merchandise. Once the mail-order house issued its catalog, however, whatever space it accorded to a merchandise item was lost for that season to alternative use. And because Spiegel, like Sears, Ward, and other mail-order sellers, dealt almost exclusively with populations that were either rural, or rural small town, it was forced to live with the habits and tastes of populations that did not have the same stimulus to adopt new products which characterized urban populations.

But even granted these conditions Spiegel seemed to be extremely conservative. At Sears, to return to that illustration, very aggressive methods were introduced to market bicycles, sewing machines, men's suits, certain types of light agricultural equipment, and lines of hardware, tools, heating and plumbing supplies, and even books.[25] And in Kansas City, National Bellas Hess, steadily developed its reputation—and sales volume—by specializing in ladies' apparel, acquiring a unique position in the market for fashion merchandise through imaginative selection and styling, and appealing prices. In marketing apparel, Spiegel, May, Stern's merchandising—more properly that of the affiliates—reflected the changes in fashion, styling, and color which characterized the industry; nothing particularly distinctive, never avant-garde, but following regularly the fashions of the previous year. Yet, compared with the merchandising which characterized the furniture and house furnishings lines, that of apparel was sheer poetic imagery. Again, there was real justification for the relative immutability of product-line and item merchandising. Tendencies toward a better taste in America proceeded unevenly. One inevitable result was that there was no strong demand by consumers for products of simple and clean design. Given this condition and the state of industrial organization then existent, there was little pressure upon manufacturers to innovate new materials, or to engage in expensive research to guide the development of fresh substitutes, or the utilization of the arts in design. Thus, in general, little change took place in furniture, heating and cooking apparatus, and house furnishings. Because this was so, the mail-order distributor was relatively safe in continuing to use the same illustrations year after year, to repeat the same copy points in advertising. And even when some new departure began to gain consumer acceptance generally, the temptation to amortize the expense of woodcuts and plates for still another year was frequently sufficiently strong to hold back a merchandise change longer than was absolutely necessary. Thus the catalog for any one season tended to differ from its predecessor only imperceptibly, although a comparison of two catalogs issued fifteen years apart revealed some significant changes. Not all changes, unfortunately, were aesthetic improvements.

Judged by the type and quantity of promotional literature employed and by the space allocations of catalogs, the principal merchandise concentrations of Spiegel, May, Stern until 1914 were in furniture, floorcoverings, stoves, refrigerators, domestics (linens and bedding), watches and jewelry. After 1914 more extensive coverage was given kitchenware and tableware, small appliances, laundry and cleaning equipment, paint and decorating materials, with a corresponding diminution in the importance of the older lines. Houston Landis devoted close attention to the productivity of catalog pages, so it is reasonable to assume a fairly accurate correspondence between promotional effort, catalog pages, and sales volume. Representative of the furniture lines were the three-piece bedroom suites, with cheval dressers which sold for $24.85 in the 1907 catalog; the oak-finish kitchen cabinets, which ranged in price from $8.75 to $15.75 in 1907–10; the four-piece Mission library sets that sold from $11.75 up to $19.95 from 1907 through 1915, thereafter more than doubling in price by 1920. Exemplary also were the varieties of rocking chairs, the plain oak rockers priced at $6.85 in 1907, and the fabricord and Turkish models ranging from $5.70 to $10.95. Dining room furniture, while showing some variation in style, was invariably stolid, with round and square tables of oak or birch, sometimes with "mahogany type" finishes, always with heavy chairs, bulky sideboards, china closets, and cabinets. Bedroom furniture featured both wood and brass beds, and while flat springs and stuffed cotton mattresses seemed to be the favorite models, these were interspersed with early variations of coiled, innerspring types.

Beginning in 1920–21, a significant change in styling occurred, with Queen Anne, Chippendale, and Louis XVI introduced to supplement basic Mission. Whatever their qualities of durability, and however they satisfied the customer's sense of receiving value, such styles were lighter and more graceful, as they combined an element of good design with the earlier functionalism. During 1920–21, also, overstuffed chairs, sofas, and couches, upholstered in velour, tapestry, wool, and other materials appeared. While these were unquestionably significant advances in user comfort their aesthetic superiority was questionable.

Heating and cooking stoves as well as refrigerators remained standard features of the product line but after 1914 the company reduced the absolute amount of promotion devoted to such articles by terminating its policy of publishing separate catalogs. Until then, a stove book was prepared and distributed annually, with refrigerator books appearing occasionally, and, in addition, some or all of these special books were combined with the house furnishings catalog in what was termed a "consolidated catalog." Refrigerators varied in size and construction depending on unit size, weight, and ice capacity; with barely perceptible modification, they underwent no change until 1920–21. In 1907 the company carried a broad line of refrigerators, their fifteen models ranging from a 95-pound box priced at $5.85 to the de luxe 350-pounder at $29.65. The ice capacity varied from 36 pounds for the smallest to 175 pounds, with exterior housings of birch, ash, and oak, and interiors finished in galvanized iron with or without white enamel finish. Refrigerators, on the average, rose about 50 percent in price between 1907 and 1917, followed by a further increase of 50 percent by 1920. After 1910, however, the company sharply reduced the depth of the refrigerator line, holding about five or six models as a general practice, and concentrating its purchases from one or two manufacturers who could guarantee supply and undertook to perform inventory stocking and drop shipping for the company.[26]

Heating and cooking stoves weighed more heavily in the company's merchandising and sales experience than refrigerators, and management arranged for an assured source of supply by contracting for the entire output of the Empire Stove Company. Empire manufactured a complete line of stoves ranging from the 210-pound kitchen range at $14.10 to the 590-pound "Grand Empire" which listed at $48.75. In subsequent years, and apparently under a different source arrangement, the cheapest cast-iron kitchen range, a three-hole, oven model, was priced under $12, while a huge "French restaurant" type was introduced in 1910 and priced at $89.95. Heating units, including the pot-bellied models that were such a distinguishing landmark of the American scene, were offered in a comparable series of sizes and prices, varying from a 60-pound model at $3.95 to a 525-pound type priced ten times higher, according to the 1907 catalog. By 1922, the stove line included kerosene and oil kitchen ranges, and one model of a gas stove was introduced. But the principal fuels for which the stoves and ranges were designed continued to be wood and coal, while the iron and steel monsters were intricately cast with gingerbreading and steel-coil handles which "guaranteed a vast amount of work for housewives in cleaning and polishing."[27]

Another important merchandise category included watches and jewelry. For a company so conscious of credit loss, the introduction of these items was somewhat curious. The attempts to get around this problem through the organization of subsidiaries has already been recounted. But Spiegel, May, Stern offered watches for sale in its catalogs and special mailers before either the Landis or Lincoln subsidiaries were organized, and continued to feature them long after the demise of those firms.

Successively, Spiegel, May, Stern introduced a wide variety of house merchandise after 1907, much of it purely for promotion in special literature such as Christmas catalogs and late spring-summer sales books. The company's rationale for the employment of special selling literature for such purpose rather than including this merchandise in the major seasonal catalogs was based in simple economy. Yard swings, lawn furniture, hammocks, ice-cream mixers, lawnmowers, trunks and traveling bags were items which had a limited seasonal use, with a buying season which probably did not extend over six or eight weeks. The same was true of throw rugs, cameras, toys, sleds, and games. Promotion in the seasonal catalogs would have involved the use of relatively high-cost space, which would have provided a very small yield over most of the season. By concentrating such special items in less costly literature, delivered at the beginning of the buying season, a better sales-to-space-cost ratio was obtained. But many of the above-mentioned items found their way into the major catalogs also, although with a greatly reduced space allocation, when experience indicated that demand extended beyond a certain time expectation.

Further line implementation followed from technological change and the means of manufacturing and generating power more efficiently and conveniently than heretofore. Representative of products which emerged as a result of the spread of use of electric power were washing machines, vacuum cleaners, and lamps. Spiegel first promoted washing machines in the 1907 catalog, beginning with a model which was essentially a huge, circular, wooden tub, operated with the aid of flywheels, pipes, and levers, and depending upon human energy. In 1920, a "Dixie Mammy" line was extended by the introduction of a new model, designed for electric power and priced at $124.95, or, as the advertising proclaimed, "a mere 31⅔ cents a day." During 1920, also, Spiegel first carried electric irons, and several models of desk and floor lamps, which could be had in either electric or gas types, and a few which were convertible to either electricity or oil.

It is impossible to understand the company's merchandising policies during this period without a closer look at consumer credit. The advantage of installment credit in providing the company with a protected niche in the market has been shown. Some of the difficulties which credit imposed upon management, particularly its effect in limiting the size of the potential market, and in imposing an inherently awkward and inefficient solution to the problem of expanding the merchandise line by adding apparel has also been indicated. But credit had other and subtler effects upon merchandising philosophy at Spiegel. It has been seen that it was the *raison d'être* for the company, permitting the price latitude which mail-order competition would otherwise have wiped out, and enabling management to compete instead with local merchants in its market towns, where even the prosaic merchandising and limited product line provided a competitive differential. But there is good reason to assume that the protection supplied by credit was destructive to the development of other bases which could have helped differentiate Spiegel from other sellers. The company did not need imaginative and forceful merchandising to survive, could afford high and profitable markups simply because the credit umbrella was there. Thus merchants were robbed of considerable incentive, and what creative imagination existed tended to be channeled into credit merchandising in an attempt to strengthen the protected redoubt.

Credit merchandising, perforce, was almost inseparably integrated with sales promotion and the recruiting of new customers in the company's merchandising philosophy. The stimulation of initial interest was habitually accomplished by emphasizing the facility with which credit could be obtained. Then, once the new customer was put on the books—preferably with a moderate purchase—and had been seasoned to determine his payment habits, he was stimulated to buy more by making his terms easier.[28] These were effective merchandising techniques, and, combined with a few others, also directly tied to credit, were a dramatic contrast to the absence of imagination elsewhere in merchandising. And the record would have been considerably more remarkable had top management recognized that it had what was unquestionably the most brilliant single idea to appear in credit merchandising in that generation. This was the simple "add-on" plan which, as will be seen, Edward L. Swikard tried out in 1918–20, and which evolved into the lucrative revolving-credit scheme which later became so popular in the United States.[29]

Spiegel's credit umbrella would have afforded little protection were it not for a fundamental change which occurred in consumer attitudes toward installment buying. For the most part, this revolution in buying behavior may be traced to the automobile,[30] but in its own way, at a much slower pace and on an infinitely smaller scale, Spiegel, May, Stern Company contributed to the spread of installment credit buying, and provided a very useful vehicle for the credit education of American consumers over these same years. The demonstration effect provided by Spiegel customers buying necessary household goods and apparel on installment was less dramatic than was the automobile, but it was persistent and tenacious. Further, the company practiced what it had learned from its own early experience and made its credit plan relatively simple and accommodating to a large segment of Americans. For with people it contacted, principally American families with relatively small but steadily-earned incomes, its promotional and customer-getting techniques encouraged the dissemination of credit knowledge even when this failed to produce immediate sales for Spiegel.

The techniques which the Spiegel management used to minimize fraud and establish a basis of confidence upon which it could extend credit to customers are of interest for two reasons. First, they reflect the evolution of management policy and the patterns of administrative thought during the period; second, they may well, individually, be closely similar if not identical to the practices of other merchants in America who employed installment credit. Men who were active in management during these years insisted that some of the small mail-order houses in Chicago which offered time-payment plans nakedly emulated Spiegel methods; to the extent this is true, it indicates that the company was considered worth copying, and hence that its procedures were relatively effective.

The merchant's need to protect himself from fraud and loss leads to the development of criteria upon which credit decisions can be based. Such criteria are partly based on the willingness to pay (character), partly on the ability to pay (income and resources), and partly on the individual's life station (moral and social pressures). The credit problem, however, is complicated. Once such general principles are accepted as valid, there arises the question of what kind of information is valuable, and the further question of how it is to be obtained. Beyond this there is a need to weigh information according to its relative importance and provide some means for validating both the information and management's own criteria.

The experience of the house prior to 1907 provided certain valuable guides to the extension of credit to new applicants. Several of these, such as the relationship between house furnishings goods and moral and social pressure, and perhaps character, have been discussed. But as of 1907 the company still operated largely on a basis of "feel" and of trial and error, both uncertain and both particularly fraught with risk in the new merchandise areas of apparel. The managers of that era apparently believed that there existed a correlation between such variables as occupation, length of residence in a particular community, marital status, and residence in an apartment or house, and willingness and social pressure to repay; further, that ability to pay was correlated with occupation, wages, and the number of days worked per week. They considered ownership of real property a positive factor, and attached some weight to the relationships between the credit applicant and other merchants with whom he had dealt, particularly if these were on a credit basis.

Little attempt was made to employ anything like scientific validation techniques to determine the relative importance of any of these variables either in granting credit or establishing credit limits. Thus, although the stability factor was regarded as important—and the length of time the applicant had resided in a community and at the same address was an indicator of stability—there was no certainty as to what weight should be attached to this characteristic. With respect to income and resources, there was the nagging question of how much was enough, and when family size should cease to be regarded as a virtue and recognized as a factor which increased the risk of nonpayment.

On yet another level was the practical matter of how the information should be gathered on the large number of applicants. The applicant himself was in the best position to know certain facts and to supply information directly to the company by means of a questionnaire. Simultaneously, he was in the best position to supply misinformation. To protect itself, the house could seek to verify information provided by applicants through recourse to supposedly objective third parties, such as local bankers, other businessmen, or attorneys; or to obtain all information it sought from these sources or from some professional credit investigator. Here, however, three factors had to be considered: (1) the expense involved, (2) the availability of efficient sources of intelligence, and (3) the climate of opinion existing in the towns that comprised the market.

A credit investigation by an agency tended to be expensive, even where such agencies existed, if it was carried out by the agency's own personnel. If another source could be substituted which could supply the needed data for less it was obviously preferable. Local bankers, for example, with their reputation for honest objectivity, were considered ideal informants. To a lesser extent, local attorneys were also regarded as reliable informants, while local merchants, particularly those whose names had been supplied by applicants on request, were splendidly situated to give information regarding the applicant's record for honesty and responsibility in meeting obligations. But in the climate of opinion which existed in those years there was substantial reason to question the advisability of seeking data from bankers and local merchants. The virulence of the anti-mail-order movement was approaching its crest, and mail-order executives had few delusions about the emotions of local merchants or the closeness of the ties between different members of the local business communities. Thus, whatever information might be supplied by these sources had to be skeptically regarded. They could well imagine the dark delight of the local merchant, struggling against mail-order competition, who could warmly recommend for credit the town's most flagrant deadbeats!

Furthermore, there were real problems connected with getting information directly from credit applicants themselves. Partly this was because many people, while not completely illiterate, had no real familiarity with written communication, and little understanding of the merchant's motives for requesting information. Even more important, however, was a reluctance to disclose what was highly private information to an alien and unknown organization. People in that era had not been subjected to the experience of mass disclosures of private information through personal income tax forms, social security forms, and job and credit application questionnaires which later formed such a familiar part of the social landscape. Further, mail-order customers living in towns swept by anti-mail-order sentiment could not be blamed for not wishing to have neighbors, employers, and local merchants know they were ordering merchandise from mail-order houses. Thus requests for the names of local merchants with whom they did business, or the identity of employers, and one or more other references, were almost certain of a suspicious reception.

In view of the environment in which they were forced to operate it is not surprising that Spiegel, May, Stern did not seek credit information from applicants until fall 1909. Throughout the period 1907–9, local attorneys constituted the prime source for credit data, bolstered when possible by information from banks. In 1913, Arthur Spiegel claimed that in each of the towns from which the company solicited business, "a local agent of good standing supplies detailed information concerning the financial worth, habits, and character of each customer applying for credit; and by this method the advisability of accepting or rejecting credit is easily ascertained."[31] Since this claim was advanced to investment bankers in a letter soliciting new financing, the president was possibly putting the brightest face on this technique. For in practice the system was inherently weak. Other executives were more reserved in their endorsement, one cynically observing that

too often it was just a joke. Either we, or one of the little, two-for-a-nickel outfits that had been set up to get credit information, would get the name of some lawyer in a town and offer to pay him to get us some information about people who had ordered from us. Now, we couldn't pay much for this or our investigation costs would go up so fast we couldn't have stayed in business. So we should have known those guys weren't going to do much of a job for us. Hell, I wouldn't be surprised if some of them didn't invent the answers themselves! And why not? Look, if the account that we opened on their recommendation went bad and we had to try to collect on it in the field, who do you think we'd hire to do that? These same lawyers who sent us the information in the first place. When you think about it, they would have been pretty stupid to have advised us against giving a man credit. Because if they got an account to collect they had a chance to make some money out of it, oh, maybe a quarter, maybe even half the amount owed us.[32]

Management's first attempt to obtain information directly from applicants came with a special gramophone booklet—this was relatively high-priced merchandise—soliciting the patronage of people with whom the company had no previous experience. Space was provided on the order form for three references, preferably merchants. In the editorial itself information was requested with respect to occupation, age, marital status, type of income, the time-

85

length of residence in community and at the given address, whether a future move was contemplated, and, if so, when and where. Solicitees were also invited to reveal the names of employers, and, if they owned real estate, "you might tell us where and how much." The language in which this request was couched unmistakably demonstrates management's uncertainty of its reception.

> We aren't asking for a guarantee or bond . . . we want to know if you are responsible. . . . You are a stranger to us . . . no way in which we can find whether or not you will keep and pay for the gramophone according to our terms unless you tell us something about yourself. [This is] no challenge to your honesty . . . but there are, unfortunately, some people who would take advantage of us. . . . [There is] no way to detect the honest from the dishonest except in asking information . . . honest and responsible persons . . . give us the information, while the dishonest, of course, cannot furnish . . . [it] . . . and consequently do not reply.

It also demonstrated, self-evidently, some naïveté if management actually believed these statements. But of much greater significance was the temerity of the approach, the fact that it was tried first on a small, specialty mailing rather than in a major effort with a large distribution, and that management felt compelled to offer some bona fide of its own. This was a listing of its banking sources and various claims to prominence and economic importance.

Between 1909 and the war years, management continued to employ variations on this same technique in soliciting credit information, and an examination of various credit letters sent out to catalog inquiries and various new mailing lists reflects a growing confidence of approach and a continued dependence upon the device of exchanging references. It is worth noting that Sears, Roebuck, which had first permitted installments on a tentative basis in 1910, did not ask any questions of a credit nature on its catalog order blanks until 1917, and then requested only the disclosure of occupation, length of time at present address, and the names of two references. It required two more years before Sears asked as many as seven credit questions.[33] Spiegel, in fact, did not presume to include credit questions on the regular catalog order blanks until the early war years, and then steadily increased the number of questions. By 1920 applicants were routinely requested to supply answers to the following:

86

1. Occupation.
2. Length of time employed.
3. Weekly earnings.
4. Number of days worked weekly.
5. Address.
6. Length of time lived at this address.
7. Previous address.
8. Length of time lived at previous address.
9. Age.
10. Married or single.
11. Number of children living at home.
12. Color.
13. Credit accounts carried with other merchants, including Spiegel affiliates and subsidiaries.
14. Obligations owed such merchants.
15. Real property owned, and amount.

The expanded questionnaire and its inclusion on the order blank indicated that (1) management tended to rely more upon information submitted by the applicant than in the past, (2) that some method of relating payment performance to the answers to these questions had been adopted and was considered viable, (3) that customers had become more accustomed to providing such information without irritation or fear. Further, that race had been formally adopted as a criterion for credit extension. In earlier years, according to one company executive, if management suspected an applicant was a black his order was ignored and his name removed from further solicitation lists.[34] In light of the criteria for credit extension described earlier, this was hardly surprising since blacks suffered notoriously from insecurity and discrimination in employment. Management was also unquestionably wedded to the stereotype regarding the black's character and attitudes toward the responsible settlement of commitments.

Given the importance of installment credit in the marketing plan and the need to add new customers, both to replace normal attrition and to grow, the house had few alternatives to the techniques it followed. It could have reduced risk by toughening the credit criteria, by increasing down payments and installments, and by shortening maturities. It could also have narrowed its so-licitation efforts to persons in high income, occupation, and life-station strata. Such a program would inevitably have doomed the firm to relative stagnation if not early extinction. Further, as Sears, Montgomery Ward, and other distributors discovered, credit or-ders tend to be larger than cash orders, and credit customers tend to buy more frequently than do cash customers. Such tendencies naturally spread overhead costs, build volume, and add to profit-ability, and Spiegel managers would have been remiss not to have sought both replacement accounts and net increments by aggres-sively merchandising credit rather than maximizing security. If the deficiencies in credit screening encouraged some attempts to defraud the company, and increased credit loss and collection ex-pense, they simultaneously encouraged responsible people to trade with the house. And in the environment in which the house op-erated, and given the state of the analytical arts then available to business, management decisions tended to be conservative rath-er than lax.

During 1907–8, years of economic recession, Spiegel, May, Stern credit policy was characterized by a flat set of terms and conditions of sale. Orders in amounts under five dollars were refused, includ-ing cash orders which were encouraged in 1907 by the offer of a 5 percent discount from list prices; down payments equal to roughly 15 percent of the dollar value of orders were required, and provided from eight to twelve months for the liquidation of re-maining balances. In addition, customers paid freight charges, al-though the company guaranteed reimbursement if the merchan-dise was returned. The typical period for liquidation was from nine to eleven months, the variation resulting from setting down payments and installments within ranges of dollar values, and from granting slightly more extended terms for larger orders. In the smallest order range, $5 to $6.24, the terms were $0.95 down and $0.50 per month; if paid out without incident, a $6 order thus had an eleven-month maturity, while that of a $5 order was nine months.

By 1909, however, this uniformity of treatment was eased to permit differentiation of terms to correspond with company ex-perience with customers. Customers who had demonstrated will-ingness and ability to carry out the terms of sale were accorded more liberal treatment than customers who had caused collection difficulty or persons who were being solicited for the first time. Active customers, or "live accounts," were divided into three groups, each receiving different treatment both with respect to terms of credit and to amount and type of sales literature they received. The "elite" class, those with accounts in current balance who had given a minimum of trouble, were "Preferred Customers," eligible to consistent differential treatment as to terms, exposed to the full battery of mailing promotions. Customers below this class, ordinary live accounts, were treated according to account status. If they were lagging in payment, but still were not considered delinquent, they received some promotional literature but not necessarily catalogs. They could buy only at regularly published terms, and new orders from this group were carefully scrutinized and frequently cut back in amount or refused outright. Management saw little sense in increasing the amount of potential loss by encouraging further business from this group, but not wanting to cut them out as a class encouraged submission of orders so that individual screening could be applied.

New accounts were classified according to their medium of entry into the house, and retained such classification until they have been seasoned, that is, until they had demonstrated their willingness and ability to pay and were reclassified into one of the above groupings. For example, if the company advertised in consumer magazines, inviting readers to write for a catalog, any orders received from such inquiries were accorded a higher status than were catalog requests which came in unsolicited. Further, when customers were asked to recommend friends to the company, or were stimulated to obtain orders from such friends by offers of premiums and prizes, such "Friends" were generally accorded slightly differential treatment in terms and literature than were other new accounts.

In August 1909, the company first offered No Money Down terms to preferred customers in a small sales flyer, and repeated this offer three months later in its Christmas Sale book. Since monthly installments were unchanged, the effect was to lengthen maturities by from one to two months while still compressing the maximum maturity on most orders to within one year. For the remaining years of this period, no-money-down terms were an integral part of credit policy for preferred customers, although there was variation in the intensity and frequency of its use.

Other techniques of merchandising terms developed included the Free Trial Offer, One-Dollar Down, and Friends' campaigns. In each case the purpose was to lengthen the payment period by reducing or postponing the down payment, while maintaining monthly installments at a constant level. The effect was to encourage business while not seriously reducing the rate of liquidation.

The free-trial offer encouraged the prospective customer to comfort himself with the illusion that he was only testing the merchandise which he would return, if not satisfied, within the trial period, and that if he kept it his payments would not start with the day of his order. Since customers always had the privilege of returning goods with which they were not satisfied, within a reasonable period of time—usually about the same as the free-trial-offer period—the actual liberalization of treatment was confined to the postponement of down payments; when in addition the company did not require customers to pay freight until after they had decided to retain the merchandise, the postponement of any cash outlay for the trial period provided a strong inducement to order. Free-trial-offer privileges, however, were inherently dangerous unless restricted to merchandise whose likelihood of being kept by customers was high. The company had to guarantee the freight on deliveries and absorb it on returns, so that a sharp rise in return rates, such as could be expected under this plan if merchandise was questionable, would effectively increase costs and reduce net income. Spiegel first introduced the free-trial offer in 1909 when promoting the sale of sewing machines, gramophones, and pianos, permitting a ten-day trial for gramophones, and thirty days for the other items.[35] Sears, Roebuck, incidentally, had been using the free-trial offer for several years prior to this in promoting the sale of durable goods.[36]

"Dollar Down" was a variation of free-trial-offer merchandising, which provided approximately one additional month for orderly liquidation of balances. First attempted in fall 1912 to encourage orders from persons to whom catalogs had been sent on request, this technique was steadily employed for the remainder of this period. Originally, $1 down was required for orders up to $26 in value, $2 down for amounts above that up to a maximum of $50. But these terms also were manipulable in response to company experience and business conditions. During the expansion of sales volume in the years 1917–20, there was some contraction of the use of dollar-down, but it was sporadic and somewhat inconsistent.

Spiegel, May, Stern initially employed the technique of Friends' campaigns in 1913, although it had been used by Sears, Roebuck for at least a decade.[37] But because it was being used as an instrument of credit merchandising, Spiegel supplied a novel variation. Customers were urged to secure orders from friends, exactly as at Sears, by offering premiums whose value was related to the number of orders they initiated. The innovation was that the new customers were also encouraged by being offered terms which were somewhat more liberal than those which applied to other classes of new customers. For example, the dollar-down privilege was submitted to Friends before being extended to new customers generally.[38] Thus, the company assumed that friends of customers who had demonstrated responsibility and the capacity and will to honor their commitments would tend to resemble them to a greater degree than would some randomly selected group of strangers.

One result of the early Friends' campaigns was a disastrous rise in collection troubles and bad-debt losses, the investigation of which uncovered the operations of cliques of frauds. The locus of the swindling rings was centered principally in southern states, although the company also identified operating nests in northern counties.[39] Alarmed, management did not abandon the Friends' technique, but acted to protect itself with more *ad hoc* methods. Counties extending over a broad area of the South were blacklisted, as were selected counties and towns in the North. By 1915 unsolicited catalog requests from below the Ohio River were ignored, the period of validation of southern customers was lengthened before preferred status was conferred, and the names of customers recommending friends were posted to the new account ledgers to facilitate quick identification of sponsors in the event the new accounts immediately defaulted.

The most engrossing venture in merchandising installment credit was the introduction of the add-on in 1917 and again in 1920. This plan was doomed to abandonment because of management's shortsighted refusal to recognize success when it was thrust upon them. In all fairness, the first trial of add-on occurred in 1908 and must be credited to Arthur Spiegel. The company was promoting the sale of watches in the Christmas Sale and it occurred to the president that this merchandise might be purchased by active customers in profitable volume if they were not forced to open a separate account. He therefore offered to merge the installments on watch payments with those on existing balances, that is, the customer could make the down payment on the watch, then send in monthly remittances to cover both installments on a single account. That he failed to understand what he had stumbled upon is reflected by the failure to include merchandise other than watches, and by the quick renunciation of the technique in favor of standard methods.

This was not true of the later sorties in revolving credit. In 1917, although sales volume and the size of the average order were rising comfortably in the swelling wave of wartime inflation, Edward L. Swikard, sales and advertising manager, was experiencing one of his periodic waves of restlessness, seeking to develop something fresh and appealing from the background of company problems and previous experience. Whether he obtained the idea from an examination of the 1908 Christmas Sale book and grasped the potential power of the idea, or whether it sprang from his imagination is both unknown and unimportant. What did occur to him was that Spiegel customers might resist buying from 1917 sale books not because they had no need for merchandise or did not want to trade with the house, but simply that they had no wish to get tangled in the problems of multiple accounts and their own bookkeeping, which was imposed on them by company policies adopted in 1908. For in that year Landis and Innis had introduced a system which had two effects: first, it eliminated monthly billings to customers, thereby saving a vast amount of labor and expense. Customers received, instead, the original bill of sale with merchandise, and were expected to keep track of their own accounts, and remit monthly installments on the date specified by the company. The second effect was much more subtle, and was not fully appreciated and acted upon by management for fifty years. This was, simply, that every mail contact with customers provided an opportunity to sell merchandise, and when monthly billing disappeared so did from eight to twelve opportunities to include small promotional pieces and reminders that the company was still in business and anxious to accommodate customer requirements. But the immediate effects of the Landis-Innis system were to conserve company capital resources and complicate both the handling of customer relations and the impact of sales promotions.

If people were discouraged from patronizing Spiegel because of these conditions, Swikard's plan would simultaneously reduce this obstacle and ease some of the problems of customer accounting. For he proposed to allow customers to buy new merchandise and add the amount of their purchases to the remaining outstanding balances on existing accounts. The preferred customers were accorded no-money-down treatment anyway, and the amount of the down payment could either be exacted from other active customers or forgiven, which in itself would have been a sales inducement. The amount of the installment required on the combined obligation was readily determined by reference to current tables of terms which specified the installment due on different balances. How he managed to slip his idea past the upper echelon of management is a secret which Swikard carried to his grave. It was probable that in the warm climate of rising sales and profits top management was somewhat somnolent and would have agreed to almost anything. Swikard himself was sufficiently skeptical to confine the experiment to one mailing piece and await results. They were not long in coming, even if more encompassing than Swikard had anticipated. He always believed that the sales volume produced from his special promotion was greater than anticipated, but he was not given a chance to test the concept further. For top management peremptorily ordered a halt; if they could not appreciate the technique as a sales builder, they had little difficulty understanding that for at least some accounts the combined new balance required a smaller installment than the customer had previously been paying, and if anything was likely to incite top echelon to a state of near rage it was a reduction of liquidation rates.

But if Swikard did not fight this decision directly it was not because he actually gave way; he operated by indirection, on the principle that it was simpler to slip into an open window than to break down a door. His idea fascinated him and in 1920 he was ready for a new trial, this time with a modification designed to overcome the fundamental objection of management. Instead of allowing the amount of the monthly installment to be set by the table of terms rating for the combined balance after add-on, the customer would have to pay installments at least as great as those which applied on the old balance alone. For most orders which the company would receive under the modified plan, there would be an extension on the liquidation of the old balance which would be more than balanced by a contraction of the allowed maturity on the new purchase. The Swikard compromise would have reduced maturities by one month as compared to the earlier plan, and actually tended to be less liberal with the added balances than an original purchase from a new customer would have been. And this argument appealed even to top management. The plan was again extended to a group of preferred customers in the fall 1920 campaign, with the apology that the previous trial had been curtailed by management "due to wartime conditions."[40]

Wartime conditions were quite evidently at an end in that autumnal season, and in fact the five-year boom was beginning to come apart at the seams. Perhaps this was the principal reason why this experiment with revolving credit flickered and died out. For management had the problems of slumping sales, falling prices, and mounting collection troubles to contend with for the next twenty months, following which it faced problems of reorganization and refinancing. But Swikard never quite believed this; he had evidently suffered a rebuff over and beyond the impact of depression, and in later years, when a colleague "rediscovered" add-on and approached Swikard with the suggestion, the sales manager was pessimistic, observing, "they'll never let you get away with it."[41]

The reasons why management failed to find revolving credit attractive are difficult to discover. As a credit house, credit merchandising was the real bread and butter, and the add-on plan not only was a tremendous tool for building sales and retaining customer loyalty, but it simplified the problems of accounting for both customers and the house. But Arthur Spiegel was five years dead in 1921, and none of the remaining executives in the upper management level were ever successfully accused of being imaginative. In this climate of opinion Edward L. Swikard was simply fifteen years in advance of the times.

The Spiegel management exercised a variety of more traditional means calculated to preserve their customers' willingness to pay. One means, of course, was the insistence upon liquidation within twelve months, because relatively short maturities, unless they impose an excessive burden upon the incomes of customers, set up attainable goals (full ownership) while the merchandise itself is still relatively new and attractive to the buyers. Still more subtle was the secondary effect of an overall merchandise and selling policy. For if merchandise was selected to maximize the design, style, and fashion durability rather than to feature fashion variation and change, the desire of purchasers to continue to use (and continue to pay) would be intensified. And if Spiegel merchandising was not brilliant in these years, it certainly possessed this characteristic: it tended to sell the same things year after year.

But such factors are difficult to check and provide small consolation to executives confronted with customers who do not honor obligations, and more obvious and pointed techniques were required to prod lagging willingness to pay. Each customer account was assigned a date upon which a remittance was due in Chicago, the dating being scheduled on a state-by-state basis so as to stagger the burden of mail opening and remittance posting over the month. Procedure in the clerical-operating departments required that each ledger (customer file) be checked monthly so that delinquencies could be promptly identified. If remittances had not been received when the account was reviewed, a sequence of standardized actions was automatically set in motion, consisting of a graduated series of reminder and dun letters prepared by specially trained correspondents. The standard system was applied as long as no response was forthcoming, but was abandoned in favor of *ad hoc* correspondence depending upon the nature of the delinquent's response. For as long as concrete action was forthcoming, such as part payments, accepting excuses, and other grounds, such as complaints about returns, allowances, and proper crediting of accounts, the consumer remained in an acceptable, if not good, status. The ledger remained in the customer accounts department and the customer continued to receive promotional literature which varied by type and quantity with the status of his account.

When, however, accounts became seriously delinquent, that is, when the debtor had not made payments for a period—usually about three months—the ledger file was removed, transferred to another collection section called the "Attorney's Department," and the customer subjected to much rougher handling. Initially, the stiffer duns were written on Spiegel letterheads, then, when such treatment proved fruitless, the account was given to a collection agency. In fact, however, this transfer was largely fictional; Spiegel, May, Stern had organized several corporations for collection purposes, purely paper organizations, with individual firm letterheads. When the new dunning efforts failed to produce results, however, accounts were given out for collection, sometimes, as has been observed, to attorney-correspondents in the delinquent's community, sometimes to authentic collection agencies.

Incompleteness of collection and loss data renders impossible a definitive evaluation of the company's credit record for these years. Still, surviving records provide some opportunity to analyze aspects of performance and to offer a tentative appraisal. The amounts charged off as a percentage of the sales of the year in which they were charged off varied from 1.7 percent in 1908 to 20.3 percent in 1914, but in most years for which data are available they were substantially under 4 percent.

Losses, of course, are but one element in measuring the costs of installment credit, with investigation and collection charges, together with the interest on money borrowed to carry receivables, comprising the rest. No record exists for such expenses at Spiegel during these sixteen years, but it is probable that the total of such charges were at least equal to debt losses, or, in other words, that total credit costs were in excess of 8 percent of net sales, quite possibly as much as 10 percent. This amount was obviously in excess of the small discount for cash which the house offered in 1907, somewhat above the rates directly charged by Sears in 1919–21, and probably about equal to the discount for cash which Montgomery Ward allowed when that company began to use installment selling.[42]

In summary, the company's credit experience suggests that the costs of catalog selling on an installment plan while high were also well within gross margins which permitted substantial rates of profit. Further, the prices which permitted the incurrence of such costs—and the profits—were only made possible by installment credit. For without the screen which credit provided, Spiegel would have been confronted with the direct and unrestrained competition of Sears and Ward, and survival would have required quite different bases than those which were employed. In addition, it cannot be forgotten that in mail-order selling Spiegel was the credit pioneer, and that a considerable proportion of the losses and expense entailed in credit selling should properly be assigned to investment—the investment in consumer education, in experimenting with different market segments, and in overcoming consumer reluctance to buy on credit. How effectively they could recover this investment depended upon managerial efficiency in learning from the initial experience and applying the best techniques and analytical methods available to provide for better customer selection and increasing the annual volume sold to those select customers.

All questions of installment methods and credit losses, of course, would have been academic had the company failed to attract customers. This promotional activity was primarily the responsibility of Edward Swikard. While his productive and often brilliant campaigns of the 1930s will be examined in some detail later, it is important to note the foundation he constructed during this period.

Arthur Spiegel, who had originally been responsible for promotional efforts, focused his attention on overcoming the reluctance of small-town people to buy on credit. This depended upon impressing readers of catalogs with the respectability of installment buying as well as its convenience. Although there were alternative approaches, the one he selected was that of building an image of the company that reflected institutional size and economic power. In an era of "trust-busting," when the public investigations of life insurance companies were still vivid, and a wave of reform was continuing to place various segments of economic enterprise under certain minimum controls such as the Pure Food and Drug Act, this image building may seem questionable, but Americans have always had the ability to excoriate certain types of behavior while retaining a pronounced respect for agglomerations of power. And under Arthur Spiegel and Edward Swikard the company's sales pages emphasized both economic power and respectability and a sort of big-brother concern for the little consumer whose interests it appeared to champion.

The implications of size and power appeared in the first Spiegel, May, Stern catalogs in 1907. On the inside front cover were illustrations of the "twenty-five mammoth stores located in the principal cities of the United States," and the statement about $7 million of aggregate capital.[43] The facts were quite at variance with this representation; the capital was less than 5 percent of this figure, and Spiegel, May, Stern possessed no stores. But the impression was there, and who was likely to confuse a back street borax installment operation with $7 million? Nor was this impression conveyed alone by sketches and dollar statements of capital. The company, it was claimed, "bought and sold more goods than any [other] three concerns in our line . . . [which] means that we can practically control the output of every factory with whom we contract . . . ." The 1907 sales editorial, which was repeated in theme and variation for the next seven years, also offered all the economic advantages which large-scale distribution held for consumers, plus the facility of credit. Arthur Spiegel identified the house with the mail-order industry when he emphasized that "all mail-order houses with their enormous buying capacity" could price below conventional retailers, but Spiegel offered much more than cash houses or local dealers who "cannot offer you anything in the way of credit which this house cannot . . . [including] . . . all the time you need to pay, sure of prompt, courteous, and liberal treatment."

Vital though the credit theme had to be for Spiegel, Arthur Spiegel lost no opportunity to build his house-image along all lines, particularly with respect to merchandise quality and styling. In sales messages covering the years 1908–11, he pointed out that "the largest and finest stores in Chicago [Spiegel]" purchased furniture of style and construction at least a year ahead of that which other dealers dared to introduce. This, it was generously admitted, led to imitation, but what imitator could effectively compete with a firm which employed "a staff of the most experienced and skilled designers in the country."[44]

In a previous section, dealing with credit screening, the company's practice of soliciting information from applicants by offering to exchange information was emphasized as a means of educating consumers in credit procedure. But the technique provided management with a further opportunity to expand the image of the house as an institution of respectability and power. Letters from bankers who endorsed the company's reputation were diffi-

cult to improve upon as testimonials, particularly when repro-
duced upon pages which appeared to provide objective statements
of capital position, the number of active accounts being serviced,
and references to "the company's own quarries" and the "output
of our factories."

After Swikard's advent, a new dimension of professionalism began to appear in the development of the educational campaign
to make installment buying respectable, tying the desires of work-
ing- and lower-middle-class families to the consumption behavior
of the wealthy. A 1913 sales letter to householders who had received a catalog but placed no order is representative of this attempt to identify social status with installment buying. Professing
anguish at the failure of consumers to take advantage of the opportunity which trading with Spiegel afforded, Swikard claimed
to have analyzed the responses of a sample group of nonbuyers,
and discovered that the typical reason given was a reluctance to
make use of credit. But this, protested Swikard, made no sense.
Wealthy people, regardless of place of residence, bought consumer goods on credit, viewing the practice as normal and convenient.
Why, he asked, should not less fortunate, but equally honest and
respectable people, those who needed the accommodation of installment credit more than the rich, take advantage of the ease
with which credit could be obtained at Spiegel, enjoy the open-
ness of company policy, and the confidence with which the house
treated its customers?[45]

A second, and important, dimension to the campaign for making
installment buying respectable was the development of the theme
of the big and economically powerful company acting to advance
the interests of the powerless consumer. In the Spiegel adaptation
of this thesis, the house was pictured either as employing its own
bargaining capacity to reduce prices to Spiegel customers, or defy-
ing the ruthless power of monopoly. An example of the first form,
that of countervailing power, was provided in the Spring Sale
book, 1909, when the company's buyers were portrayed as having
exercised every energy and wile to obtain merchandise on the best
terms possible, a version which included the portrayal of Sidney
Spiegel as a sort of high-principled Machiavelli. Adamant in his
determination to get prices down for customers, he was supposed
to have gathered the three largest manufacturers of chairs to-

gether in his office, and set them bidding frenziedly against one another to obtain a lucrative contract. When the dust had settled from the resulting donnybrook, "we had entered into a chair agreement that secured these chairs at a lower price, by at least 35 percent, than [such] chairs . . . . ever before cost us."[46]

Left unexplained is the question of why the manufacturers permitted themselves to be so manipulated. Was it high-minded devotion to the competitive ideal which restrained them from entering some collusive arrangement? Was it stupidity? Or was it rather Sidney Spiegel's shrewd refusal to allow them opportunity? The hyperbolic arts lost nothing in Swikard's hands two years later when Spiegel gave up on the last of its watch subsidiaries. In announcing the plan to purchase the Lincoln Company, Swikard warned his readers that the intention to sell the acquired inventory at bargain prices was fraught with hazard. The plan, he confided, had been leaked to the "strongest monopoly on earth" despite every security precaution, and had resulted in a visit from a representative of the trust who counseled abandonment of price-cutting schemes. But when management indignantly rejected this advice, "we got a touch of the Trust Methods. If we did not raise our prices . . . the Trust would stop at nothing to blow our business to pieces."[47] Happily for Spiegel, May, Stern, the Watch Trust proved to be a paper tiger which slunk pitifully into the shadows under the scornful eye of a management which refused to be intimidated!

Such fictions and exaggerations by a business organization appear unbelievable, ridiculous in the light of modern advertising sophistication. But the techniques and methods of communication are functions of their times and conditioned by their environment and the levels of expectation and credibility of recipients. As he was later to observe, Swikard never knew which message, or which aspect of a message, touched a responsive chord in his readers. One result of this uncertainty was an unwillingness to abandon any particular approach. He was selling to a small-town audience, to people conditioned by a fanciful and romantic literature, exposed during those years to reports and rumors of concentrations of economic power and its abuse. If some readers gave credence to his *opéra-bouffe* contrivances, if some found them lightly entertaining, Swikard had little to lose. Those who would scorn them were, almost without exception, unlikely to buy from mail-order catalogs, and in this group he had no interest. But Edward Swikard's contribution to mail-order selling and to the advancement of a distinctive image for Spiegel, May, Stern was not confined to such concepts as the above.

Of a more enduring character was the sober symbolization of power, respectability, and protection which he contributed in the spring of 1911 with the introduction of the term "Buying Power." This name he gave to a romantically idealized young giant whom he clad in Greco-Roman costume and posed standing astride an equally idealized representation of the company's plant, past whose sandaled feet bulging freight trains sped, and from whose outstretched hands merchandise tumbled as from a veritable cornucopia. In later catalogs and selling pages the symbol was tied to the credit theme, and although Arthur Spiegel's name appeared on the editorials it was the personalized Buying Power who promised no collectors, no rigid rules, no extra prices or interest charges, and who guaranteed that in the event of personal misfortune payment terms would be extended, and who expressed disdain for repossessing merchandise.[48]

The development of a market position through consistent efforts to enhance the respectability of credit buying was the natural legacy of the installment sales plan, and the policies which stemmed from this plan consistently shaped all other aspects of company selling behavior. As a general-line house, Spiegel, May, Stern Company followed the same generalized patterns of marketing which characterized Sears, Roebuck and Montgomery Ward. That is, the big business-getting instrument was the catalog, but the catalog was supported and complemented by a variety of selling literature, each element of which was designed to accomplish one or more tasks, and the combination of efforts were aimed at maximizing company sales and profits. Thus, for all general mail-order houses, sales management involved the development of two major campaigns each year, each of approximately six-months duration, each requiring the preparation of a major catalog and such auxiliary efforts as were deemed necessary. The kind of supporting literature resorted to by a given management varied with the general and special objective sought. For example, if a management sought to reduce the amplitude between seasonal peaks and valleys in sales, such as that which exists between pre-Christmas and pre-Easter maximums, a special sale could be held in January. The nature of the mailing efforts involved would vary with the objective. Thus, in the previous example, a sales bulletin might confine itself to white goods only, or a more ambitious effort might feature a richer variety of merchandise.

For the mail-order house, the seasonal catalog is the "store." In it are displayed the overwhelming proportion of all merchandise the company has in stock available for sale. And, as is true in retailing generally, its space is organized and exploited through the use of line, light, and color to display the merchandise to advantage, to invite consumers inside the covers and encourage them to explore. The costs of layout of this store are high because of the extent and richness of the merchandise lines carried, and the number of units distributed. Thus the mail-order house, like the department store, seeks to attract as many potential buyers as possible, and to increase to the maximum the volume of business which the store can produce. Pressing the analogy further, the mail-order catalog, like the department store, benefits from repeat calls, from having customers return to satisfy more of their consumption needs. This they seek to accomplish not only by stocking an immense variety of goods, but by urging a buildup of orders or order size through the utilization of promotions designed to bring to the attention of customers the availability of certain kinds of merchandise.

But while there are strong analogies between mail-order and department store marketing, there are simultaneously major differences. One such difference is that whereas the department store has available not only the demonstration effects of its advertising, its window and interior displays, its sales clerks who, ostensibly, are able to satisfy customer requests by further demonstration, exhibit, and persuasion, the catalog, on the other hand, must rely exclusively upon layout and copy to attract attention, to stimulate interest, and to sell. It must inform precisely, whether the information pertains to price, color, material, construction, or size; it must display all available goods—even at the risk of overwhelming readers with the sheer volume of such displays; and it must provide a reasonable correspondence between goods as they will be received by customers and goods as they are illustrated and described. If it fails to perform these functions with the required accuracy the firm will not only lose sales but will suffer the additional losses of high rates of returned goods and corresponding transportation charges. Thus, in mail order, a variety of controls are desirable which are not required in conventional retailing where customers have opportunities of judging by inspection before purchasing, and the larger the scale of operations the more necessary these controls become. Thus at Sears, where sales rose to close to $250 million in 1920, substantial strides were made to provide for scientific testing and inspection of merchandise, specification buying, comparative shopping, and improvement in the production of catalogs.[49]

Since the catalog comprises the mail-order store, it follows that in the hands of active customers and prospects alike it constitutes the best appeal the house can provide and will, other things considered equal, promote orders whose dollar value will tend to be higher than those stimulated by some other form of promotion offering more limited arrays of goods. But distribution of catalogs to families with whom a company has no experience can be ruinously expensive unless undertaken on a selective basis. For the going concern, the recruiting of new customers can be most economically undertaken from among people who tend, in attitude, attributes, and characteristics, to closely resemble current customers. Therefore, it is advisable to recruit new customers from the same type of localities, occupations, income groups that characterize active patrons, and to ignore the rest.

Spiegel, May, Stern first attempted to make use of active customers as salesmen in 1908, with a plan strikingly similar to that employed by Sears, Roebuck several years earlier. Spiegel proposed to a comprehensive list of active customers that they accept ten general catalogs, distribute them to friends and neighbors whom they believed would become customers, and supply the company with the names and addresses of such distributees. Sears, more ambitious and with more capital, had provided their customer-salesmen with twenty-four books.[50] The incentives provided by Spiegel were two sets of premiums: the first set, of limited value, were distributed according to the number of names returned to the company; the second set were graded according to the volume of business received from those to whom catalogs had been given. Apparently the experiment was unproductive. The company's experience with the customer-salesman plan, however, was sufficiently favorable to encourage the adoption of the modified program previously described, the Friends' campaigns. Under this version, which continued to be employed over decades, customers were encouraged by the offer of premiums to solicit orders and/or inquiries from their friends.

In addition to the Friends' campaigns, Spiegel resorted to a variety of methods for obtaining lists of names suitable for solicitation with catalogs. One method was through advertising in magazines with national or multiple-regional circulation, offering either a gift of a catalog for those who would send in requests, or promoting a specific item of merchandise. The limited program of national magazine advertising, however, could not provide the numbers of prospects which the company required to build replacement customers and increase its net growth. To develop additional customers, it purchased name lists from commercial suppliers, postmasters' wives (it was illegal for their husbands to give out such information), labor unions, and fraternal organizations. Former customers or "paid-ups" were also aggressively recruited.

By the onset of the American entry into World War I, the average order size was rising rapidly, building to a level near $38; the result was fewer efforts to recruit replacements or new customers, but with a substantial increase in the number of individual pieces dispatched per effort. Swikard was able to establish tighter restrictions upon circulation of catalogs, which in fall 1919 were sent to over 280,000 names, and he culled the inquiry list rigorously; his largest mailing in 1919 was 522,000 announcements of the fall catalog, almost half of which was comprised of old paid-ups and new 1919 inquiries, combining the Spiegel and Martha Lane Adams lists. As a slow paralysis of economic activity began to overtake the country in the latter half of 1920, there was a sharp contraction in the average order size being received, and the sales department went quickly into action. The fall catalog announcement went out to 918,000 names, 75 percent more than the 1919 mailing, new customer lists were built up through more aggressive Friends' solicitation, and nearly 500,000 fall catalogs were distributed, the list covering inquiries, paid-ups, Friends, and active customers, with nearly 60 percent of the circulation being directed to reviving old and developing new accounts. Even this paled in comparison to 1922, when a combination sale and fall catalog announcement for Martha Lane Adams went to 3 million names, followed by half-a-million copies of the subsidiary's fall catalog. The Spiegel September sale went to over 1 million names, and the fall catalog to over 324,000. Other major distributions in fall 1922 included the Christmas Sale book, to 1,575,500 persons, and two other special sales, in August and October, to over 900,000 names each.

The company's success in wooing these customers was strongly influenced by distance and freight rates. Prior to the passage of the Parcel Post Act in 1912, the geographic limits of the market were essentially fixed. In terms of population concentration, the number of small communities, and transportation costs, the prime territories were the East North Central, West North Central, and Middle Atlantic regions, where over two-thirds of the dollar value of sales were registered over these years. It is notable, however, that although the gain was moderate, the states of the South and Southwest steadily increased in market importance for the company, their share of total sales rising from 21 percent in 1907 to over 25 percent in 1911. While there was a slight relative improvement in the volume forthcoming from the extreme reaches of the transportation limits, New England and the Mountain and Pacific states accounted for less than 8 percent of business in 1911.

Although data as to geographical distribution of sales after 1911 are inadequate to form valid judgments, there is small reason to doubt that the Parcel Post Act stimulated the southern and western markets. Prior to 1913 the rate for fourth-class mail in the United States had been one cent per ounce, with a maximum weight limit of four pounds, and relatively serious restrictions regarding the matter which could be shipped. Thus, except for relatively light articles of high value, parcel post had been prohibitively expensive as a method of transportation, regardless of the convenience of door-to-door delivery and the relative speed it afforded. Instead, express was recommended by Spiegel (and other mail-order houses) for shipments of under twenty pounds, if value, speed, and weight conditions warranted, but the overwhelming proportion of company shipments went by ordinary freight. Freight rates varied with weight and distance, but one feature that was employed to the advantage of mail-order sellers was the flat charge for all weights between ten and one hundred pounds.

Spiegel, like Sears and Ward, had long urged customers to build up orders to the maximum weight so as to reduce the ratio of freight charges to value of purchases. One effect of this had been to raise the level of an average order size, while another had encouraged the sharing of catalogs with friends or relatives so as to obtain for the houses more profitably sized units of business. But parcel post, bitterly fought by independent retailers and associations of salesmen, brought about far-reaching and important changes in the mail-order industry. The basic Act, which became effective in 1913, provided that parcels weighing up to eleven pounds with a combined length and girth of 72 inches would be delivered by the post office wherever carrier service was provided directly to the house or mailbox of addressees, and imposed a zone system (at the insistence of foes of the Act) whereby parcels of comparable weight would be charged greater postage the further removed from the sender the recipient resided.[51] The success of the Act in stimulating postal revenues and expanding markets led to successive modifications of the basic law, such that by 1914 the weight limit had been raised to fifty pounds for the first two zones from the sender to twenty pounds for further zones. The length and girth limits were also liberalized, permitting parcels up to a combined 89 inches to be sent. The basic 1913 legislation had made no provision for catalogs under the fourth-class rates, and the existing third-class charges for printed matter were a penny and one-half for each two ounces of matter (or fraction thereof), or, in terms of the standard one-pound book of Spiegel, a minimum of twelve cents per copy. But in 1917, the Act was again amended to permit the application of the fourth-class rates to printed matter weighing over eight ounces, and threw wide the doors for the distributors of big catalogs. Even the smaller Spiegel catalog could be shipped by parcel post at prices approximately 20 percent lower than the third-class rate, while the savings to a firm like Sears, Roebuck, with their multi-pound books was around 67 to 70 percent.[52]

The value to mail order of the parcel post legislation cannot be overestimated, despite the fact that, for the most part, the various managements at Sears, Ward, National Bellas Hess, and Spiegel avoided backing the legislation or supporting it in Congress. Even the zone system, intended to be restrictive to mail-order distribution, was amenable to treatment if multiple shipping points could be established and catalogs or parcels could be sent in bulk to these points by freight for quicker and cheaper reshipment through the mails from points closer to the homes of customers. Among the mail-order companies, however, only Sears and Ward effectively utilized this method on a large-scale basis, just as they were doing for general distribution through the establishment of branch plants after 1905. For Spiegel, the rate of saving on their smaller books was considered inadequate to finance the establishment of redistribution systems. This factor, of course, tended to exaggerate the disparity between Spiegel and the bigger firms in terms of market shares. The company was able to employ the quicker, more convenient, and less expensive means of fourth-class delivery to handle an increasing share of its shipments, particularly of apparel, domestics, and lighter household items, and extended the reach of the company into the further corners of its market during the years when speed of delivery tended to count more in competition than had been true during the opening years of the period.

Operations, Financing, and Reorganization 1907–1921

Chapter 5

Any number of standards may be used to measure the relative success of an enterprise. One can refer to the growing ingenuity and sophistication of its management, the efficiency of its operating techniques, and the more common financial indices such as sales volume and earnings or rate of return on investment. Measured against these and other standards, Spiegel, May, Stern experienced a period of general though uneven progress between 1907 and 1921. Having already viewed the company's merchandising activities, it is important also to review the operational side of the business and its financial ventures during this volatile period of the company's history which ended with the reorganization of Spiegel, May, Stern.

Without question the most unfortunate event of this period was the death of Arthur Spiegel in April 1916. The passing of the young and dynamic creator of the Spiegel mail-order venture was a severe blow to Spiegel, May, Stern. Arthur Spiegel's drive, in fact, was largely responsible for his untimely death. Not content with the challenge of directing his fast growing mail-order business, Arthur had expanded his horizons to include a major venture into the newly emerging motion picture industry. In 1913 he founded Equity Films in New York, which was then the capital of the industry. His prompt success with this motion picture company

108

led to the formation in 1914 of the first publicly financed film company, World Films Corporation.

The young enterpreneur at first tried to manage his three companies simultaneously, traveling to New York every weekend and returning to the Spiegel offices in Chicago early Monday morning. The strain of constantly traveling and working eighteen to twenty hours a day soon began to show. Therefore, Arthur took a temporary leave from Spiegel in 1915, but still hurried home almost every weekend to spend his few moments of relaxation with his family.

In less than a year his movie companies became major powers in the industry, but this quick success had a high cost. A very tired and weakened man, Arthur died of pneumonia at the Plaza Hotel in New York at the age of thirty-two.

The shock of Arthur Spiegel's death was not readily shrugged off within the company. On April 25, 1916, a special meeting of the directors elected Modie J. Spiegel as the new president (he continued to serve without salary), and Sidney Spiegel became, in effect, the resident partner in mail order, being elected a director and treasurer. But, as has been shown, Modie Spiegel's first love was not mail order, and the actual direction of the Company was left to Landis for the remaining years of this period. Following Arthur Spiegel's death, Frederick L. Innis returned to the company and quickly found himself appointed to the position of assistant general manager, principally concerned with the operating divisions and with seeking to improve Spiegel's service to customers.

Although the company made money in 1915, following a poor performance in 1914, it became very profitable only with the war-induced economic expansion of 1916–20, when its aggregate net earnings exceeded those of the previous decade by more than 40 percent. This, of course, was largely accomplished with inflated dollars and did not represent a proportionate improvement in the real elements of business growth, such as increased numbers of active customers or reduction of operating expenses to increased sales. Nevertheless it was the type of performance which gratified Aaron Waldheim and the Spiegel brothers if only because of the opportunity afforded to declare and receive dividends.

Waldheim's influence in management increased with Arthur

Spiegel's death, and the methods of compensation set for Landis strongly reinforced this influence. The compensation system encouraged the general manager to hold down expenses and capitalize upon increases in prices which exceeded increases in costs. During the years following Landis's appointment as general manager, his base salary moved up from $15,000 to $25,000 per year, and his incentive pay was raised to 2 percent on the net profits of Spiegel, May, Stern, and Martha Lane Adams.[1] Furthermore, even in the event that substantial dividends and bonuses reduced the improvement in surplus and reserves and deprived the corporation of the investment funds which could have gone toward building a more substantial base for growth, Landis stood to lose little. A downturn in economic activity after the war would—and did— hit the company hard if the inflated average order size collapsed and the company was left with insufficient customers to cushion this shock. But with what amounted to absentee top executives and owners who possessed complete confidence in his capacity to run the operation, even this possibility offered small potential risk.

Thus the upper structure of management at Spiegel during the period after Arthur Spiegel's death consisted of a board of directors whose objective was profit and generous dividend distribution, operating through the agency of a trusted general manager who, by compensation plan, training, and a highly developed set of responses, executed the type of program which maximized the satisfaction of his employers. To carry out the program he had skilled and highly professional subordinates in sales and operations, both of whom were tied to his own interests by generous salaries and bonus plans based upon company profits. If the buying functions were less ably performed under Sidney Spiegel's direction, this did not seem very important during the inflation years when demand for all goods was brisk. There were, of course, problems to be faced, such as improving service through more adequate order-handling and upgrading merchandise quality standards. There were other problems, also, more dimly perceived, such as the effects of the rapidly growing demand for automobiles and the implications of this new mobility factor for mail-order marketing. But the first sets of problems appeared manageable with the organization which Arthur Spiegel had built with Landis's help, and the second set would be met as they materialized.

The organization of Spiegel, May, Stern as a separate mail-order corporation with optimistic prospects for expansion had required a plant adequate to handle the operations on a basis more efficient than that afforded by the Sangamon Avenue warehouse. Shortly after the incorporation, therefore, management had decided to construct a plant in an area which afforded some opportunity of gaining a labor force and in which land values were sufficiently low to hold occupancy costs at reasonable levels. Following a careful survey, real estate was purchased in the old Bridgeport section of Chicago's southwest side. Here, on 35th Street, a block west of Morgan, construction was begun in 1907 on three buildings which were ready for occupancy early the following year.

The new plant consisted of an administration building of one story, with basement and mezzanine, and two six-story and basement warehouse and merchandise-handling buildings. All were of mill construction, providing 123,558 square feet of merchandising and 35,928 square feet of office floor space. They were constructed on 33,500 square feet of land area, complete with railroad sidings and landing docks, and serviced by a belt line.[2] Modie and Sidney Spiegel were sufficiently farsighted to acquire several parcels of land immediately adjoining the Spiegel, May, Stern real estate, and within two years another 23,000 square feet of land were purchased on the north side of 35th Street upon which was erected the North Building, a four-story and basement structure possessing 88,428 square feet of floor space, 11,572 square feet of dock area, and was designed for both warehouse and clerical use. This building was completed in 1910 and became the headquarters for Bernard Mayer & Company before 1913, and thereafter housed the Martha Lane Adams subsidiary. Except for the construction of two additional floors on B-Building, one of the original warehouses, in 1913, and the lease of additional space nearby, this was the company plant for the remainder of the period. It was within this physical setting that Landis and Innis and their associates carried out the daily operations of the company.

The functions and organization of the merchandising and sales promotion divisions have been analyzed earlier, and a similar description and analysis provided for the operation of credit management. The remaining functions—in mail order these are termed *operating*—performed by the company included the handling and filling of customer orders, correspondence, customer and corporate accounting, shipment of orders, warehousing and stock maintenance, and the mechanics of checking customer accounts and prospect mailing lists, necessary in selecting names to receive specific mailing efforts.

Technically, clerical operating divisions were responsible for the functions of mail opening and routing, order entry and adjusting, customer accounts handling, routine collection activities, preparation of sales slips, billing, posting of remittances to customer accounts, all correspondence dealing with orders, complaints, adjustments, and credits, and, at that time, with traffic functions. The latter included the scheduling of physical orders out of the house, preparation of waybills, shipping documents, and other papers necessary in freight and express transportation, and following up claims on shippers and common carriers. Physical order-handling was performed in the warehouses and on the order-filling floors, and involved handling, selection, scheduling, assembly, packaging, and other movement of physical merchandise from stock to shipping dock. The warehouse operating groups were also, of course, responsible for the receipt of merchandise from sources as well as returned goods, for its storage and movement to bins and open stock locations available to order pullers and fillers. The physical order-handling operation was also responsible for the use and maintenance of all equipment necessary to the movement of merchandise from reserve stocks to bins and pits on the stock-pulling floors, and the flow of such goods to the order assemblers and packers.

With different floors in the warehouses handling different classes of merchandise, and with final assembly and packing confined to the main floor, with ready accessibility to shipping docks, it was necessary to develop systems of moving goods from dispersed to centralized points of concentration cheaply and quickly. Moving belts, chutes, and conveyor chains were introduced during the period, although because of the importance of heavier and bulkier furniture in Spiegel sales patterns such systems and equipment were used much less than was to become the case in later years. During this period, in fact, PIT items—Pieces Individually Transported—outweighed in importance merchandise which could be assembled in a single package or shipping container, with correspondingly less weight attached to assembly and routing functions. This was less true in the physical handling of apparel merchandise, the result being separate order-filling systems and relatively greater importance attached to techniques for assembly and packing at Martha Lane Adams and Clement Company than at Spiegel, May, Stern. Further, during the first decade of operations in particular, the preponderance of PIT merchandise at Spiegel placed nowhere near the importance upon close scheduling of orders through the house that later came into being, and there was a resultant indifference to customer service. There are no surviving data, for example, concerning the time required for an order to pass through the house from the moment the order blank was opened to when the assembled package was dispatched from the shipping dock, but according to men who were active in management during those years the interval was considerably longer than in the middle 1930s, when the company became actively concerned with poor service and undertook vigorous actions to reduce the time to twenty-four hours.[3]

In part, a basic cause for relatively poor customer service stemmed from management attitudes about customers on the one hand, and a lack of appreciation for the problems of order handling on the other. For despite the problems of sales promotion in persuading the markets of the respectability and convenience of buying on installments, members of management tended to think of customers in somewhat disparaging terms. That is, such patrons needed to buy on credit because they did not have the means to pay cash, and Spiegel offered them credit; thus, if orders were filled more slowly, with considerable delays due to deficiencies in back ordering ready stocks, customers would standstill for it since they had few alternatives. Further, management was, with few exceptions, not organization minded, and a wide gulf separated the front office executives from the men responsible for warehouse and physical order-handling operations. The latter were regarded, as a subsequent chief executive officer of the company pointed out, "as plumbers. We thought that any plumber could do the job, and as a result we usually got plumbers to do it."[4]

This was much less true of the organization of the clerical operating functions during the period. One reason for the difference in attitude was the proximity of top management to the per-

formance of clerical operations in order receipt, payment of remittances, credit investigations, sales promotion control, and
collections. Another reason was that the early professionals in
management had been trained in these functions, and were given
the responsibility for their structure and operation. An obvious
result was that soon after Landis and Innis joined the company in
1907 marked improvements were made in the systems in force and
in the equipment and procedures used in carrying out the complex tasks of handling the paper flows. Equally obvious was the
caliber of personnel employed in positions of responsibility in the
clerical operating areas. Selection and training of personnel was
more carefully performed in these sections than among the warehouse labor force and supervisory staff, and while this difference
was not fully reflected by the wage scales existing for clerical and
warehouse labor, it certainly existed in the middle segments of
management.

The point of entry into the whole complicated machinery of
mail-order operations was, and is, the mail-opening division. Here
all incoming mail was received, opened, sorted according to the
nature of content, and routed to the indicated departments. Other
than communications pertaining to matters not concerned with
direct relations with customers, a relatively unimportant quantity,
incoming correspondence was sorted into five major classifications: remittances from customers on account; credit investigations; complaints and indications of customer dissatisfaction,
including return of goods purchased; responses to collection efforts; and new orders.

The nature of the order form received in mail-opening varied
with the effort which had produced the order. The company early
adopted standard order blanks which were enclosed with regular
catalogs, and later distributed special order forms for Friends'
business and other special promotional efforts. Some of these were
of different colors, or printed in distinctive styles or with different
inks to facilitate their identification. In addition, orders were received on coupons that had been included in magazine advertisements, and many came in with no form but written as part of an
ordering letter. In the event a down payment was included or a
dollar-certificate received, record of the remittance had to be
made. In the case of no-money-down orders, of course, only a

record of the order was necessary, to be sent to customer accounts for posting to ledgers.

But with respect to orders two courses of action had to be followed, depending upon whether the order was from an active or a new customer. For new customers, the order itself was sent to the credit department for investigation, a process which might require little or much time, depending upon whether a field investigation was required or further information was to be requested of the applicant. When the order had been approved for credit it was returned to the order entry sections for processing, and a new ledger would be prepared upon which was entered identifying information, the amount of the order together with the transportation charges (which were supposed to be included by the customer), the amount of the down payment received, and the record of the effort which had prompted the order. Once an order was received and approved, it went to a section that in today's terminology is called *preadjusting*, where it was analyzed for accuracy. Here a check was made to see that the remittance had been correct, including the charges for outbound transport; that the colors, sizes, and specifications had been filled in accurately; and that the prices were entered and extended to account for the number of units of different types of goods ordered. Unusual or difficult cases were referred to supervisors for action. The routine cases, however, received standardized action. A duplicate order form was made up and sales slips for the individual components of the order prepared. Although in later years the slips, or "tickets" were preprinted, requiring entry only of the quantity, during that era they were written in full by the clerk. Then the order form went to a billing operator for totaling and subsequent ledger entry, while the original order form and its accompanying tickets went to a scheduling desk where the date and time for physical order-filling to be completed was entered. These documents then went to the warehouse and were assorted according to the different departments from which merchandise stocks would be drawn.

In the warehouse, the individual department supervisors assigned tickets to stock pullers who moved up and down aisles selecting merchandise and removing it to stations to be ready for placement on belts that would carry it to the packing and assembly stations already assigned. In the event merchandise was out of stock decisions were necessary as to whether the goods would be back ordered, or whether that portion of the order would be canceled, or some substitution made. A back order was a matter of reordering identical merchandise from the source, and keeping proper records of missing items on customer accounts so that when the goods had been finally received by the house they would be sent to customers. In such cases the customer received the total bill with his order, including a notation that the missing parts would be available in some estimated future. For goods that would not be back ordered, either cancellation would occur, or some substitution might be attempted. Substitution, unless authorized by customers, was dangerous since it tended to add to returns and reduce sales and profits.

The changes which were introduced into clerical order divisions during this period by Landis and Innis were designed to reduce the opportunity for errors, improve the speed and efficiency of handling orders and customer account posting, and eliminate the performance of functions considered unduly expensive. Innis, for example, reported that when he joined the company he was impressed by the tremendous waste of labor entailed in sending receipts to customers for installments. As he recalled,

They used the old gelatin roll duplicator in those days, and they had to be kept moist in order to make out the receipts. It was a slow, dirty, and laborious job. They were using those things when they sent out receipts for payments and they were sending out receipts for every payment. It was very costly and it was very unnecessary. We could always tell people to send only money orders for which they got a receipt when they purchased it. This seemed to me a useless waste of money and I put a stop to it in a hurry.

This move reduced expenses, of course, and greatly reduced contacts with customers. Thereafter, the only acknowledgment customers got from the house (except in case of delinquencies or mail promotions) was the return of their original order form, duly completed, with sales slips. While unquestionably economical, this method surrendered the opportunity of mailing a selling piece each month with receipt of payment. Whether this would have occurred to sales management, however, is questionable. It was not until fifty years later that the adoption of new methods and new criteria in credit selling stimulated Spiegel executives to use monthly statements as a means of aggressive merchandising.

The second obvious improvement in clerical operations was contributed by Houston Landis, and involved the form of customer ledgers. Prior to 1909 all documents and records pertaining to a customer's account were kept in a large individual envelope which was filed in wood or metal cases according to state and community of residence. All entries regarding orders, remittances, collection activity, correspondence, complaints, returned goods, and the mailing of promotional pieces were kept, entered on ordinary sheets of ledger paper. Since the accounts were handled at least once monthly, for collection follow up or remittance posting or both, the physical maltreatment and ordinary wear resulted in a high rate of replacement of envelopes and ledger sheets, with resultant expense for paper and for recopying. Further, since the accounts were so frequently out of file, moving to correspondents, to posting clerks and billing operators, to other departments, the sheer size of the packets imposed a heavy and clumsy burden upon operatives. Landis disapproved of the system and with Innis's help conducted a series of experiments with alternative techniques and materials. Finally he adopted a cardboard ledger form measuring 15½-by-8½-inches which, when twice folded, comprised a neat and durable packet within which could be kept copies of correspondence. The form was printed with sections cleanly delineating space for recording data for identification, current balance, credits and charges, memoranda, and code numbers and letters corresponding to the dispatch of various pieces of sales literature. Among the advantages of the new ledgers was the elimination of cabinet filing. The new packets could be filed in open trays, easily accessible and demanding less precious space and lost employee time.

The critical importance of this modification becomes clearer when the number of accounts is considered. By mid-1913, for example, Arthur Spiegel had reported that the company had approximately 250,000 active accounts, with more being recruited. This would have required, on average, 10,000 accounts to be handled each workday which, under the old system, would have in all likelihood doubled the labor and depreciation expense in the department. While essentially different systems were in vogue at Sears, Roebuck and Montgomery Ward during this period, these being cash companies, the Landis innovation was apparently far ahead of the field for purely credit mail-order firms. Innis recalled:

In later years I had the opportunity of visiting Straus & Schram [located next door to Spiegel on 35th Street] and do you know that they were doing exactly what we had done before Landis had this brainstorm. They kept every piece of correspondence, stuffing it in big envelopes and keeping everything in file drawers. And they were bulging at the seams! I asked one of their officers how they managed to do business at all that way, and he replied that he didn't know how they could stay in business without it.

The third major improvement, contributed by Innis, occurred in the company's billing and posting operations, and resulted in the development of special-purpose posting machines by National Cash Register Company for Spiegel. During the years leading up to World War I, posting of payment media, cancellations adjustments, returned goods, and extension of account balances were done by girls operating Elliot Fisher billing machines which were cumbersome and heavy. As Reuben Don exclaimed, "If a girl worked one of those machines all day, believe me, she did hard physical work." Not only were these units slow and lacking flexibility, but they were complex, typically requiring weeks of training before an employee could attain reasonable efficiency. This was a decided disadvantage in a business so subject to seasonal variation as mail order, where November sales volume—November then being the busiest month—could exceed by sixfold that for the slowest months, with the commensurate needs to have sufficient trained personnel on hand to take care of the peak volume.

After Innis returned to the company in 1916, he arranged meetings with sales representatives of most of the major manufacturers of office equipment, Remington Rand, Burroughs, and National Cash Register, and explained and demonstrated the deficiencies of the Elliot Fisher machine. He asked them if the firms they represented could devise equipment which would be easier to operate and more flexible, permitting, for example, the posting of remittances, extension of balances, and the distribution of charges over multiple headings such as merchandise prices, transportation charges, and the like. Remington, then a typewriter manufacturer, could offer nothing helpful; and Burroughs, while offering to consider the problem, proved no more effective. Then, Innis recalled,

I made some arrangement with a National Cash Register salesman. They had a machine which they used in some of the furniture stores, but it was slow and not very flexible. It didn't serve our needs but I talked with him and another representative and they took the problem back to Ohio. It took them about eighteen months to develop something we could use in recording those remittances, but they finally produced a machine for the job and from that developed the bookkeeping machines the N.C.R. is manufacturing today. This all stemmed from the effort they made to help us solve our problem. The machine they developed for us cost about $450.

The machine was basically a cash register, without drawers and other mechanical devices useful in cash transactions, but with feeding devices and other controls so that it could post numerical data to customer ledgers and provide a means of distributing accounting data to the proper classifications desired by management. Although awkward by today's standards, the unit was a definite improvement over the machine it replaced. It was possible to train operatives on it in a fraction of the former time; better control of data was provided which permitted a tape-printed control against which the payment media could be compared at the close of a day; and it reduced the amount of exhausting labor involved in the posting process. Equally important, it was much faster in operation, thereby enabling the saving of important quantities of labor and subsequent improvement in customer service.

The substructure of the operating organizations during these years had attained a reasonable degree of uniformity with respect to supervisory personnel and numbers of workers responsible to them. As Innis remembered—no organization charts or work records were maintained—each division was headed by a manager with one assistant, and

we tried to have a supervisor for every twenty-five employees on the average, although this didn't always work out. The manager, assistant manager, and division head were supposed to see that the employees were properly trained and oriented, look after the quality of their work, recommend them for advancement; things of that sort.

The men responsible for the operating organization were confronted by a problem which is common to all such executives in mail order. That is, twice each year, with the approach of the seasonal peaks in March–April and November–December, temporary personnel had to be added to the work force, both in the warehouse and in the offices. This, of course, entailed anticipating the number of people who had to be added to each department and division, hiring these in sufficient time to provide some basic on-the-job training so that a fairly efficient ready-state could be reached by the time the flood of orders peaked, and achieve this without excessive spending. According to H. George Meinig, who became manager of the customer accounts department in 1920, top management provided for a considerable degree of individual initiative among department heads at the time, but with certain caveats.

They knew pretty well how much business was going to be produced [based on past buying behavior and the volume of sales promotion effort being planned] and how fast each department would have to act to prepare for it. At least I assume that other departments were prepared like mine was. We could make our own plans, *but you had better be prepared!* And, of course, you had better not spend too much money.

Then, following the peaks, the expanded structure had to be sharply reduced, temporary workers laid off.

These problems were intensified by the firm's location, by relatively ineffective transportation facilities for employees living outside the area, by low wages, and by long hours. Reuben Don, catalog production manager, recalled something of the wages paid when he was first employed by the company in 1907:

I started at eight dollars a week. The girls used to get raises of fifty cents a week, and they had to wait months to get one. I got up to fourteen dollars a week and then was offered a job with Chicago Mail Order Company for two dollars more. I put in my resignation and Mr. Landis called me in and told me what a wonderful opportunity I had with Spiegel; that they would meet this amount but he couldn't give it to me then because of the rule that an employee had to wait six months for a raise.

According to Innis, starting wages at Spiegel were typical of that era for the kind of skills the company required. Office workers, such as file clerks and mail openers, began at seven dollars a week. An experienced office worker earned fifteen dollars weekly. In the physical order-handling departments the starting wage was ten to twelve dollars, but raises came even less rapidly in the warehouse.

In addition to low wages, Spiegel employees worked long hours. Typically, the average work week for full-time employees was over 57 hours during the years up to 1916, falling thereafter to around 50 by 1920–21. The work week amounted to six full days beginning at eight o'clock in the morning, except for special workers in particular departments who were required to begin earlier, and ending at six in the evening, with one-half hour for lunch. During the hottest summer weeks, however, the company closed at one o'clock Saturdays. But for considerable portions of the labor force the day did not end at six o'clock. Grimly remarking upon the period, Innis said:

I remember we used to work nights. I know I wasn't home for one night for two years before ten o'clock. This was before 1914. The girls used to work three or four nights a week, and we didn't even pay them for it. They were given thirty-five cents for supper money and they had to find their own way home on the street cars.

Apparently, hours of work for employees of mail-order companies in Chicago during these years were well standardized. The nine-and-one-half-hour day, with several nights and Sunday overtime—the only pay for the latter was dinner money—was in practice at Sears, Roebuck,[5] and differential rates of pay and hours were highly unlikely at the other important companies, such as Ward, Chicago Mail Order, or the smaller ones which clustered nearby Spiegel, such as Elmer Richards and Straus & Schram. Hours tended to be even longer during periods of seasonal peaks, when the labor force was pressed to the edge of exhaustion.

In common with most enterprises of the period, management at Spiegel tended strongly to paternalism. There were amateur theatricals for employees, company sponsored athletics, picnics, and outings. Management also undertook to pension worthy old employees, but this was a gratuity, there being no organized pension system. Few members of the permanent labor force who accepted the conditions of labor and performed their jobs with the required diligence and loyalty were fired, but there were no standardized provisions for job security. Department managers and supervisors could dismiss people in most cases without recourse. Despite small pay, long hours, hard conditions of labor, the threat of unionization never seriously arose for Spiegel, not even during the troubled months of 1919 when Chicago, like other centers of American industry, was torn by strikes and lockouts. From time to time management suffered some inconvenience as the result of strikes of teamsters in the city, but since it received and shipped most merchandise by rail directly from its docks these imposed no serious hardship.

In addition to Spiegel, May, Stern's operations, the financial aspects of the company's development deserve special attention. The scale of the company's capital requirements during the years 1907–21 tended, generally, to vary with sales, although not linearly. That is, a growing body of assets were required to finance growing sales over time, but an increment in sales did not always require a matching increment in assets. For example, in 1907 and 1909 $1.00 of sales were obtained by assets of $0.73 and $0.80, respectively; but in 1912 it required $0.90 and in 1914, $1.08. During the years 1913, 1916, and 1921, $1.00 of sales required from $0.84 to $0.87, while in 1920 it needed only $0.75. It is probable, however, that the ratio of sales to assets for the years 1907–12 was also in the range $0.84 to $0.90, but because of the absence of real estate and plant data on the surviving financial records a more accurate statement of total assets can not be made. The total corporate sales shown in table 3 include Martha Lane Adams after 1913, but exclude other affiliates, while the total corporate assets include investments in all affiliates and subsidiaries. The assets for the years 1907–10 are understated for the reason given above.

3. Total corporate sales and corporate assets, in thousands of dollars, 1907–1921

Year	Assets	Sales	Year	Assets	Sales
1907	$1,102.6	$1,517.2	1915	. . .	$3,592.8
1908	1,532.9	1,933.9	1916	$3,859.4	4,441.8
1909	1,968.6	2,452.1	1917	3,856.9	4,777.5
1910	2,523.9	3,008.1	1918	. . .	5,502.2
1911	. . .	2,779.7	1919	. . .	6,794.7
1912	2,876.5	3,300.9	1920	5,447.9	7,302.4
1913	5,794.9	6,849.1	1921	3,978.0	4,690.7
1914	3,237.0	2,977.4			

Source: Corporate records, 1907–21.

In addition to providing a relationship between total assets and sales volume, the tabulation clearly reflects the very modest growth which Spiegel, May, Stern enjoyed over this period. It can be assumed that the asset account for 1910 is understated by $200,000 (a reasonable value for net land and plant). There was a compound rate of growth of slightly under 9 percent per year in assets between 1910 and 1920, and an overall gain in sales volume of about 130 percent. According to a definitive study of the development of American distribution systems, mail-order retail sales rose from $165 million in 1909 to almost $543 million in 1919, a gain of nearly 230 percent.[6] During these same ten years Sears, Roebuck increased its sales by nearly 359 percent, and its 1919 sales were over thirty-five times greater than those of Spiegel compared to the 1909 ratio of 21 to 1. Thus, except for the single year 1913, Spiegel sales (and assets) increased gradually with the national economy, reflecting the management attitudes earlier described as well as the relative efficiency with which administrative functions and promotion were performed.

It must be noted that even a moderately respectable growth requires financing, and Spiegel, May, Stern provided the preponderant share of capital formation by plowing back its own earnings into reinvestment. During the fifteen years, 1907–21, total Spiegel earnings, including the company's net income from its investments in its subsidiaries and affiliates, amounted to $4.8 million, before provision for federal income taxes. Of this amount $1.07 million was distributed in dividends, while stockholders' book equity rose by almost $2.96 million. The remaining $776,000 is impossible to trace in the absence of reliable financial records, but it is clear that income taxes could account for only a relatively small share of this difference. The growth of net worth and its relation to income is represented in exhibit 1 (see Appendix). In addition to reflecting the degree to which the company provided its own long-term capital increments out of earnings—only $60,000 in cash dividends were paid stockholders during the first ten years of operations—this exhibit indicates the highly respectable rate of net earnings to equity capital.

Information with respect to the year-end volumes of credit supplied by manufacturers and banks, together with the company's trade receivables and merchandise inventories, is provided in table 4. Suppliers' extension of credit, typically on a thirty to sixty-day basis, accounted for a relatively small proportion of short-term borrowing, with bank loans comprising the major share. The degree to which such short-term funds financed inventories and receivables varied from 32 percent to 55 percent for the years for which data are available, and that after 1913 long-term capital increased in importance in such financing. The 1921 results can probably be disregarded as atypical. The ratio for the first four years would be higher than shown if inventories had included the value of returned goods in transit and freight claims which had been done for the years after 1910. Even with such inclusion, however, it is obvious that management followed a more liberal inventory policy after 1915, although company records fail to indicate whether the reason emerged from growing inflation and a disposition to buy ahead to anticipate price changes, whether for speculative reasons or to dampen the company's own price changes, or to provide better service through reduced back orders and cancellations of customer orders.

Prior to October 1910, Spiegel, May, Stern depended upon two Chicago banks to supply the credits it required for short-term financing purposes. One of the banks was A. G. Becker & Company. In October 1910, however, with sales rising toward the $3 million level, additional funds were necessary and a special meeting of the board authorized management to extend the line of credit which had been negotiated earlier in the year with National City Bank of New York City.[7] The amount of the line or its terms were not disclosed. When a big sales drive was launched by Arthur Spiegel in 1913 and the company ran out of working capital, Ladenburg, Thalman & Company and A. G. Becker & Company guaranteed to underwrite and place promissory notes and bills of exchange for the company up to a maximum of $2.5 million. In effect this meant that the bankers would find commercial or private banking sources for company paper at regularly prevailing interest rates for such risks which, during 1913, would have been in excess of the 6.2 percent then being charged for prime commercial paper accepted on a four-to-six-month basis. The $2.5 million limit was set to restrict company activities in such a way that the estimated net worth of June 30, 1913 would not be impaired. The bankers

4. Year-end volumes of credit, receivables, and inventories, in thousands of dollars, 1907–1921

Year	Receiv-ables (1)	Inven-tories (2)	Col. (1) + Col. (2) (3)	Credit Supplied* by Manufac-turers (4)	Banks (5)	Total Credit Col. (4) + Col. (5) (6)	Credit as a % of Receivables and Inventory Col. (6) ÷ Col. (3) (7)
1907	$ 743	$202	$ 945	...	...	$ 346	36.6%
1908	993	240	1,233	...	...	671	54.4
1909	1,340	183	1,523	...	...	778	51.1
1910	1,624	178	1,802	...	...	927	51.4
1911	...	...	...	...	...	...	...
1912	1,939	280	2,219	...	...	...	...
1913	4,379	569	4,948	$776	$1,945	2,721	54.9
1914	1,895	286	2,181	134	950	1,084	49.7
1915	...	...	...	...	...	...	...
1916	1,914	608	2,522	205	610	815	32.3
1917	1,618	693	2,311	289	580	869	37.6
1918	...	...	...	...	...	...	...
1919	...	...	...	...	...	...	...
1920	2,471	939	3,410	128	1,234	1,362	39.9
1921	1,674	461	2,135	178	100	278	13.0

*Breakdown by source unavailable for 1907–1910, but aggregate data available as shown.
Source: Corporate records, 1907–21.

imposed a charge of 0.25 percent for this service. In November 1914, the company renewed its agreement with the bankers, which provided that effective December 1, 1914 the latter would place or sell notes to mature during the first six months of 1915, for a special commission of 1 percent plus the previous 0.25 percent charged. While the maximum amount of new money it guaranteed to seek placement for was $1 million, the underwriting group offered the company the option of extending the covenant until June 1, 1915 for the same commissions on the full maximum of $2.5 million.[8] After June 1915, the agreement was apparently not renewed, probably because the reduction in volume during 1914–15 diminished the company's dependence upon such accommodation.

The company's overall performance with respect to rate of growth and the rate of change in mail-order sales has been indicated. Discounting for the problems associated with installment selling, this relative performance was not particularly impressive; taking such factors into account, it was probably a good record. In terms of more conventional criteria, however, the record was nothing for which management needed to apologize. Total sales for the years 1907–21 amounted to $62.4 million and net income from all sources was $5.2 million, before the deduction of *any* taxes, yielding a profit rate on sales of 8.33 percent. Total taxes for the period, federal, state and local, amounted to $1.14 million, leaving a net profit available to management of almost $4.06 million, for a rate of 6.51 percent. A comparison of the yearly profit rates and the company's net worth after taxes is given in table 5. With respect to return on investment, a fundamental measurement of performance, the record was even more favorable. The relationship between net profit before taxes to both year-end and average net worth is shown in exhibit 1 in the Appendix. The rate of return on year-end worth after taxes, given in table 5, is without taking into account what effect the addition of real estate might have had upon net worth during the years 1907–10. For the years following 1911, however, the net worth statement included all land and plant. The notable characteristics of this aspect of financial performance are that in seven of the fifteen years the rate of return was over 20 percent, in four it was between 13 and 20 percent, and that in only one year, 1914, did the company suffer an unusual loss. The magni-

5. Annual profit rates and net worth after taxes, 1907–1921

Year	Before Taxes	After Taxes	After Tax Profit to Net Worth
1907	9.5%	8.1%	16.7%
1908	6.9	5.9	13.5
1909	15.2	12.9	27.6
1910	13.4	11.4	22.1
1911	3.9	3.3	5.7
1912	15.3	13.0	20.5
1913	10.8	9.2	22.9
1914	(28.6)	(32.9)	(50.6)
1915	4.6	3.9	6.7
1916	18.0	15.3	24.5
1917	8.9	7.6	13.0
1918	13.3	11.3	22.2
1919	17.7	15.1	28.5
1920	9.0	7.7	14.3
1921	(7.3)	(8.4)	(11.0)

Source: Corporate records, 1907–21.

tude of the 1914 disaster was rooted in the credit losses created by the marginal accounts created during the 1913 drive for expansion. The 1921 loss was moderate considering the sharp contraction of general economic activity in the United States. In comparison, Sears, Roebuck during these years was averaging substantially better than 20 percent on investment, and until 1921 profit to investment was never under 12.7 percent from 1909 forward. Montgomery Ward profit rates were somewhat below Spiegel's for the period 1914–21, and although they suffered no loss in 1914 this advantage was offset by substantial losses during the years 1920–21.

The company's utilization of earnings has already been generally indicated. During the first five years of operations all earnings were reinvested and the book value of equity rose by $996,900. At the end of 1909, however, with unapportioned surplus amounting to $580,000, the stockholders-directors voted to increase the number of capital shares to 10,000 and distribute $500,000 of surplus in a stock dividend. Distribution of the additional shares duplicated the 1907 pattern, Waldheim receiving 2,000 shares, the Spiegels

127

3,000.[9] Prior to the stock dividend the book value per share was $317.76, an increase of $199.32 over the value at the time of organization of the company.

The results for 1912 were sufficient, however, to cause the directors to declare the company's first cash dividend at their meeting in January 1913. The amount voted was 12 percent, payable in equal monthly installments during the year.[10] But, as has been noted, the rate of new account formation and commensurate selling expenses placed a heavy strain on working capital resources before the close of the spring season. With the unofficial approval of the directors, Arthur Spiegel halted dividend payments at the end of June after $60,000 had been distributed; this was formally approved the following January.[11] The restrictive covenants imposed in the financing agreement with the bankers in 1913, the heavy losses in 1914, and the modest profits the following year precluded dividend considerations, but the agreeable upturn in sales and profits in 1916 signaled a return to cash dividends. In January 1917 the directors voted an 11 percent dividend and the following year in two separate actions provided for the distribution of 18 percent, payable from 1917 earnings and surplus.[12] The dividend rate was increased again in January 1919, this time to 24 percent, and this rate was maintained consistently through June 30, 1922 despite the 1921 losses.[13]

As can be seen in table 6, the percentage of after-tax profits paid in dividends from the net earnings of 1916–20 amounted to 31.1 percent. If 1921 losses and the $120,000 in dividends paid during the first six months of 1922 are included, the rate of dividends rises to 39.5 percent of after-tax income. For the entire period through the 1922 dividend payments out of 1921 year-end surplus, however, the dividend rate was 29.2 percent. In addition to the cash

6. Dividend rates by percentage, 1907–1921

Period	After Tax Net Profits	Cash Dividends	Dividend Rate
1907–1915	$1,208,900	$ 60,000	4.96%
1916–1920	3,249,800	1,011,000	31.10
1916–1921	2,856,700	1,130,000	39.55
1907–1921	4,065,600	1,190,000	29.27

Source: Corporate records, 1907–21.

dividends received, which amounted to $238 per original share, the value of the outstanding stock per share was $354.99, or $709.98 on an original share basis. To the extent to which Spiegel shares were salable, an original $100 of stock had produced cash and book increments representing almost 848 percent.

In general, Spiegel, May, Stern and its associated affiliates and subsidiaries performed with reasonable effectiveness during the first fifteen years of their operations, making a small gain relative to total mail-order sales. In terms of profits the results were again reasonably satisfactory, although insufficient information respective to the mail-order industry prohibits drawing valid comparative conclusions. With higher prices than the cash houses, Spiegel nevertheless managed to approximate Montgomery Ward profits on investment, but fell well behind Sears, Roebuck according to this criterion and in terms of profit rate on sales. As noted earlier, the results from the individual stockholder's point of view were quite good. Although the company had suffered losses in volume and a reduction in surplus as a result of the vicious 1921 depression, it concluded the year in a relatively strong cash and working capital position with inventories worked down to manageable levels without serious speculative losses entailed. In terms of management the organization contained a small but experienced and skilled trio of managers in Landis, Innis, and Swikard, with a highly professional selling and circulation control organization operating with proven techniques. The most serious deficiencies within the organization, divided top-level direction, merchandising, and split structure for the distribution of apparel, were correctable, provided management possessed the will to improve. As the company moved into 1922 circumstances were changing rapidly for the owners and these provided the opportunity for new developments.

As the country began edging out of depression and the red ink ceased flowing so thickly on the operating statements of business firms, the Spiegels found themselves presented with an opportunity to buy out the interest of Aaron Waldheim. Waldheim was apparently pressed for cash in early 1922 as he struggled to hold together his various business and philanthropic interests. In addition, he desired to concentrate his still considerable vigor upon matters closer to his heart and home than the Chicago enterprise.

The Spiegels were delighted at the chance of acquiring complete ownership of mail order, particularly since it would permit a re-integration of that business with the Spiegel House Furnishings Company. The main obstacles were the costs of acquiring Wald-heim's shares and the means of financing the purchase. On the basis of the company's 1921 position, Waldheim's 40 percent inter-est entitled him to a claim of almost $1,420,000, and although indi-vidually the Spiegels had grown wealthy during the years since 1906 they were in no position to make such a payment from their own resources. As they had so often in the past, the Spiegels turned to A. G. Becker & Company. After a careful audit of Spie-gel, May, Stern and Spiegel House Furnishings, conducted by Price, Waterhouse & Company, and consultation with other bank-ing organizations, Becker & Company worked out a plan for finan-cial organization which was approved by all parties.

Essentially, the reorganization arrangement provided for the sale of debentures, the organization of a new corporation, a re-appraisal of physical assets, and the liquidation of all doubtful assets. Accordingly, $2.5 million in 6.5 percent gold sinking-fund debentures were purchased by the underwriters at a discount of 10 percent from face value. Of the $2.25 million which Spiegel, May, Stern received, $1,574,000 was paid to Waldheim in exchange for his interest in the company, the remaining $676,000 being re-tained as new working capital. The increase in the price paid Waldheim over the original estimate was based on the rise in sur-plus during the first half of 1922.

Simultaneously, the company's attorney obtained an Illinois charter for a new corporation which retained the old mail-order name of Spiegel, May, Stern Company, with an authorized capital of $3,000,000 of 30,000 shares, $100 par value per share. In Sep-tember the stockholders of both companies went through the for-malized routines of approving the reorganization and dissolving the old firms. The new board of directors consisted of Modie and Sidney Spiegel, Houston Landis, and Frederick L. Innis. Modie Spiegel was named president, Sidney became vice-president and treasurer, Innis was named secretary, and Harry A. Welsher, who then headed the old Spiegel, May, Stern accounting and auditing department, was named a vice-president, purely for the sake of convenience in the signing of checks and documents.[14] In keeping with their positions in a larger and ostensibly more profitable institution, both Spiegel brothers were voted salaries of $60,000. The 30,000 shares were divided equally among the four principal branches of the Spiegel family.

As can be seen in exhibit 3 (see Appendix), although the total assets of the new corporation were increased by $1,019,761, the value of net worth was diminished $740,343. And, assuming the appraised values of the Westminster building investment and the company's physical plant and realty represented market values, the new company was in a strong position. Net working capital amounted to almost $4.2 million, retail sales were strong and climbing, and Edward Swikard was busily preparing new promotional campaigns which gave management sound grounds for optimism. Indeed, the directors were so optimistic by October 1922 that they voted a dividend equal to two-thirds of 1 percent for each month in the final quarter, or $60,000 in all.[15] The only cause for sobriety was the presence of the $2.5 million debt with its annual interest charge of $16,250 and the necessity of setting aside $100,000 per year for the sinking fund. A. G. Becker and the other underwriters had not, however, imposed the burdensome restrictions with regard to maintenance of ratios of quick assets to total liabilities which had proved so embarrassing to Sears, Roebuck in 1921,[16] and the other covenants, such as forbidding of additional funded debt without the underwriters' permission, were not considered onerous in view of the company's plans at the time. There was further reason for optimism among the owners in that Sidney Spiegel, Jr. and Modie J. Spiegel, Jr. had joined the firm during the year and were gradually being introduced to the intricacies of the business. Frederick W. Spiegel, the president's oldest son, had already gone through this orientation and was currently occupied in merchandising and operations at Martha Lane Adams.

The interests of the Spiegel Brothers were not, however, modified by the reorganization. Modie Spiegel, as president of the corporation, was naturally involved in the major decisions affecting mail order, and continued to participate with Landis and Innis in negotiations with bankers for credit lines. In fact, with the termination of Waldheim's influence, the top executives quickly moved to open up new lines of credit in anticipation of a more aggressive push for additional sales volume. And as Innis later recounted,

Modie was fine at that. We went together one day to the Corn Exchange Bank. In our discussions with their president, Modie was wonderful; seemed to say just the right thing at the right time. . . . Finally Modie said, "You know what we are here for. We need some more money to keep the business going." The business was going well, but we wanted money to expand. Their president scratched his head and then said, "Well, I'll loan you a million dollars." We had gone in with the hope of getting half that. But Modie was the same whenever he went with me to New York. That time we arranged to get a line of credit of $7 million from the banks, and in every case he was polished, urbane, and impressed those he talked to.

The buying out of the Waldheim interest also revealed that the professional managers had felt constrained in earlier years, after the 1913 debacle, from being aggressive. Charles Folger recalled that when the news became general of the Spiegels' decision to buy out the Waldheim interest Houston Landis said to him, "Now we're really going to have to go out and get some volume." It was ironic that Arthur Spiegel, who had struggled vainly against the restraints, was not there to benefit in the atmosphere relieved of having to make every decision under the Waldheimian admonition, "How much do we owe the bank?"

As for Waldheim, he could not have cared less. In return for his initial investment of $225,000 he had, inside of sixteen years walked away with $1,574,000, or a capital gain of 600 percent, plus taking $476,000 in cash dividends. Even in Waldheim's world, in that low-tax, wide-open, blue-sky atmosphere of the early twentieth century this was rather fair earnings for a man whose major contribution to the enterprise had been to counsel caution. But now he was gone from Spiegel and in the more relaxed atmosphere the corps of professionals moved quickly to inaugurate plans by which they hoped to recover some of the opportunities for expansion that had been lost with Arthur Spiegel's passing.

The Fat
and Lean Years
in Mail Order
1922–1932

Chapter 6

The optimism which permeated the presidential office of Spiegel, May, Stern on a bright October morning in 1922, as the Spiegels gathered to celebrate the integration of their income producers and to elect a management to direct the reorganization, was well founded. Mail-order sales were being recorded at a rate approximately 45 percent above those of the year before, and gratifyingly better than the spring results. Retail performance was improving at an even sharper pace, moving up at a rate which would more than double the level of 1921. Further, the entire economy seemed to have passed the bottom of the depression and started the long climb up to prosperity and full employment.

At the beginning of the fourth quarter of 1922, the United States had shaken off the more ominous symptoms which had marked the postwar irritability and disillusionment. The Treaty of Versailles was history, the irrational fear of imminent bolshevism which had generated the "Big Red Scare" was fast ebbing, Sacco and Vanzetti had apparently been safely convicted, and the excesses of the Ku Klux Klan were waning.

There were, however, the automobile and the radio to bring about other kinds of revolutionary changes. The public's ownership of automobiles and use of trucks and buses had swelled enormously since the eve of the war. Total private automobile registrations in 1914 were 1.66 million plus roughly 100 trucks; by the end of 1921 registrations were 9.21 million and 1.28 million, respectively, and record production levels during 1922 would raise them to 10.7 million and 1.57 million. During the six years 1923–28 the automobile industry would produce nearly 21 million passenger cars and over 3 million trucks and buses. There was an automobile, on average, for three out of every four American households.[1] The astonishing influence of radio upon the living habits of Americans was only beginning to be felt in 1922, but even so it was developing into a craze which kept people glued to the headphones of the crude apparatus to listen to the few programs offered. And the $60 million that Americans spent in 1922 on sets and parts increased during the next six years to an aggregate of $2.5 billion.[2]

There were other things being manufactured which also strongly influenced the lives and attitudes of Americans. For example, mechanical refrigeration companies which produced 5,000 units in 1921 were manufacturing over 390,000 refrigerators annually by 1928.[3] And Americans were demanding and getting new homes and apartments at an astonishing rate. Residential, nonfarm construction in 1921 was valued at $2.1 billion, climbing to $3.36 billion in 1922. Thereafter it soared steadily to reach a peak of $5.6 billion in 1926 before falling back to $4.77 billion in 1928.[4] Nor was the building boom confined to private residences. Between 1922–28 total construction of all types in the United States amounted to over $99 billion as new commercial, governmental, and industrial buildings were raised throughout America. To this record-breaking volume was added the massive outlays of state and local governments for new highway construction and improvement, and for surfacing streets to handle the ever-growing motor vehicle population.

Certainly the new mobility which private automobiles provided profoundly affected old patterns of consumption and buying practices. Not only did people substitute automobiles for other types of durable goods, but the added mobility encouraged a steady movement of population away from the city into suburbs which ringed the major urban centers. Because of the use of the automobile and the advertisers' frantic sales messages appearing in magazines and newspapers and stridently issuing from radios, traditional habits of shopping changed quickly. Shopping centers which had grown up in railroad towns withered as the improvement of old roads or the construction of new, permitted shoppers to move conveniently to alternative sources of goods and services. As Frederick Lewis Allen observed:

Villages on Route 61 bloomed with garages, filling stations, hot-dog stands, chicken-dinner restaurants, tea-rooms, tourists' rests, camp sites, and affluence. The interurban trolley perished, or survived only as a pathetic anachronism. Railroad after railroad gave up its branch lines, or saw its revenues slowly dwindling under the competition of mammoth interurban busses and trucks snorting along six-lane concrete highways. The whole country was covered with a network of passenger business.[5]

With these changes came new patterns of retail distribution, responding to altered buying behavior which in turn was changing in response to extensive use of advertising, and to the increasing attraction of installment buying. Chain retailing spread rapidly into the small and middle-sized communities, providing fewer services to consumers but offering them standardized, nationally advertised goods at lower prices than could the traditional independent. On the other hand, advertising and effective demonstration persuaded millions to desire refrigerators, electric vacuum cleaners, toasters, radios, automobiles, new furnishings, and sporting equipment, and a more sophisticated apparatus for financing purchases sprang up to permit their acquisition on easy-payment terms. The continued development of the cinema strongly conditioned Americans to new standards of beauty, personal grooming, apparel, and consumption. What the "stars" wore, what cosmetics they used, the kind of cigarettes they smoked, and the products they recommended provoked young and old into emulation. Bobbed hair, regarded as a wartime craze which would wane when the hysteria was spent, confounded the style experts by becoming fashionable. So, also, did short skirts and sheer silk or rayon stockings. The rapid growth of the popularity of slender, youthful figures swept away earlier patterns of feminine apparel.

These changing patterns of consumption were influenced greatly by the mounting Harding-Coolidge prosperity. The gross national product, after stalling through 1922, picked up steam and by the end of 1926 was $97.7 billion, a rise of 32 percent over that of 1921.

Personal disposable income went up also, but at a somewhat slower pace, 28.6 percent for the five years, amounting to $77.4 billion in 1926. By that year unemployment had fallen to under 900,000 persons, or under 2 percent of the labor force. Further, there had been a gain in real income for most Americans. The national population rose by 8.2 percent for this period to 117.4 million, and wholesale prices, after rising to an index level of 103.3 for 1925 had fallen to 100 in 1926. All this meant, according to Department of Commerce estimates, a rise in per capita gross national product, measured in terms of 1929 prices, of almost 25 percent since 1921.[6]

Furthermore, this very substantial growth in national product and wealth was not all flowing into just a few pockets. The American rich, particularly in that low income tax era, were doing very well indeed, but there were substantial gains registered also by the middle classes and the members of the working classes. There were, however, some members of the community who were not enjoying this prosperity, farmers and blacks in particular, and some independent merchants also suffered as they experienced the hard edge of chain store competition. Perhaps a broader distribution of income would have helped, but business investment in plant, capital goods, and inventories was going at full speed, and business and the American economy were both doing very well without a "share the wealth" program. And after all, the business of America was, as Calvin Coolidge observed, business.

The business community had its detractors, H. L. Mencken and Sinclair Lewis being among the most listened to, but it was achieving for Americans more in terms of standards of living and physical comforts than any other modern economy had for its citizens. Some of the value system which had grown up around the business and moneymaking ideal was dubious and business could not duck the responsibility for it. And business institutions and techniques and businessmen themselves contributed to abominably poor taste, such as Bruce Barton's likening of Christ to the world's greatest salesman. But one could not have everything, and there was always the hope that people would tire of Rotary, Clara Bow, and the Charleston and would move on to something else. At least the economy was providing the money for any kind of taste indulgence. That, in fact, was what was intriguing to the Spiegels. Was the America of the 1920s going to continue buying from places like

Spiegel? Was the automobile going to make the mail-order market as obsolete as the horse and wagon? Were people, with larger incomes and greater shopping alternatives, going to continue to buy the kinds of things Spiegel sold at the kinds of prices Spiegel charged? Or were changes in incomes and consumer attitudes going to place new strains upon management and call forth new and creative responses?

The responses made by the company's management were, indeed, creative at times, but on other occasions they bordered on the absurd. Such wide variations in the courses pursued suggest the lack of direction in company policies which characterized the period. Business decisions were mixed with serious family rifts which also led to major changes in the company's financial structure. This financial reorganization in turn led to the addition of bankers to the board of directors and a series of muddled decisions regarding Spiegel's role in retailing and mail-order apparel sales. Certainly when the euphoric bubble of the 1920s burst, the Spiegels wished their efforts during that decade had been more soundly planned and more carefully implemented, for with the advent of the Great Depression the company was confronted with an unparalleled threat to its existence. We will first review the company's mail-order efforts and later turn to a discussion of its ventures in retailing. Both of these areas of Spiegel's operations were greatly influenced by a growing struggle between Sidney and Modie Spiegel.

The 30,000 shares of common stock issued upon the organization of the integrated company in October 1922 were originally divided so as to provide equal shares for Matilda Spiegel, her two sons, and Arthur's widow, Mae O. Spiegel. Between then and 1927, however, 2,700 of Matilda Spiegel's shares were disposed of to the other three in an interfamily arrangement. The effect of this distribution was to provide Modie Spiegel with 8,550.5 shares, or one more than his brother, Sidney, while Mae Spiegel's holding was increased to 8,100. Matilda Spiegel, of course, was by this time beyond the age where she would take any active interest in the operation of the business and Mae Spiegel, involved in her children and her community interests, was concerned only in safeguarding the value of her investment and the stream of dividends which it provided. Direction of the company was the concern of the Spiegel brothers, and as long as harmony existed between them the distribution of voting shares was unimportant.

And during the first several years following 1922 this was, in fact, the case. The division of particular interests between the brothers remained unchanged, with Sidney Spiegel headquartered at 35th Street as the resident partner in mail order, while Modie Spiegel made his office at 115 Wabash Avenue, in the main store of the small retail chain. But although both took an active interest in the direction of the enterprise, neither concerned himself with the everyday operation of the component elements of the company, at least to that degree which the literature and folklore of entrepreneurship implies. The organization of the new company resulted in the continuation of Houston E. Landis as general manager, but except when consulted about retail problems Landis restricted himself to the direction of mail order. Modie Spiegel had, since his early thirties, demonstrated an indifference to the routine concerns of a general manager and had worked through professionals whom he selected and appointed to the major administrative and branch manager positions in the retail organization.

Sidney Spiegel, on the other hand, participated somewhat more closely in the overall supervision in mail order, particularly in the areas of merchandising and operations. Officially he was head of merchandise and warehouse operation, and the mail-order general manager consulted him on policy matters which lay between routine and upper level decisions which required the attention of the president. The routines of merchandising and buying were delegated to Charles Folger, who had been with mail order since 1904 and had been a buyer since the early years on 35th Street, while direction of the warehouse was delegated to a superintendent. Sidney Spiegel took part in what planning went into the development of the various mail-order selling campaigns, including the assignment of catalog space to various categories and articles of merchandise. He was apparently also final arbiter regarding the choice of hard line goods for selection and the responsibility for such selection, including the styles, quality, and price, was invariably his. This meant a considerable latitude within which buyers and Folger and Swikard could exercise influence, but the areas of freedom had to be carefully explored and were never certain.

Sidney Spiegel was by no means unintelligent and had a rather

138

clear insight into his own limitations. At the same time, he was painfully aware of his somewhat subordinate position to his elder brother in the family and the company hierarchy, an awareness that resulted in his insistence upon being continually informed of everything and led to explosive outbursts of temper when he considered his status and prerogatives slighted. All of which was scarcely conducive to a warm, open relationship between himself and the professionals on 35th Street, or to the development of an area of security for the latter in the performance of duties over and beyond routine execution. Furthermore, Sidney Spiegel was deliberately kept apart from certain of the more sensitive zones of corporate business, particularly contacts with suppliers of capital funds. An ex post explanation, perhaps jaundiced, was that Sidney's personality and propensity to colorful language were such as to make exhibiting him to bankers somewhat risky.[7] Since he also held the title of treasurer in the corporation this was, to say the least, extraordinary.

Below the Spiegel brothers, the organization of the combined company was cleanly separated into mail-order and retail divisions. The term "integrated company" has been employed to describe the procedure wherein the family consolidated their commercial enterprises, but the term may be overstrong. Each division maintained its own identity, sharing only the common firm title. No attempt was apparently made to combine buying, credit, warehousing, selling, or general administrative functions. Overall policy and the allocation of investment funds were handled on an integrated basis. In retail, between 1922 and 1926, Albert Baum was general manager under Modie Spiegel, with a manager for each of the three branch stores appointed by the president. When the chain was expanded additional managers were appointed but their responsibilities and the chain of command through the general manager and the president remained unchanged. Within the organization there was a credit department with a retail credit manager and subordinates who handled credit passing in the branches. Handling of accounts was centralized in the main store, as were all credit review and collection activities. Retail buyers were lodged in the main store and the warehouse, such men being responsible for merchandising the departments for which they bought, for hiring sales personnel and setting wages within the range of overall retail policy. There was a central warehouse, but inventories were maintained in the branches as well, and, in addition, retail maintained its own small fleet of trucks for hauling between stores and for customer delivery.

The managerial structure in mail order, except for changes in personnel, retained the organization which had been developed after the death of Arthur Spiegel. Landis continued as general manager, with Innis in general charge of clerical-order operations, including credit and traffic. Swikard was advertising manager and responsible for catalog production, circulation, and new customer recruiting. The merchandising and warehouse operations were the responsibilities assigned to Sidney Spiegel and his assistants. But shortly after the reorganization Houston Landis suffered a paralyzing stroke and after a brief, lingering illness, died. Frederick L. Innis was appointed general manager in January 1923. Innis had excellent motivation to make Spiegel, May, Stern a profitable operation. His salary was $27,500 plus 3 percent of after-tax profits, and by 1926 the base pay had been raised to $35,000. Swikard was also placed on an incentive plan and its amount reflected the value management set upon his contributions. For 1923 his base salary was $22,500 plus 1 percent of net profit, and during the following five years this rose to $25,000 and 1.5 percent of net earnings.[8] In view of the firm's net earnings such terms could have provided an annual bonus for Swikard for the years 1923–27 of from $6,000 to $30,000, and for Innis from $19,000 to $60,000. The Spiegel brothers limited themselves to salaries of $60,000 annually during these years, deriving their share of profits from dividends.

Following the death of Landis and the promotion of Innis to general manager, a restructuring of the clerical operating hierarchy took place. To succeed him Landis chose John Cheshire, who had grown up in the customer-accounts division, and whose position there was taken by George Meinig. The credit office was directly responsible to Cheshire and was soon headed by Duncan Ferguson. The general accounting office was the responsibility of Harry A. Welsher. The reorganization had resulted in the divestiture of the Clement Company, which became the property of Modie Spiegel, but Martha Lane Adams remained a separate operation within mail order until it was liquidated in 1927, and during the remainder of its life it was directed by William A. Garvey. There were thus five strata of management within the mail-order company. Immediately below the Spiegel brothers was Innis, and in an uneven ranking below Innis were Swikard, Cheshire, and Folger, together with Garvey and Welsher. Below this rank came the various departmental managers and buyers, the warehouse superintendent and traffic chief, and then a final ranking of assistant managers and supervisors. There was, however, little comparability between the ranking of Swikard and that of Cheshire, Folger, and Garvey. Swikard was responsible to the general manager and the owners, but his unusual talents and unique contribution to Spiegel's development placed him in a separate universe, a fact attested to by his salary and profit-sharing contract. The other members of the administrative hierarchy were competent men, trained in a limited number of functions, with limited experience and perspective.

Three men in the organization were in a distinctly separate category during these years. This group was composed of the sons of Modie and Sidney Spiegel. Frederick Spiegel, the oldest son of the president had been in mail order since 1919, following a brief spell in retail. He had been pushed through what amounted to in-plant training in that period and then had been put into the Martha Lane Adams organization where he specialized in physical order-handling and its associated activities. Frederick Spiegel was ostensibly responsible to Garvey but in fact enjoyed a broad latitude commensurate with his status as the eldest son of the eldest son. Modie Spiegel's second son, Modie J. Spiegel, Jr. ("M. J." to distinguish him from his father), had joined the mail-order company just prior to the reorganization and immediately following his graduation from Dartmouth College. He had, in fact, worked for several summers prior to that for Clement Company, but in mail-order operations of a somewhat different nature than he became involved in at Spiegel, May, Stern. M. J. Spiegel was a tall, slender young man, emotionally intense, who possessed, in addition to the best education in the company, imagination and a driving energy which had not been experienced on 35th Street since the death of his uncle Arthur, whom he had revered and physically resembled.

During the first phases of his orientation M. J. Spiegel had been treated most gingerly by the various managers and division heads into whose departments he was sent. As he later recalled, he believed he was there to learn and observe, and nobody suggested that he do any work. Nobody, that is, except George Meinig, manager of customer accounts and correspondence, to whose department M. J. eventually proceeded. Meinig observed that he was not sure how the matter should be handled, but acting on his conviction that you could best learn by doing he promptly assigned M. J. to various tasks. There was an immediate clash of wills, but young Spiegel was determined to work it out himself without taking refuge in an appeal to Innis or his father. He began to work as Meinig wanted him to, and was soon completely absorbed in the methods which were being developed for reorganizing the work flows within the department. He worked with Meinig in a spirit of complete harmony and developed an association which would prove mutually beneficial a decade later. He worked with such absorption, in fact, that he developed nerve and stomach disorders and was forced to take a leave of absence which lasted almost a year. Following his return to the company he was asked by his father to direct the affairs of Clement Company, which was experiencing difficulty, and after trying to run that operation at night and on weekends while holding down a full-time position at Spiegel during the day, he left the company to assume the management at Clement until that firm was liquidated in 1927.

Sidney Spiegel, Jr. was eighteen years old when he was brought into the company by his father in 1922. Sidney, Jr. had been raised by his father and sister after his mother's death and he had apparently grown up with only sporadic control. School bored him, whether at New Trier High School or in the private eastern preparatory school to which he was consigned by his exasperated parent. Dramatics, on the other hand, fascinated him, and at a very tender age he helped organize an amateur theatrical company on the North Shore and worked in this group with actors. Unfortunately, however, his father was unsympathetic with this interest, largely because he wanted his son in a secure occupation and because he was unhappy with the prospect of his brother's sons growing up in a business which they would inevitably take over unless his own child could be brought in to play an important role. Thus Sidney, Jr. found himself part of the Spiegel, May, Stern organization and went through the processes of learning to which his cousins were exposed. But there was one exception to this, and an important one. Sidney, Jr. received his training in the areas where his father was dominant, especially warehouse operations. Unlike his cousins, he apparently never gained any direct experience in merchandising and selling, but instead confined his attention to order handling and in assisting in the development of a new method for manufacturing customer stencils that were a vast improvement in terms of the ways they could be used than alternative systems in credit mail order. Furthermore, Sidney, Jr. had inherited some of his father's personality characteristics to which he had added a substantial stock of his own. Whereas Frederick Spiegel was affable and friendly, and M. J. Spiegel possessed a charm—when he desired to use it—which was difficult to resist, Sidney, Jr. had much of the appeal of a first sergeant.

The presence of three young Spiegel males in the organization, all of whom could be expected to move into positions of real authority in the future, would probably have had harmful effects upon morale among the officers of a larger, latter-day, corporation. But, as has been pointed out, the middle hierarchy at Spiegel, May, Stern was not comparable to its counterparts at, say, Sears or Montgomery Ward, and with the exception of Swikard, who was a specialist, the only position which could be jeopardized in the top echelon was that of the general manager. And if Swikard felt any qualms about the future he did not express them. This problem, in fact, was more acutely felt by Modie and Sidney Spiegel. It was not particularly difficult for the brothers to decide that a professional manager was indicated when considering their own abilities and limitations, but the problem of trying to assess the roles to be played by their children was another matter and one which tended to produce much more heat than light between them. Adding to this highly combustible fuel was a substantial disagreement regarding the performance of the furniture stores. Baum had been succeeded by Donald Folger as manager, and when this had not turned out well, Sidney, Jr. was picked for the job and sent into retail to work under Modie. While his relationship with his cousin, M. J. Spiegel, had always been friendly, no such feeling developed between Sidney, Jr. and his uncle, a fact which deepened the growing estrangement between the Spiegel brothers.

These disagreements became so general and so acrimonious, in fact, that Matilda and Mae Spiegel found themselves more and more involved in the brothers' clashes. Since they held, between them, the balance of power within the organization, their support was being constantly solicited, a situation both embarrassing and disruptive. By 1927, Carl Meyer, a personal friend and long-time counsel for the Spiegels and their companies, was consulted. His recommendation was to have the company issue a special preferred stock which could be exchanged for the common shares of the two widows, after which the common could be retired or rendered nonvoting by agreement of the Spiegels. The effect would be to provide a steady and secure income to the widows and let the brothers work out their own solution to their disagreements. Meyer's plan caused the organization of two corporations, the M-S Company and the May-O Company, capitalized for $1 million and $1.4 million, respectively, whose assets were the 4,800 and 7,500 common shares owned by Matilda and Mae O. Spiegel.[9] The directors of Spiegel, May, Stern then issued 24,000 shares of what was called "first preferred stock," requiring a 6 percent return and carrying a cumulative provision.[10] Matilda Spiegel received 10,000 of these shares, with Mae Spiegel acquiring the rest, and Spiegel, May, Stern, in return, obtained the capital shares in the two *ad hoc* corporations.

Following the issue of the 24,000 shares of first preferred stock and the effective retirement of 12,700 voting shares which resulted from this action, a virtual managerial stalemate existed. As will be seen in the next chapter, the situation was particularly distressing in the Chicago retail operation which was a prime bone of contention between the brothers. The mail-order operation, however, continued to boom.

Well before spring 1928, and by common agreement with the other members of the family, the Spiegel brothers were looking around for a means of switching Spiegel, May, Stern from a tightly held family enterprise to a public corporation. This had to be done in such a way that the public disposition of a part of the family holdings would provide a large quantity of cash while still permitting the family to retain control of the company. This arrangement would permit the liquidation of fixed obligations and the development of additional sources of short-term capital such as to permit the continued expansion of sales and the company's share in mail order. The company's excellent earnings record was a solid

Joseph Spiegel, founder

Left to right:
Modie, Sr. and Arthur,
sons of Joseph Spiegel

Original Spiegel & Co. building
on Chicago's Wabash Avenue

The 1,000 Best Fall Styles
Selected by Martha Lane Adams
Charge Account—A Year to Pay—No References Required
Stylish Skirt, Waist and Petticoat
Only $5.48
Send Only 50c
50c Monthly If You Keep It
This 3-piece outfit—skirt, waist and petticoat—will give you wonderful wear. It will be sent you on approval, to be returned if you don't like it. The Skirt is made of heavy-weight men's wear, all-wool serge, cut with a Princess top. It is scissored down the front into an open welt seam, ending in a diagonal-cut effect. Beneath this diagonal effect are three wide plaits, giving the skirt plenty of fullness. The skirt front is also nicely trimmed with four silk soutache loops and cloth buttons. Comes in blue and black serge only. Be sure to mention color wanted. The Waist is strictly man-tailored of fine linene. The front is plaited in groups and closes by means of loops and buttons. Waist is also finished with standing collar and turned-back cuffs. This style is all that possibly could be desired for Fall. The Pretty Petticoat is made of fine mercerized sateen, has a deep flounce, which is made by means of shirring and tucking. This petticoat is guaranteed to give excellent wear. Comes in black only. In ordering from this paper be sure to give bust measure, waist measure and skirt length.
Outfit No. C4G470. Postage prepaid. Price $5.48
Spiegel, May, Stern Co
3412 Wall Street, Chicago
(494)
Mrs. Adams, who has charge of our Women's Wearing Apparel, has prepared the finest Style Book that ever was issued.
A thousand new styles, with fabrics in colors. 140 pages filled with new ideas for women.
Suits—Coats—Skirts—Waists—Dresses—Furs—Corsets—Hats—Shoes—Hosiery—Underwear—Children's Garments.
Piece Goods, Cotton, Wool and Silk.
The book is free. We ask you to write us for it.
Credit to All
Mrs. Adams is also offering terms which never before were offered. And she is here to see that you get them.
A charge account will be opened with you the moment you write for our Style Book. No references required.
A year to pay is allowed on every order. No extra price.
We quote wholesale prices, saving an average of 33 per cent.
We give free delivery.
We ship on approval, allowing return at our expense for any reason whatever.
We make to measure without extra charge. All suits, coats and skirts are made to measure and a perfect fit guaranteed. Suits made in this way are sold by us from $12.95 up.
This is a $7,000,000 concern, the largest of its kind. With Mrs. Adams in charge, we intend to make this the best shopping place in America.
Write for this mammoth Fall Style Book. Note the countless styles, the bargain prices and our matchless terms.
Fill out and mail us the coupon now.
MAIL THIS COUPON
Cut out this coupon so you won't forget. Mark the books you want. Send us the coupon and the books you want will be mailed at once, postpaid.
SPIEGEL, MAY, STERN CO.
3412 Wall Street, Chicago
Mail me your Fall Style Book. Also the books marked below.
....Furniture Book.
....Stove Book.
....Dress Goods Book.
....Jewelry Book.
Name
Address

Spiegel fashion advertisement from the Gibson Girl era

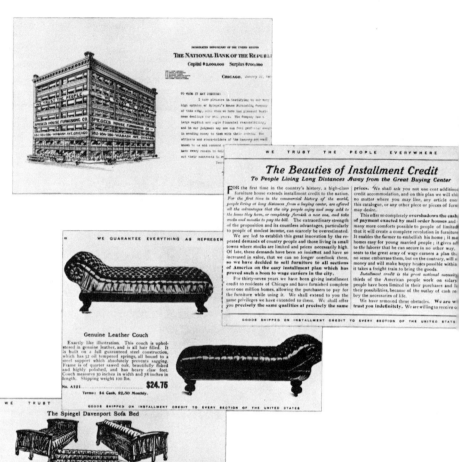

Pages from a 1905 Catalog

Modie J. Spiegel, Jr.
Photograph by Halsman

A 1920 Catalog cover

Page from a 1923
Spiegel Catalog

Spiegel Congoleum promotion
of 1926

The 1932 Fall
and Winter Catalog

A 1934 Catalog cover

Present-day Chicago headquarters building

inducement for investment bankers to undertake a public underwriting even though Spiegel was not entering the chain store field,
a factor which made Montgomery Ward so popular in financial
circles. Modie Spiegel and Innis found themselves handsomely
received in New York. The general outlines of an agreement were
arranged with the Chatham-Phenix Bank of New York, which arranged, in turn, a syndicate of other banking and financial houses
to provide the purchase price of the securities from the company
and members of the family, and for the eventual sale of securities
to investors. A new firm was incorporated in Delaware using the
same name, Spiegel, May, Stern, and on May 11, 1928 the directors
voted to turn over all assets of the old company in exchange for
the newly issued stock of the new corporation.[11]

The terms of the underwriting and the value placed on Spiegel,
May, Stern were generous. The stated net worth of the company as
of December 31, 1927 was $9,439,336, projected forward onto a
pro forma balance sheet basis as $13,092,133. The capital structure
of the new company was to consist of 70,000 shares of 6.5 percent,
cumulative, preferred stock (par value $100 per share) and 175,-
000 shares of no-par common. According to management, the company valuation of the common stock was $53 per share, which,
combined with the $7 million par value of the preferred, would
have meant a new worth of $16,275,000. This was a neat turn even
for the standards of financing in 1928 (see table 7). Because of

7. Conversion of stock, 1928

Stock	Old Shares	New Shares	Conversion New for Old
1st, 6%, preferred	24,000		
		70,000	2.333
2nd, 7%, preferred	6,000		
Common	17,700	175,000	9.887

Source: Corporate records, 1928.

the need to provide the new corporation with funds sufficient to
wipe out the existing fixed obligations and reduce current bank
loans, however, a lower rate of conversion was established with
respect to family stock holdings. According to agreements worked

out through the company's attorney the exchange of stock by members of the Spiegel family was on the following basis: 1.07527 shares of new preferred per 1 share of old 1st preferred, 1.075253 shares of new preferred per share of old 2nd preferred, 8.4954 shares of new common per share of old common. The new distribution is shown in table 8.

8. Distribution of stock, 1928

	6.5% *Preferred*	*Common*
Company	37,742	24,638
Family	32,258	150,362
Total	70,000	175,000

Source: Corporate records, 1928.

The bankers received, according to the agreement, all 70,000 shares of preferred stock, for which they paid $93 per share, and a total of 70,000 common shares which included all originally assigned to the company plus 45,362 shares from the family. At the specified price of $53 per share for the common, the amount paid Spiegel, May, Stern for these securities was $4,815,820. The various members of the Spiegel family, in turn, received $2,999,994 for their preferred and an estimated $2.4 million for their common. Of the 105,000 shares of common which remained in possession of the family, Mae O. Spiegel owned 5,096 shares with the rest divided almost equally between Modie and Sidney Spiegel or members of their respective families.[12]

The family retained the controlling interest in the company (60 percent) and the relative position of the Spiegel brothers was unchanged. The basic difference imposed by public ownership of the preferred shares and 40 percent of the common stock was that account thereafter had to be taken of what the financial community was pleased to call "the public interest." Wallace T. Perkins, Chatham-Phenix Bank's voice on the Spiegel board, in theory represented the public view. In fact, however, he represented a much more concrete group of financial middlemen, who had a keen interest in seeing that Spiegel, May, Stern made profits and paid the kind of dividends that enhanced market values and their opportunity to unload their inventory of securities at comfortable margins. Therefore, company operations had to become more formalized and be provided with a good set of manners in keeping with the new image, and managerial performance had to be tightened to impress the bankers' representative.

The new financial arrangement placed other kinds of pressures on management. The proceeds of the public sale of stock had permitted the retirement of Spiegel's fixed obligations and the reduction of current bank loans, but the company was now committed to annual outlays of $455,000 in preferred dividends. In addition, the company had incurred a noncontractual obligation to maintain earnings of at least $7 per common share. This obligation was because of a dividend policy adopted during the first meeting of the board of the new company. Thus it was hardly surprising that management was eager to undertake actions which met with the bankers' approval.

The composition of the board of directors following the public underwriting and reorganization was, in addition to Perkins and the Spiegel brothers, a mixture of Spiegel sons and management professionals. Frederick W., M. J., and Sidney M., Jr. were members as were Innis, Swikard, and Charles J. Folger. The company officers and their respective titles had remained unchanged. Thus, the 1928 board represented the major functional areas of management for the first time, and these men, also for the first time, were brought face to face with the bankers' representative, aware that he would report his own reactions to them to his associates.

The company's board and management structure soon underwent a major change, however, because of the internecine struggle between Modie and Sidney. Upon the suggestion of Wallace Perkins a study was undertaken by Innis to determine the desirability of Spiegel following Sears' and Ward's aggressive move into chain retail stores. In conducting the study Innis requested the assistance of M. J. Spiegel. M. J., while willing to assist, was highly sensitive to the interfamily relationships at the time, and since Sidney Spiegel really represented the family interest in mail order he asked Innis if his uncle had approved of this. Innis, reportedly, replied that he was the general manager and would clear it with Sidney. This, apparently, failed to mollify Sidney Spiegel who, when M. J. had returned from a field trip, berated him for going over his head and demanded an apology. This was not forthcoming, but it did prompt the suggestion that with the relationship so strained it might be better if one of the brothers bought out the interest of the other. Sidney Spiegel apparently had other wounds to lick, one of them concerning his son, and at the board meeting which followed he unaccountably burst into a furious denunciation of everything and everybody who troubled him. Wallace Perkins, initially stunned, showed a banker's urbanity, or at least the kind of urbanity the fraternity were reputed to possess before October 1929. He was reported to have quietly asked Sidney Spiegel what he proposed doing, and being told that he was about ready to sell out and get out, Perkins then said, "I think you can get a deal, Mr. Spiegel. When you are next in New York come to see me and we'll work something out."

A telephone call a few days later brought Sidney Spiegel to Chatham-Phenix and a sale was consummated for a price estimated to have been nearly $60 per share. Sidney Spiegel resigned his directorship and vice presidency, and terminated his thirty-five year association with the company in bitterness. Some of this bitterness may have disappeared after October 1929 when the price of Spiegel common began to slide, but he never could bring himself to make up his differences with the older brother and his nephews.

The final family split put a significantly different picture on the equity and management situation in the company. Instead of having a comfortable control assured by family common stock, Modie Spiegel now could command less than 35 percent of the equity. While this assured the maintenance of his position, the possession of big blocks of stock by investment firms and banks which could be mobilized in the event that the bankers became dissatisfied with the conduct of the company's affairs was a source of great concern. The departure of Sidney Spiegel and his son—the latter's resignation quickly followed his father's—left two positions on the board open, positions which were promptly filled by the election of H. G. Keogh and J. N. Darrow, two more representatives of the underwriting syndicate. The influence of the financial group could be felt in other ways, also: no overt flexing of muscles, of course, but suggestions of a type which the Spiegel inside directors found awkward to reject.

While the bankers' influence was to be felt more keenly in the company retail activities, it was also felt in mail-order operations. However, Spiegel's policies in mail order were designed to increase sales volume through a more intense use of the technique which had been employed successfully in the past. In view of the fact that the level of mail-order sales declined nationally by an estimated 16.4 percent between 1919 and 1929, this objective was by no means an easy one.[13]

During the years 1922–32, merchandising and selling in mail order were marked by four fundamental characteristics. The first was the integration of all product lines and selling effort within the company and the elimination of the last vestiges of the decentralized organization which had included subsidiaries such as Martha Lane Adams and the Clement Company. Corollary to this development was a rather confused and unsuccessful policy of abandoning apparel lines only to reintroduce them after a brief period. The second characteristic was the introduction of new products into existing lines only after their popularity had been proven. Third was the continuous search for merchandising devices capable of making a dramatic impact sufficient to increase greatly the number of active accounts and raise the value of the average order. Finally, Spiegel continued to rely heavily on its reputation as a credit house.

Before turning to a discussion of these mail-order strategies it is necessary to review briefly the market conditions of the twenties and the general attitude of Spiegel's management toward its changing environment.

Mail-order sales between 1919 and 1929 declined by $89 million, according to the estimates of Harold Barger in a National Bureau of Economic Research study, while Spiegel, May, Stern mail-order sales increased by 204 percent. Management found itself competing more directly against the dominant mail-order firms than had been the case prior to the war. A principal reason for the more generalized competition was the adoption by Sears, Roebuck and Montgomery Ward of installment credit.[14] Both of these sellers, however, tended to demand a higher down payment than did Spiegel, and carrying charges of as much as 10 to 12 percent of purchase price, and, in general, shorter maturities. Based on Barger's estimate of national mail-order sales of $543 million in 1919, Sears, Roebuck enjoyed the dominant position with 43 percent, Montgomery Ward had slightly over 18 percent, and National Bellas Hess 7.2 percent.[15] Between 1919 and 1926, the three leaders increased their sales by 23.7 percent compared to a gain by Spiegel of 22.7 percent, a slight worsening of the competitive position of the company. But during the following four years there was a significant change in the rate by which Spiegel improved its relative ranking in mail order, even though the national sales of the three leaders increased substantially. The reasons for this change are attributable to the move by the two biggest houses into direct retailing through chains of stores. This move was never seriously considered by the Spiegel management prior to 1929, and then only because of its banker-directors.

As noted earlier, the period from 1919 through 1929 was one of near revolutionary change in the distribution of consumer goods in America. One influence in this change was, of course, the rapid adoption of automobiles, motor trucks, and buses. Other factors of importance included the continued vigorous transition of the nation from a rural to urban character, the smaller but still important centrifugal effect within major metropolitan areas of tendencies of population away from the city centers to smaller suburban communities on the perimeters, the development of new consumer durable goods, the increasing importance of installment credit, and the vast increase in consumer advertising through new and traditional media of communication. To these changes, with their effects upon buying habits and consumer preferences, a major adjustment was made by the distribution system, particularly in the acceleration of retail chains and the development of branch outlets by department stores. All these factors had an important effect on mail-order distribution and the strategies of Spiegel, May, Stern.

Unfortunately, the strategies devised by the company's management paid too little attention to these major environmental forces. In the face of mounting chain store competition, the decline of rural population and small communities and their adverse impact on mail-order sales, Spiegel relied on periodic merchandising coups rather than a systematic program of creative response and adaptation.

While a very fortunate and well-timed merchandising triumph indicated the methods whereby a substantial improvement in market position could be attained, insufficient analysis of its implications and inadequate exploitation of the new customers which it attracted threw away much of the opportunity. Top management, as a result, tended to become overly concerned in a search for similar "gimmicks," although at least one member of the younger group was convinced that it was futile to expect luck to become incorporated as an operating parameter. Further, gratifying profits between 1926 and 1929 removed considerable stimulus for keeping management alert, driving, and restless. Several company veterans noted the growing tendency for the upper echelon executives to extend the lunch hour, or not to return to their offices after the midday break. Liberal incomes and low personal income taxes provided for numerous diversions and distractions. Swikard could afford to indulge his inclinations by acquiring a modest string of racehorses, and the stock market, rising to awesome heights in 1928–29, claimed the attention and money of members of the upper management group. This is not to begrudge these men their indulgence of time and attention to other matters, but only to emphasize that such characteristics were at variance with the tightly paced, forced draft behavior of executives of other large organizations of the period.

There were, of course, exceptions to this prevailing tendency. M. J. Spiegel, when he returned to Spiegel, May, Stern in 1928 following the liquidation of Clement Company, threw himself into various company problems with tremendous energy. He was particularly fascinated by an astonishingly successful 1926 campaign, and sought to identify the reasons for its success and develop these into patterns which could be followed systematically. When these interests failed to excite the sympathy of Innis and Sidney Spiegel, he succeeded in persuading them to introduce apparel into the merchandise line, and with a few catalog pages and some imaginative merchandising borrowed from his Clement experience, produced a volume of sales which astonished everyone.

But such exceptions merely highlighted the otherwise pervasive sterility. For example, despite the pleading and feverishly cunning devices resorted to by Swikard for its preservation, management junked Martha Lane Adams and its feminine apparel lines in 1927. With the exception of one year when prices were marked up only 90 percent of cost, management tenaciously adhered to 100 percent markups, in virtual ignorance of or contempt for variable pricing techniques being successfully employed by other merchants. In general, management relied upon the policies and patterns of past years as their guide for the 1920s. There was little room for what could be called effective organizational thinking in management, for the application of systematic analysis of business problems, or for the development of organizational framework capable of being expanded and directed to the achievement of company objectives which would change as an increasing share of the market and competitive pressures mounted. Unquestionably the management of the 1920s had profited from their own earlier experience in credit mail order and effectively performed the routine functions which had emerged from that experience. It failed, however, to demonstrate that it had learned that prior experience is useful principally when it is continuously reexamined within the context of contemporary change and the challenge of competition. Even more pertinently, the Spiegel management of the 1920s would be called upon to demonstrate whether it had developed, by intent or by luck, a resilience sufficient to absorb a major crisis and survive. The depression ushered in by the stock market disaster of 1929 would put it to just that test.

One of the major characteristics of mail-order policies was an outgrowth of the sterility of management's thinking. With the exception of Arthur Spiegel and Edward L. Swikard, Spiegel's management traditionally had little enthusiasm or respect for soft goods in general and for apparel in particular. Thus when the reorganization of 1922 occurred, the directors lost no time in disposing of the interest in Clement Company. Of the 250 shares which Spiegel, May, Stern owned of Clement stock, Mrs. Matilda Spiegel, Mae O. Spiegel, and Sidney M. Spiegel each acquired 83.33 shares. Modie Spiegel, immediately moved to acquire complete ownership of Clement, buying out the Regensburg interest in 1923 after Waldheim's claims on the company had been satisfied in the general settlement of 1922. He brought his two sons, Frederick and M. J. into the firm, the former as vice president, the latter as secretary and treasurer. Although Frederick's position was largely honorary, M. J. became directly involved in 1925 when he became general manager. The sale of Clement to Modie Spiegel took Spiegel, May, Stern out of men's wear and, except for the occasional offer of such goods in special merchandising efforts, no attempt was made to reenter the field until M. J. Spiegel returned to the company in 1928. Thus, in 1923 the company was left with only Martha Lane Adams to distribute feminine apparel and other soft goods.

From the beginning in 1922, Martha Lane Adams found itself struggling against two formidable obstacles. The first of these was the stiff competition being offered by competitive changes which affected the retailing of women's wear, particularly the inroads of the chains into the company's traditional small-town markets, with the improved merchandising, fashion and style emphasis, and low prices which characterized integrated retailing. Data for earlier years are lacking but by 1929 multi-unit organizations were distributing 28 percent of total retail sales of women's dress and accessory shops, with integrated department stores and mixed apparel chains accounting for important proportions. The swelling tendencies toward centralized apparel distribution, with its accelerating tempo of fashion change and style consciousness, pressed hard on the hitherto more leisurely pace of mail-order distribution, broadening the avenues for error in merchandise selection prior to the distribution of the seasonal catalogs, and placing new pressures on buyers and merchandise management. One indicator of importance in the otherwise scant company data for the period reflects the magnitude of this problem, the ratio of returned and unsold goods to net sales. In 1922 this ratio was 24 percent, 28 percent in 1923, 25.6 percent in 1924–25, and 36 percent in 1926. The situation was not helped by the stubborn refusal of management to meet the new competition, much of it based on price, by modification of the traditional markup policy. Whereas the estimate of retail margins for all apparel sales (no separation into men's, women's, and children's lines is available) was 31.8 percent in 1919 and 34.1 percent in 1929, Martha Lane Adams gross margins hovered around 50 percent of net sales for 1922–25, and fell to 47 percent only in 1926, the subsidiary's last full year of operation.[16] Coupled with these discouraging factors was the all too evident attitude of top management that apparel was living on borrowed time.

Yet despite elements which could hardly encourage a high morale among buyers and second-round officers at Martha Lane

Adams, the subsidiary's sales contributed importantly to overall volume for the company through 1925 and the operation more than broke even for the five years 1922–26 (see table 9). The 1926

9. Martha Lane Adams sales and profits, in thousands of dollars, 1922–1926

Year	Net Sales	Percentage of S. M. S. Sales	Gross Merchandising Profit	Percentage of Sales	Net Profit (Loss)	Percentage of Sales
1922	$1,999.0	52.2%	$1,017.5	50.9%	($ 21.7)	(1.1%)
1923	2,437.6	31.4	1,197.4	49.1	116.5	4.8
1924	2,109.4	24.5	1,081.9	51.3	274.0	13.0
1925	1,761.9	21.1	837.6	47.5	(149.4)	(8.5)
1926	719.0	5.5	338.9	47.3	(107.4)	(14.9)

Source: Corporate records, 1922–26.

results, however, are distorted as a result of the actions undertaken to close down the operation and the increased overhead charges which were deliberately sought against a declining volume of sales.

There was little rationale for the decision to get out of the women's wear lines even though the abandonment of the subsidiary and a consolidation of merchandising, selling, and operational effort in one company under a unified management was a move too long delayed. It is obvious that even under a divided operational arrangement, with substantial duplication of functions and personnel and consequent waste, women's apparel contributed profits to the company. While an improved effort in buying and merchandising the lines was apparently called for, with better controls over quality and more careful merchandise forward planning, this appears to possess greater advantages to the organization than throwing away millions of dollars of sales and thousands of customers. Edward Swikard also was of this mind and resisted the Spiegels' decision to the extent of his influence and capacity. Even M. J. Spiegel, then immersed in trying to save the Clement Company whose future had been made bleak by a decision of Spiegel, May, Stern to withdraw the permission to use company mailing lists, was unable to influence the management. The decision to close the subsidiary was made in 1926 and in May

1927 all assets were transferred to the parent company.[17] Martha Lane Adams enjoyed a strictly formal existence until May 12, 1928, when it was officially dissolved. Thus, by May 1927 Spiegel, May, Stern Company was back in the position it had been in 1906, with a chain of Chicago furniture stores and a mail-order division specializing in hard lines and without a product representation in the important apparel and soft goods fields.

The inconsistency of management policies and leadership, however, is suggested by the fact that this withdrawal from apparel was short lived. When M. J. Spiegel returned to full-time duty at Spiegel, Innis assigned him to the men's wear area. Management had been persuaded by Swikard to offer some men's clothing in the June 1928 sales book. Not much merchandise, of course, a few shirts and hose, a few pairs of shoes, some undergarments and work pants, but it reversed the decision made in 1927 to abandon apparel entirely. Thus, M. J. Spiegel was appointed merchandise manager for men's wear and he was given an office in the old Martha Lane Adams building. His response was much beyond Innis's expectations, or M. J.'s own expectations for that matter. Six pages of men's and boys' wear were included in the fall catalog, with a few models of suits and coats, jackets, sweaters, and ties added to the June coverage. There were also a few pages of women's articles, dress goods, handbags, and some jewelry items. The merchandise had been carefully selected from the point of view of M. J. Spiegel's concept of the Spiegel customer group, and sales of over $1 million were produced, approximately 6 percent of annual volume in return for slightly over 2.2 percent of annual catalog pages.

Based upon this triumph M. J. could successfully claim additional catalog space in 1929 for men's and boys' wear—twenty pages—and in addition there were thirty-six pages of women's articles and five pages of girls', children's and infants' wear. The women's line was broadly comprehensive, including dresses, suits, and coats, sports and smallware, shoes and hats.

In the fall 1929 catalog women's lines were expanded to fifty-four pages, to which were added four pages of cosmetics and beauty aids. These items, together with several models of women's coats and dresses, were illustrated in good three-color print. The fall book also featured a complete line of winter coats, mostly wool but including various types of fur. There were standard muskrat ($197.50 with a raccoon collar), coney, lamb, and opossum at $159.50 and up, but smaller budgets had their choice of such exotic offerings as "Iceland beaver" or "chinchilla coney" at $19.95 and $21.85, respectively, or "Manchurian wolf dog" for $37.95.

This, of course, was the peak. With the coming of depression the catalog was itself reduced in size and all apparel space contracted with it. But apparel had proved itself and by the late years of the period was commanding 40 percent and more of total catalog space.

While the Spiegel executives were slow to recognize the importance of apparel and soft goods, they had thoroughly learned the basic mail-order lesson that it was not their function to pioneer new merchandise or to waste precious catalog space introducing new product ideas and educating customers as to their advantages. And this was the second major characteristic of the company's mail-order efforts during this period. When new products were featured in the catalogs or special sales efforts, it was certain that a substantial degree of acceptance had already been achieved as a result of the work of other merchants and the investments of manufacturers in national advertising campaigns. This phenomenon was readily observable in the timing of the products which entered the catalogs after 1922. In keeping with national consumption trends these were mostly confined to the automobile, radio, and light appliance fields. Within the latter the tendency was to introduce equipment of a household work-saving nature.

Although there were in excess of 17.5 million automobiles registered in the United States at the time, Spiegel did not offer its first automobile accessory until April 1926, and then in a sale book rather than a seasonal catalog. The item was a six-volt, eleven-plate, 110 ampere automobile battery priced at $14.95, which offered the additional advantage of being adaptable to radios. Two months later, however, the company was sufficiently aware of the automobile revolution to offer in its "Good Luck Wishbone" sale a broader variety of auto accessories.

The lag between the first general consumer acceptance of the product and the date when it was introduced into the company's merchandise line was much shorter for radio than for automobiles. The initial units of radio equipment promoted by Spiegel were a

24-inch loud speaker, a 14.75-inch bell-type speaker, and a receiver headphone set in the "Bull's Eye Sale" of April 1926, an
effort sent to a list of 1,667,000 names. In the fall catalog of that
same year, these same items were included in addition to cabinet
speakers, charges, static eliminators, tube "rejuvenators," cable
units, home soldering kits, serial wire, receiver cabinets, and dry
and wet batteries. But no receiver sets. These were not introduced
until fall 1929 when they were featured in the catalog in a special
two-page foldout promotion inside the front cover, which was
the equivalent to four catalog pages but gave the impression that
management had not quite made up its mind whether radio was
here to stay.

In the field of electrical home appliances Spiegel had a representative offering early in the period. The first electric hand iron
made its way into the fall 1922 catalog and was being offered in
several sizes and models the following year. In the fall catalog,
1924, the iron was joined by various other appliances. Noteworthy
were an electric toaster ($3.95), a waffle iron ($8.95), a small
electric stove and a toaster ($2.50 and $2.65, respectively), an
electric curling iron ($1.98), and a room heater ($8.45). The same
catalog featured electric percolators and percolator sets, the single
units selling for $4.95 and the sets, aluminum and nickel plate, for
$11.25 and $28.95. In 1926 the company was offering a combination electric percolator, toaster, and griddle tied in with a break-
fast or dinner set, all for $17.95, but apparently enjoyed little suc-
cess with this contribution to America's dining ease.

Among the larger appliances, laundry equipment, refrigeration,
cooking, and heating units, progress took place at a much slower
pace. Management had introduced a very few gas cooking stoves
during the 1921–22 era, and continued to maintain a very narrow
selection of such units during the rest of this period. The basic
line of cooking and heating equipment, however, remained virtually unchanged from the previous decade: coal and woodburning
units predominated, with some oil and kerosene types filling out
the line. The sole improvement of these units was the simplification of design, probably in response to a growing refusal of American housewives to be burdened with equipment which was as
difficult to clean and maintain as the earlier monsters. In the field
of refrigeration the sole concession Spiegel made to the times was

in adopting a steel icebox, a clean-lined, efficient unit, but not mechanical. All the rest, as in previous periods, were the familiar wooden, zinc or metal-lined ice chests of various capacities. But, as was noted earlier, large appliances lent themselves more to retail than to mail-order distribution. The price of such merchandise was large in terms of the household budgets of average-income earners in that period, a circumstance which implied considerable consumer shopping and consideration before buying. This could be more readily done in retail stores than through investigation of catalog descriptions. Further, the problems associated with servicing and repair of large appliances inhibited customers from purchasing through mail-order houses which could provide no such facilities. Sears and Ward overcame this problem by their shifts into retail, and subsequently—Sears in particular—developed a thriving business in big appliances.

Management's failure to compete effectively in major appliances was, like many of Spiegel's other shortcomings, attributable to the company's reliance on periodic merchandising campaigns created by Edward Swikard. Prior to the reorganization of 1922, mail order had been forced to increase the pace of its efforts to obtain additional customers and augment the amounts customers spent with the house in an attempt to offset the sharp contraction of sales which resulted from the 1921 depression. Expansion of sales during the 1920s depended upon the ability of mail-order selling to overcome competitive disadvantages associated with the company's relatively narrow product line and rigid pricing structure, as well as growing disadvantages in terms of increased competition in retailing and shifting consumer buying habits.

The burden which the management decisions—both positive and negative—thrust upon the mail-order selling division was therefore immense, and the importance of Swikard in the organization was enhanced. Sales expansion in a period of relative price stability entailed adding new customers at a considerably more rapid rate than old customers discontinued buying, while simultaneously pushing up the average annual expenditure of newly added patrons as soon as they had proven themselves as credit risks. To increase the flow of new customers it was necessary to extend the market areas, to intensify the exploitation within a given area, or both. To stimulate larger orders from customers it was necessary to deliver to them a sufficient quantity of effective selling literature, and to make it effective demanded some combination of merchandising and credit appeals sufficiently attractive to counterbalance the limitations of product lines and noncompetitive prices. Installment credit continued to be the main merchandising tool. Nevertheless, management still pursued a policy which abruptly increased the down payment requirement for orders beyond a given size and continued its insistence that each order by a customer be paid for separately; in other words, the company refused to adopt the add-on feature previously proposed by Swikard. Since other mail-order competitors did not adopt the add-on until after 1929, its use could have provided the company with a significant new dimension to its advantageous installment plan, which permitted *all* merchandise to be bought on terms as long as the minimum order was five dollars.

Edward Swikard, now in his early forties, was unquestionably the most able and creative individual in the upper echelon of Spiegel management and probably one of the truly gifted figures in mail-order promotion. Except for preparing the editorials and developing the selling plan outlines, he concerned himself little with the routine preparation of copy, or other details. But he put together the overall selling themes of the catalog and integrated the campaigns, and he had an instinctive feel for the promotional capability of merchandise in terms of the audience which would receive the literature. When he worked it was with a burning intensity which seemed to consume his energies, dictating pages of material, pulling ideas out of the experience of buyers and merchandisers and the graphic artists from the commercial studios which were under contract to the company. When these outbursts were spent he seemed visibly to deflate and sink back into lethargy, reading detective stories or the racing form and stock market reports, stirring only to consult the trainer of the few racehorses he owned. His bearing in the company was lordly, earning him the sobriquet, "The Baron."

Swikard's continuing interest was in circulation, in developing means of evaluating customer productivity, and in searching for techniques which would permit more economic distribution of sales-maximizing literature. Thus he was engaged in experiments with different categories of customers and new prospects, with different geographical areas, between communities of various population sizes, and with market receptivity of different types of merchandise in promotional flyers. To provide improved controls in the distribution of literature, that is, the concentration of mailings to persons who provided orders, he stimulated the search for equipment that would permit a quick reference to customer behavior responding to various mailing efforts. This was to lead to the development of the Selectograph machine for punching indications into the frame of customer stencils. Unfortunately, Swikard had little command of accounting and particularly statistical techniques; thus, while he accumulated a substantial stock of information which was useful in the selection of names for solicitation, it was not handled on a systematic and accumulative basis.

During 1922 Swikard had relied upon the previously described attempt to develop a productive list of new prospect names by offers of free trinkets to persons who would recommend others they believed to be potential buyers. Despite heavy mailings during the year this concept proved sterile. Then, in 1923, he changed direction abruptly and launched one of the most successful merchandising campaigns in mail-order history. Instead of the trinket offer, he circulated a large flyer, 17½-by-26-inches in size, printed in two colors, offering four big merchandise promotions. These included a thirty-seven piece aluminum kitchenware set, totaling twenty pounds in weight, for $13.95; a variety of rugs in eight patterns and styles; a massive four-piece living room set for $82.20; and a 9-by-12-foot Gold Congoleum art rug. The Congoleum was offered in a blue and gray tile pattern which, with three 18-by-36-inch matching pieces, was offered for $15.95. This mailing went to 174,900 old customers in January. He also got out another large flyer a month later, featuring a 9-by-12 fiber rug for $18.85 with a small 18-by-36-inch rug free, terms one dollar down and a thirty-day free trial offer. The second mailing went to 492,675 names, combining old customer lists and catalog inquiries from the previous fall. In both cases Swikard was experimenting, testing to see whether prospects would respond more favorably to the offer of good merchandise at a bargain price than they had to the 1922 concepts.

While the response to the fiber rug offer was indifferent, the reaction to the January promotion was unexpectedly good, particularly to the aluminum set and the Congoleum rug. How consumers judged the value of the kitchenware is uncertain, but there was no mistaking the criterion for the Congoleum. Congoleum-Nairn's advertisement in a national magazine in January 1923 featured the 9-by-12-foot rug at a price of $16.20, while the small rugs were priced at $0.50, or a total of $17.70 for the same set which Spiegel offered for $1.75 less.[18] In late March and April 1923, Swikard got out another huge flyer, the Congoleum rug set featured on one side, an offer of the "Home Lover's Big Bargain Book" on the other. In addition to the approximately 2,240,000 flyers mailed, the offer was repeated in coupon advertising in several national magazines that spring, and in a small selection of trade papers. In all promotions the rugs were obtainable for one dollar down, including the thirty-day free trial offer privilege, and with each order filled the customer received a note and order blank, acknowledging receipt of the order and requesting that the blank be given to some friend who might wish to partake of the bargain.

There was no possibility of mistaking the effects of the aluminum and Congoleum promotions. With the catalog virtually unchanged over that of the previous year, monthly sales for the first three months of 1923 were more than double those of the corresponding period in 1922, and for each of the first five months were the highest the company had ever enjoyed. Unadjusted net sales for the spring were over $5.1 million, more than 34 percent above those for all of 1922. During the fall season Swikard got out heavy mailings of similar literature, including a sixteen-page booklet restricted exclusively to Congoleum products. In this booklet the offer had been somewhat modified as a result of the increase in Congoleum's selling prices. The manufacturers had increased the price of its 9-by-12 rug to $18, and maintained the price of the 18-by-36-inch rugs, making a total outlay of $19.50 when the set of four rugs was purchased at retail, compared to the price of $17.95 Spiegel charged for the set. This reduced the comparative Spiegel advantage to $1.55. Despite this, substantial volume was produced, with only August sales failing to set new monthly records. And although for the entire economy 1923 improved by approximately 16 percent above 1922, Spiegel mail-order sales increased by over 100 percent.

Extensive mailings, running from four to over six million pieces, plus favorable economic trends and liberal credit terms succeeded in pushing company mail-order sales up 11 percent more in 1924, but during 1925 the steam had gone out of the Congoleum appeal and sales in that year slumped almost 4 percent below the previous year's level. Swikard was not, however, convinced that Congoleum had suddenly lost its attractiveness to American housewives or that the market was saturated. If the price difference between what Spiegel offered and what retailers set could be made patently obvious, this type of promotion could still be counted on to bring in large numbers of first buyers and stimulate old customers to step up the rate of their regular buying. His successes in 1923–24 persuaded Sidney Spiegel and Frederick Innis to this point of view, and a price of $9.75 was set on the same four-piece Congoleum combination, but limiting it to one design and the blue and gray color pattern. By this time national Congoleum advertising had reduced the price of the big rug also, but the Spiegel price was now six dollars under competitive retail prices. In the spring 1926, backed by magazine test advertising a special mailer went out to almost 9,500,000 new prospect names. Over three million of these were R.F.D. selections, over 2,500,000 were registered owners of low-priced automobiles, and the rest consisted of inquiries, stencil-test names, and lists procured from the Polk Company. The flyer featured, in addition to Congoleum, two other items of merchandise, but this was pure embellishment. Congoleum was the bargain.

In view of the 1923 results, the buying division had set up a very large open-to-buy for Congoleum and ensured the steady delivery of products from the manufacturer. Additional warehouse help and supplements in the clerical order divisions were provided, so management was prepared for a flood of orders. They were not, however, prepared for the avalanche of business which this promotion and successive efforts, including contests, produced. The initial order to the manufacturer was for 50,000 units, but these vanished during the first few weeks after the first announcement. Thereafter the company handled deliveries on a mass scale at extremely low handling costs. Frederick W. Spiegel remembered that rugs were received from Congoleum-Nairn in freight cars.

They came in carload lots on the old Chicago-Joliet railroad, and each car had 998 rugs. The mailing labels, postage stickers, and all that were prepared for each order in the offices. Then they handed some guy from the warehouse 998 addressed labels, a pail of glue, and a brush. When a freight car arrived on the siding he went in and went to work. He didn't have to count the rugs because he knew he had just the right number of labels. As they came off the car he slapped the label on the package and it was pushed off on the dock, ready to be transported out to the freight station or post office. Not a rug came into the warehouse; we didn't have any warehousing problems and didn't have to double handle the things. If you had one label over you had a rug short; if he was a label shy there was one more rug left over.

As it turned out even, with the substantial price reduction, the volume of orders Spiegel made to the manufacturer cut the delivered price so much that the company still realized its regular markup, and with the very low handling costs entailed, the realized profit on over 200,000 transactions was breathtaking. Whereas the 1923 promotions had stimulated a sales increase of $3.9 million in mail order, the 1926 Congoleum campaign produced a rise of $4.7 million. New monthly volume records were set except for August, and the spring total of over $7 million came within 16 percent of equaling the aggregate 1925 volume.

It would be difficult to expect more from a promotional idea and its crisp follow-up execution. In the spring 1926 catalog Swikard set up a room-planning contest, the objective being for customers to offer plans for furnishing a home on an income of $20 per week. Five thousand dollars was offered in prizes, and with Congoleum rugs available at $9.75 there was a real possibility for a contestant to come up with interesting suggestions. The campaign continued into 1927, combining Congoleum with various other merchandise, rag rugs, rocking chairs, daybeds, and kitchenware sets, although the number of mailings tapered off, falling back to around six million pieces for each promotion.

It was also difficult to see how the success of the 1926 campaign and its 1927 follow-up could have led to anything except a continued rapid expansion volume of business in successive years. The Swikard achievement had provided the company with several hundred thousand new customers, patrons who, as he later recounted, were so delighted with the bargain and so afraid of losing the merchandise through some accident, such as a temporary layoff which would make it impossible to meet installments, that they paid off the purchase within a few months instead of

163

utilizing the full period of repayment.[19] The merchandise they had received was of good quality, marked well below current retail prices of alternative suppliers, and they had been able to buy on dollar-down terms without burdensome red tape, awkward minimums, and irritating delays in delivery. Thus their initial impression of Spiegel was highly favorable, and they should have constituted a huge pool of ready business, ready for effective promotional follow-up exploitation. This did not happen, or at least it did not happen quickly or effectively enough. And in itself this failure to act is almost inexplicable. Perhaps it was because top management was so busy congratulating itself and counting the profits that it had no time to consider the future business implications of the promotion.

It is equally difficult to ascertain the responsibility of individuals for this oversight. A good working hypothesis would take into consideration that sales volume was increasing steadily after 1925, that previously used ideas continued to bring in new customers and that repetitive patterns of catalog distribution, much of it wasted on former customers who had discontinued buying, brought average customer orders back over the twenty-dollar mark. Without much doubt this generated a substantial managerial complacency, but it still fails to explain why Swikard, with his keen interest in circulation and the experience of his tests behind him, failed to exploit properly the new opportunities. In view of his later actions, after mid-1932, it is reasonable to presume that the failure was less the fault of Swikard than that of his seniors in rank. For this group, there was undoubtedly an intellectual awareness of the need for building up new account openings more rapidly than attrition wore away active patrons, but this was never translated into operational terms. Not, at least, to the extent of investing in new account development on a consistent basis. Top management ideas in distribution were, as M. J. Spiegel later observed, confined to such strategies as "let's send out a million sales books to the 1920 paid-ups." Against this view Swikard was unavailing; it would require a surer and more ruthless hand at the tiller before the poverty of such thinking and such policy would be exposed and discarded.

The company achieved gains in sales and customer receivables, both as a result of the successful exploitation of Swikard's new customer recruiting campaigns and the unsystematic distribution of literature which followed these to build the size of average customer orders, and because of a continuation of the proven techniques of merchandising credit which had been developed through the years prior to 1922. That is, providing liberal no-money-down terms to active customers, particularly the segment of elite live accounts classed as "preferred customers," extended use of the thirty-day free trial offer, and low down payments to both new prospects originally contacted and to the more select lists which responses had culled from the original group of contacts. In addition, contract maturities were adjusted to correspond with experience and management objectives, being liberalized during the years 1926–30, then slowly constricted in 1931–32. Also, more aggressive techniques were utilized to stimulate consumers to buy on credit and to make more use of credit to gratify their wants.

Throughout the period management continued to demonstrate that whatever its other merchandising deficiencies it knew how and where to merchandise credit. For example, in the spring catalog 1923 the central theme impressed upon readers was the ease of opening an account at Spiegel. As a matter of fact the editorial read, "the first thing we want to impress upon you is that your *credit account* is now open. The minute we mail this catalog we enter your name on our books as a *charge account customer*. You don't have to write us or make any arrangements of any kind in advance." The charge account, of course, was the installment plan, since the company during these years did not operate the conventional charge account credit system. But this type of arrangement was coordinated with the message that "we don't charge extra for credit," and the emphasis that no discount was made for cash. Cash sales, in fact, were discouraged by every means, although when a customer insisted upon paying cash his account was treated as an installment sale and he was immediately classified as a paid-up.

There is little doubt that compared with most distributors of consumer goods with which it competed, Spiegel evolved relatively smooth, easy, and efficient handling of credit sales. During the Innis regime many of the successive series of credit look-ups and detailed entries in customer account records were simplified and eliminated. The principal source of delay in servicing a customer order was the initial investigation. In general, the house relied upon the techniques adopted in the previous period, that is, used investigation correspondents in different localities to provide management with the data upon which credit could be approved or rejected. This service was supplemented by the use of brief reports provided by one or more of several commercial organizations in which Spiegel had a financial interest. For new customer orders, generally, a delay of from three days to one week could be expected before the order was filled and shipped, or before the applicant was told that the company could not do business with him or required a larger down payment. But one element, letters of reference, was never required, and the credit application itself tended to become simpler over time.

The spring 1927 catalog is representative of the credit information sought during this period. The questions on the order form-questionnaire were:

> Have you bought from us (or Martha Lane Adams) before.
> White or colored?
> Occupation?
> Amount of weekly earnings?
> How long with present employer?
> Employer's name?
> Age of man? Age of wife?
> Number of children?
> Do your rent, board, or own place of residence?
> If not resident of present town for one year, in what town have you lived for one year or more?
> If you have moved since last ordering from us, what was your old address?

A comparison of this questionnaire with earlier models attests to the enhanced simplicity of the later type, and provides a rough indication of the relative weight of occupational, family size, income, and living condition data in the company's evaluations. Evidently, however, there was no systematic attempt to evaluate the efficiency of questions in the screening process, or to determine whether the judgment of the questionnaire was born out by experience with individual customers or groups. Objective research in credit criteria and behavior was still some years in the offing. In addition, the procedures for reviewing accounts and initiating collection follow-ups remained essentially unchanged from earlier years. Exhibit 4 (see Appendix) reveals, however, that bad debts and charge-offs were not a serious problem.

While matters of credit remained relatively uncomplicated, clerical and physical order-handling functions within the company and the detailed activities associated with customer accounting were generally more complex during this period than in earlier years. This condition resulted from the duplicate organizations in the Spiegel mail-order division, the Martha Lane Adams division, and the Chicago retail furniture division. After Martha Lane Adams was closed in 1927 and its office and warehouse functions consolidated with those of Spiegel mail order, this duplication was greatly reduced, but a venture into retailing home appliances, which was inaugurated two years later, did nothing to continue this simplification. Only in the final years of the period, when the company's retail ventures were liquidated, was a relatively simple operation worked out, but under depression conditions even this was not efficient, primarily because of the rise in fixed costs relative to total income.

During these years Spiegel's mail-order plant technology remained roughly constant, and with new customer accounts, sales, and physical inventory increasing, the physical plant quickly became a bottleneck. Ideally, additional plant facilities should have been added in the immediate vicinity of the 35th Street layout to keep interbuilding transfer of goods and personnel to a minimum. The company's property holding was sufficient for the construction of another building adjacent to the existing warehouses, or, alternatively, additional floors could have been added to the Martha Lane Adams building. But when sales jumped sharply in 1923 under the stimulus of the first Congoleum campaign, management was in no position to handle the investment which would have been required to build new facilities. The gold note indenture and the interest and sinking fund requirements of the 1922 financing effectively precluded additional long-term debt. When space limitations became intolerable the company leased 60,000 square feet of warehouse space in a building at 20th Street and Morgan, and transferred certain storage and mailing functions to that site. While this met the space needs for several years, it involved higher operating costs than would a more convenient location.

In 1928, following the public underwriting and the great surge in volume which the second Congoleum campaign had produced, management was again pressed by the physical plant problem. The margin which the temporary abandonment of apparel and the closing of Martha Lane Adams had apparently produced quickly disappeared with the reintroduction of apparel, and estimates of business for 1928–29 were such as to require a long-term solution to the problem. In June 1928 the directors were confronted by three alternatives: (a) renting additional space, (b) purchasing the Straus & Schram warehouse which adjoined the 35th Street plant on the west, or (c) constructing a new warehouse on company property.[20] The first was discarded as impractical since suitable facilities were not available on terms which would have permitted a reasonable cost operation. Apparently Straus & Schram were willing to sell their mail-order property but not on terms which management was willing or able to meet. The public financing had wiped out the long-term debt and indenture restrictions, but in its place had substituted heavy preferred stock commitments. Management, seeking to achieve dramatic improvments in sales and earnings to impress the bankers and facilitate the profitable sale of the stock held by the underwriting syndicate, was in no mood to add to its burden of fixed charges or to deplete operating capital. For the same reasons commitment to an expensive building program had little immediate appeal.

A solution was found later that year when Modie and Sidney Spiegel organized the Esem Corporation which in turn acquired a tract of land from Spiegel, May, Stern for a nominal consideration (the property had been valued on the company's books at $40,000). Upon this property the Esem Corporation constructed a twelve-story building, with basement and loading docks, which was available for occupancy by late spring 1929. Title would remain with the Esem Corporation until the final installment had been paid by Spiegel, May, Stern in January 1949. According to the terms of the original agreement which was approved by the directors in February 1929, Spiegel would advance one-sixtieth of the total costs on May 1 of that year and pay out the rest of the acquisition price at the rate of 5 percent per year. The price was to be actual cost of the building, including the cost of money advanced during construction at the rate of 9 percent per annum.

In September these terms were modified and the final price set at
$630,000. According to the final arrangements Spiegel, May, Stern
made a first payment of $157,500, equal to five years rental; there-
after it would reduce the obligation at the rate of $2,625 per month
plus payment of interest on the declining monthly balance at the
rate of 9 percent per year.[21] In the event of default Esem could (a)
repossess the building, retaining all previous payments as liquidated damages, or (b) declare the entire unpaid balance due with
interest at the above rate for the period between the last payment
and the date of notice, plus a premium on the unpaid balance outstanding at the time. The amount of this premium was adjusted
to periods such that the premium diminished from 15 percent of
the balance for the interval April 1929–April 1931 to 1 percent if
default occurred during the final year of the contract. The contract also provided for prepayment by Spiegel, May, Stern after
1936, the prepayment privilege also carrying a sliding premium.
The seller reserved the right to issue mortgage bonds up to an
amount of $625,000, providing these were paid out by April 1,
1949.

Reviewed from the vantage point of time, this decision could
hardly have been less opportune. Within a year the mail-order
division was hard put to make effective use of its 1928 physical
plant, a situation which deteriorated rapidly over the next two
years. While the prepayment of five years' rental required no
cash drain during the worst depression years, the rental was on a
plant which essentially stood empty, with consequent operating
losses. But what was worse, in terms of transfer costs, was the loss
of flexibility in the years when business recovered. In 1935–36
building costs and interest rates were considerably below the
1929 level, and a new plant which would have been better tai-
lored to the company's changed position and expectations could
have been constructed at a substantial saving. But in the year of
decision sales volume was rising comfortably and the long-term
outlook was favorable. Spiegel management could hardly have
been condemned for a point of view which generally coincided
with those expressed by most members of the business community.

Spiegel, May, Stern's mail-order operations were influenced significantly between 1922 and 1932 by internal and external factors.

Internally, the break between Modie and Sidney Spiegel and the public offering established a somewhat different atmosphere. The estrangement between the two brothers eliminated a spirit of family unity, and the public sale of Spiegel stock and the subsequent withdrawal of Sidney from the business eliminated the family's controlling interest in the company. Externally, Spiegel found the rapidly changing competitive business structure and significant social, economic, and technological changes a growing challenge.

The response of Spiegel's mail-order division to these challenges was marked by four characteristics. The campany's mail-order operations were centralized by the elimination of Martha Lane Adams and the Clement Company, and Spiegel temporarily withdrew from the sale of soft goods. Second, the company continued to offer only merchandise which had established its salability. Spiegel's mail-order efforts were also characterized by a continuing search for merchandising techniques which would offset the company's disadvantages associated with high and rigid prices. And finally, the company continued its emphasis on soliciting credit sales.

This, however, is an incomplete picture of Spiegel between 1922 and 1932. During this same period the company was actively involved in generally unsuccessful efforts to sell products directly to consumers through traditional retail outlets. Thus, we will next turn to Spiegel's retail ventures, as well as treatment of how the company responded to the initial years of the Great Depression.

Retailing and
Initial Responses
to the Depression
1922–1932

Chapter 7

The struggle confronting Spiegel, May, Stern in 1932 was made all the greater by its direct retailing efforts. During the 1920s the company's management simply lost its touch in selling furniture through retail outlets. Changes in management were made, new policies instituted, new ventures launched, but they were to no avail. The burden on mail order to support the company, therefore, became all the greater. Yet, the top echelon in mail order was precariously close to becoming infected with the same ineptitudes that had overcome retailing. A lack of direction and purpose threatened to undermine the entire company, but fortunately there were men prepared to take up the challenge.

The reorganization of 1922 brought the small Spiegel House Furnishings chain into the Spiegel, May, Stern organization, but the integration was primarily confined to a centralization of executive titles and some financing. Modie Spiegel was president of the corporation until May 1928 when he was moved up to become chairman of the board of directors, but while he performed certain essential functions of a chief executive officer he was content to leave the operating administration of mail order to Innis, with his brother continuing to act as the resident partner in the retail division. As in former years, Modie Spiegel's first love was retail, particularly those aspects of retail which he knew best and could perform without the hard attention to detail demanded of an administrator. He maintained his headquarters in the main store at Wabash and Monroe in downtown Chicago where he could keep close to the things that mattered most to him. These included his activities in the Standard Club, in politics—he had been a member of the Board of Education for years—and in the congeries of business and financial enterprises in which he was forever investing. Among these was the Gatzert Company which he had substantially underwritten after it had been launched by Walter Gatzert, Frederick W. Spiegel's brother-in-law. This was a bond house dealing principally in municipal securities. In addition, he had an avid and continuing interest in sports, and had narrowly failed to acquire a major interest in the Chicago National League baseball team—the "Cubs"—before William Wrigley acquired it. This lost opportunity, however, failed to dampen his enthusiasm for the game and he frequently could be seen on summer afternoons occupying the box which he purchased season after season.

In the retail business, Modie was concerned principally with the activities on the selling floor and the sales results. As in former years he would personally oversee the operations, striding along the aisles or riding the elevator when he was not in his favorite position on the mezzanine. Courtly as could be his appearance and manners he was never able to shake off the earlier need to participate directly, whether this consisted of the ostensible dressing down of sales clerks for the benefit of patrons or bellowing for a clerk to watch a suspected shoplifter. Obviously, this diversion of his energies left little time for what must be regarded as top executive duties, and in the actual management of the retail stores he depended excessively upon the general retail manager and the managers of the branch outlets.

In the abstract, of course, there was nothing about such dependence which was necessarily harmful, nothing which could not have been productive of excellent results. All that was necessary was the selection and appointment of effective managers and the development of controls which could have provided him with a ready guide to their performance. And such performance would have had to include a perceptive evaluation of changing conditions in the retail furniture trade in Chicago, such that the retail division could adjust to the market and maintain its local position. This, however, proved to be the overriding deficiency for Modie Spiegel. He recognized that good administrators were always scarce and he made liberal provision for attaching their loyalties through good salaries and an opportunity of sharing in the profits of the business. He did not, however, have a particularly strong record with respect to the men he selected, nor did he maintain the close controls over them which would have permitted him to take action to correct the mistakes in judgment to which all men are prone. Thus situations not infrequently got past the stage where relatively painless changes could have corrected faults, and necessitated belated and more expensive action. It was this sort of thing and its repetition which pushed up the tension between the Spiegel brothers during the 1920s and led to the transfer of Sidney Spiegel, Jr. from mail order to the position of retail general manager in 1927.

Certain of the administrative improvements which had been suggested by the company's auditors and by Houston Landis in the years before the 1922 reorganization had been developed effectively enough to provide a strong improvement in retail sales and profits in 1919–20, and the division had ridden out the 1921 slump in good condition. In fact, in 1922 retail sales improved to over $3.5 million while mail-order volume contracted below the 1921 level, and retail earnings of $215,500 amounted to 6.1 percent of sales. This improvement continued during 1923 as sales increased to $4.63 million and profits rose to $425,200. While the rise in retail volume was well below the improvement in mail-order sales, retail profits were equal to 9.2 percent on volume compared to a rate of 8.9 percent in mail order. But then conditions in the market began to close in around the retail stores. During the two years 1924–25 sales volume declined an aggregate of $1,257,000, or almost 28 percent, and although the profit in 1924 was $180,600, in 1925 there was a loss of $77,300.

There was nothing particularly mysterious about the causes of this decline in Spiegel retail fortunes. Chicago, like other major metropolitan areas in the United States, had continued to grow in population during the years after 1913, but the composition of population within the city had shifted substantially. The mixture of new immigrants from Europe into the total population had thinned as a result of the decline of immigration after 1914. For the five years 1915–19, foreign immigration to the United States amounted to a little over 1.72 million people compared to the more than 5.17 million for the preceding five years. Even after the war there was a decline, with only 2.77 million arriving in the country between the end of 1919 and 1924 when the Immigration Act went into effect with its discriminatory quotas slashing heavily into migration from the southern and eastern European countries which had supplied a high proportion of immigrants between 1900 and 1915.

In partial compensation for the reduction of European immigrants the big industrial centers such as Detroit and Chicago had become magnets attracting immigrants from other sections of America, particularly the South. During the war years tens of thousands of blacks had migrated into Chicago to be absorbed into the dirty, unskilled jobs in meat-packing and steelmaking, and the poorly paid tasks in industry and transportation. The older immigrants were making more money and changing some of their habits and preferences in the consumption of goods, but the new migrants did not fill the gaps wrought by change. In particular they did not constitute the market which Spiegel retail had formerly served so auspiciously. There had been alterations in living patterns and residential locations, great improvements in transportation, and more intensive competition in retail distribution and in the neighborhood and district shopping centers. By the mid-1920s fewer Chicagoans found the location of the Spiegel branch stores particularly convenient or the atmosphere, which had previously been one of the chain's main points of attraction, particularly enjoyable. There were many other furniture distributors in Chicago who now could compete vigorously in installment credit, many at lower prices and with outlets located in areas where customer traffic was increasing and where sturdy competition forced merchants to a keen awareness of the need for appealing merchandise well displayed and promoted. By 1925 it was no longer possible to avoid the conclusion that the Spiegel stores were beginning to die on the vine, with management which failed to move promptly with the times, with locations poorly suited to the shifting patterns of the markets.

Albert Baum had been Modie Spiegel's general retail manager for over a decade, but before the end of 1925 a change was so obviously indicated that Baum resigned and his successor, Donald Folger, was appointed in January 1926.[1] Folger had been with the retail division for many years in addition to acquiring experience in other retailing organizations, and he was given a three-year contract calling for a base salary of $18,000 annually plus 3 percent of net retail profits. Folger was apparently able to institute certain internal administrative changes, but more importantly, he succeeded in increasing the scale of operations by opening new stores and closing the old Commercial Avenue location. The growth of population on Chicago's north side and the development of the area on Broadway north of Wilson Avenue as a major shopping section attracted the company's attention. Thus in March 1926 a twenty-five-year lease was negotiated with the owners of a newly erected building on Broadway near Lawrence Avenue, and a branch store opened there that spring, with suitable advertising fanfare, new fixtures, delivery equipment, and warehouse facilities, but with a continuation of high-markup and price policies. In May 1927 another new outlet was opened in a recently constructed building on Cottage Grove Avenue near 63rd Street, in one of the heavy shopping areas on the South Side, this involving another twenty-five-year lease. These changes provided the division: the main store in the Loop, two South Side locations (including the store at Ashland Avenue), the Milwaukee Avenue store, and the Broadway outlet. Management was pleased with the 1926 results to which the Broadway store contributed importantly. Sales climbed back to $3.79 million, a gain of over 12 percent, but the most obvious source of satisfaction was the profit picture. The 1925 loss changed to a profit of $490,800, equal to 12.9 percent on sales, and only the astonishing mail-order record borne on Swikard's Congoleum achievement caused it to lose in relative significance. Yet this did not prove to be a turning point for an aggressive reinvasion of Chicago retail furniture markets and exciting new profits. In 1927 sales fell back again by over $250,000, while profits slumped to $179,900 or 5.1 percent of sales.[2]

The contrast of the furniture store deterioration with the rapidly booming fortunes of mail order provided Sidney Spiegel with more than sufficient ammunition for his demands that a major change be undertaken in retail. The increasing friction between the brothers involved their mother and sister-in-law, and this led to the mechanics, already described, which took them out of the line of direct fire and provided an income commitment upon the corporation which practically compelled a more harmonious solution to the brothers' disagreements. The exact nature of the compromise is not recorded, but Sidney Spiegel, Jr. abandoned his work in mail order, where he was currently involved in the experiments with the Selectograph machine, and was named general manager for the retail chain, directly responsible to Modie Spiegel.

All things considered the change was not particularly fortuitous for Spiegel, May, Stern or for the family. In one sense there can be little doubt that Sidney Spiegel, Jr. found himself doing things that he enjoyed more than anything he had been charged with in mail order. While retail merchandising is not necessarily equated with showmanship, young Spiegel found some opportunities to indulge his desires for the theatrical, particularly in opening new stores. During 1928–29 the retail division opened large new outlets in the booming shopping districts of Madison and Crawford on the West Side and near 61st Street and Halsted on the South Side. In addition, small outlet stores for the disposition of mail-order merchandise and special purchases were opened on South State Street, Blue Island Avenue, and Halsted and 79th Street. This provided three outlet stores and six large branches in addition to the main downtown store.

For Sidney Spiegel, Jr. the new openings were unadulterated pleasure. A carnival atmosphere attended the openings of the new stores, with hired brass bands tooting in the street, premiums for children, and brightly colored banners hung in the interiors. Furthermore, nothing but the best was good enough for fittings, decorations, and furnishings. The customers were offered modern-looking furniture at prices which tended to be marked up at least 100 percent on cost, and frequent daylong sales were utilized more and more to attract them to the stores. The same tendencies were noticeable in the chain's newspaper advertising, described by one veteran as "arresting." "Oh, they could attract attention, all right, but we were selling furniture not attention, and I never noticed that the damn' ads produced much in the way of sales." Young Spiegel had a propensity for premiums, or special merchandise sold at low prices if customers bought something else. For example, he tried to sell sugar in the stores which carried only hard lines.[3]

But whatever could be said for his showmanship qualities—that these were considerable was to be demonstrated during the next decade when he became proprietor of a substantial chain of motion picture theaters in Chicago—he was completely deficient as a merchant. And his deficiencies were nowhere more pronouncd than in the important area of human relations. That is, it would have been difficult to find an executive who was so completely insensitive in the handling of customers and employees. A nervous man, who, as one former store manager described him, "was ill at ease, who tended to get rattled easily," young Spiegel was "ruthless in his handling of people. He talked to them as if they were animals, and this wasn't an act with him; he meant it." This attitude not only extended to customers, whom Sidney Spiegel, Jr. regarded as an evil which had to be borne, but tended to permeate retail during the last years of its existence. Meinig, who had come into retail in a special capacity during 1928, pointed out:

A customer to Sidney Spiegel was just somebody to be damned—and often where he could hear it. But whether they could hear or not wasn't the main thing; the whole organization had been permeated with this attitude—to hell with the customer! And I mean this was not just the sort of thing you often hear expressed by some employee who is disgruntled. Everybody I contacted, buyers, salesmen, they all not only talked that way, they behaved that way. It wasn't any wonder they lost customers.

However, retail did not lose customers more rapidly than they found new ones in the freshly opened outlets on the West and South Sides during 1928, for sales boomed up by $657,000 and yielded profits of $194,300. That this was again but a temporary spasm was borne out in 1929 when volume fell by more than $800,000 and the loss incurred was $175,600. By this time, however, the retail losses included Sidney Spiegel, Jr. The 1928 results, in the estimate of management and the directors, had stemmed largely from the losses incurred in the downtown store, and even before the February 1929 directors' meeting a search was on for a buyer to take over that property and its lease. The directors were less than pleased with the low rate of return on the retail assets which were close to $4 million at the time.[4] Several, in fact, were in favor of disposing of the stores entirely except for their interest in the success Sears and Ward appeared to be making of their retail chains, and the possibility that the Chicago stores could constitute a nucleus for a possible extension of retail throughout the mail-order territory. By now the board no longer included Sidney M. Spiegel who had resigned from the company and was in process of disposing of his stock. With his father gone and his relations with his uncle already seriously strained, Sidney Spiegel, Jr. also resigned, and another reorganization was under way in retail.

As the 1929 results indicated, this was not immediately productive of improved results, although Modie Spiegel was able to promise the board in April 1929 that steps had been initiated to reduce salaries and rentals during the year by $100,000 and held out hope that the 1930 retail profit would approach $400,000.[5] Even this prospect dissolved in the losses that mounted in retail during the second quarter of the year and by the July meeting the directors voted to have the management take whatever steps were required to dispose of all the Spiegel retail stores.[6]

It was much easier, however, to vote for dissolution than to find commercial buyers sufficiently strong and optimistic to purchase the whole chain, and the effects of a piecemeal liquidation upon the prices and terms for each subsequent unit were greatly feared. The other Chicago furniture chains who were approached, such as Hartman, were uninterested at the prices Spiegel wanted, or were disturbed at the lease commitments that would have been required. However poor performance had been in 1929, it looked like the pinnacle of achievement when the results for 1930 were known.

By the end of February 1930 management was sufficiently desperate to consider favorably a proposal brought to them by Harry Fish, a member of the family which operated the Fish Furniture Company, a low-priced furniture operation which had existed in Chicago for as long as the Spiegels had been in house furnishings. When the highly reputable Burley Company found itself in serious financial trouble after the stock market collapse, Fish had acquired control of that company and apparently held the idea of combining it with other home furnishings firms whose economic distress put them in jeopardy, and building a powerful chain of stores in the city. Harry Fish was a hardheaded businessman with extensive experience in cheap furniture retailing and a reputation for shrewdness and tough dealing. To the Spiegel management, looking for a way out of retail and not having the personnel in their own organization who they believed could dispose of the stores at reasonable terms, Fish appeared as the man of the hour. He was retained to liquidate the organization, but almost immediately suggested to the Spiegel management that a reorganized Burley Company be established to which Spiegel would turn over its retail assets in return for two-thirds stock interest. In terms of the reputation of the old Burley Company for fine merchandise and indisputable quality, the combination of these two operations were analogous to a merging of Tiffany & Company with a chain of cheap, credit jewelry shops. Yet, at the strong urging of Modie Spiegel, the directors voted to turn over to this new organization, which later was incorporated as the "Yelrub Corporation," assets worth $4,047,957 and current liabilities of $205,504, and to convey to Yelrub all store leases on the condition that the new company perform all obligations required by the leases. In return Spiegel, May, Stern received 20,000 out of a total of 30,000 capital shares in Yelrub. Harry Fish was elected president of the new firm and Spiegel took out insurance on his life for $500,000.[7] On July 1, 1930, Fish confidently reported to the Spiegel board that Burley (Yelrub) had "succeeded in the greater part of the liquidating business," and that "on the basis of the current rate of volume" the company stood to lose no more money.[8] It is somewhat difficult to determine just what was meant by the greater part of the liquidation, perhaps it was the outlet stores; it is just as difficult to evaluate the basis for Fish's optimism regarding retail losses. When the books were finally closed in 1930 total retail sales were $1.94 million, a reduction of almost $1.4 million from 1929 volume, but the loss was sensational, $1,632,300, or almost eighty-four cents for each sales dollar!

Apparently the directors could stomach no more. Spiegel owned all the Burley (or Yelrub) stock and Fish was eased out of control of the retail liquidation proceedings. That the company was reduced to conducting this procedure with its own personnel was attested to in April 1931 when the directors voted to give Modie and Frederick W. Spiegel authority to "investigate the possibility of getting an expert merchandiser with real estate and accounting knowledge" to examine the retail situation and recommend whether it should be continued on its current basis, or steps be taken to

sell or write it off.[9] Two months later the directors voted to liquidate Burley, and H. George Meinig was effectively, although without official titular authorization, given the task of negotiating for
the disposition of inventories, settling the termination of retail
employment, and arranging for lease settlements.[10] When it appeared that a more wholesale disposition might be affected, with
the Hartman Furniture Company taking over several units in the
chain as the Tobey Furniture Company had done with the outlet
stores and one larger store the previous year, the unit-by-unit
method was held in abeyance. The negotiations with Hartman
continued through the fall and into spring 1932, before a settlement was reached. This, however, did not extend over all the
Spiegel outlets. Hartman, with the permission of the owners and
with Spiegel guaranteeing the rental, accepted the leases on the
properties located on East 47th Street, at 4042 Madison Street, and
4832 Broadway, and paid Spiegel $32,500 for the inventories
stocked in the latter two sites.

In the settlement of two other leases, however, including that
for the main store at Wabash and Monroe, it proved impossible to
negotiate take-over terms with merchants acceptable to the owner.
Particularly difficult was the main store, which had proven a white
elephant to Spiegel even during the prosperous years of the 1920s.
The collapsing real estate market in downtown properties made
the owner completely unamenable to accepting a weaker name on
the lease; only a cash settlement was possible, and in November
1931 an agreement was reached involving $108,787 for the main
store location, supplemented four months later by additional
amounts which raised the final settlement price to $168,000.[11] This
sum was payable in thirty-six monthly installments; and Spiegel,
May, Stern had to pledge its guarantee in order to release the personal guarantees of Modie and Sidney Spiegel, given when the
lease was originally signed. By the end of 1932 the Chicago
furniture stores had been completely liquidated except for the unsettled leases on four properties still under negotiation, the contingent liability on transfers made earlier. During 1934 a final
settlement was arranged on leases which involved purchase by the
company of three properties with an assessed value of $300,000;
and as late as 1939 two of these were still in the company's
possession.

The liquidation expenses and ultimate losses from liquidation were formidable for a company as deeply immersed in the depression as Spiegel. The company's annual report for 1931 specified liquidation expenses as $1,236,854 in addition to the net operation loss in retail of $672,600. During the next two years almost $300,-000 more was added to these losses and expenses, principally in settlement of the leases.[12] This aggregate, however, was not chargeable solely against the Chicago furniture stores. Approximately one-half of the total losses were incurred in the ill-fated venture launched in 1929 known as Standard Home Utilities. This case provides a good example of opportunity costs.

Following the public underwriting in 1928, and the election of Wallace T. Perkins of the Chatham-Phenix Bank to the board of directors, a growing concern developed with maintaining satisfactory prices and adequate dividends. These objectives placed a premium upon Spiegel's expanding sales at profitable rates. Perkins reflected this financial community concern in January 1929 when he expressed an interest in the chain store development then being vigorously pushed by Sears and Ward. At the time, Innis and the Spiegels were fully inclined to undertake whatever action the bankers seemed to favor, providing it seemed within the competence of the organization and would produce profitable results. There was not, however, much enthusiasm shown by members of management for getting into direct retailing of a general line of goods to compete with their large and well-financed rivals, or for invading the Canadian mail-order market, another possibility suggested by the banker. Innis, as the newly elected president and general manager, inaugurated studies of both possibilities, although he was personally interested in neither and was much more intrigued by another alternative. His assignment of M. J. Spiegel to make a brief field survey of the Ward and Sears stores led, as has been seen, to the crisis which resulted in Sidney Spiegel's resignation from the company and the disposition of his common shares to members of the original underwriting syndicate. One result of the resignation was the election of two other financial representatives to the board, replacing Sidney Spiegel and his son and strengthening the influence of the bankers on management.

Innis's reports on the feasibility of getting strongly into retail on the Sears and Ward plan were unfavorable, as would be his later evaluation of the recommendation to invade the Canadian market. But in the interim he was steadily pushing for adoption of his own plan: to limit the extension of credit sales and switch the emphasis in mail order to a cash plan. By April 1929 Innis had won sufficient support for his proposal to obtain a board resolution to the effect that there appeared to be a ceiling of $3 million to the profits which credit mail-order selling could produce and that the company should therefore gradually begin converting to a cash basis. But although Modie Spiegel, as chairman, proposed the resolution, there was by no means real assent to the proposal. M. J. Spiegel in particular was skeptical of the capacity of the current organization to begin converting to cash; the entire company experience had been in credit and nobody in the company had cash experience except Innis, and his had been limited and was long out of date. Further, the costs of setting up a duplicate organization to handle cash selling would have been high, how high nobody in the company knew. Although they had voted for the resolution, neither Swikard, Charles Folger, nor Frederick Spiegel were avid supporters of conversion. With this nucleus, M. J. Spiegel began to devise some proposal which would attract the interest of the banker-directors and divert their attention from cash mail order. The result was Standard Home Utilities.

The basic plan upon which this venture was founded had the advantage of appearing soundly geared to the steadily expanding market for household appliances and of having already attracted the attention of highly reputable organizations. One of these, Public Service Company of Northern Illinois, had organized a chain of outlet stores to distribute a wide selection of home appliances, including kitchen ranges, mechanical refrigerators, heating and cleaning units, lamps, toasters, and electric irons. M. J. Spiegel's idea was to set up a group of similar stores in medium-sized towns in several states in the Midwest, with centralized merchandising and operations controlled in Chicago. Terms would include both cash and credit, and an experienced appliance merchant would be employed and be made responsible for the selection of locations, negotiation of leases, employment and training of personnel, and development of an effective merchandising and store operation plan. According to his estimates the total investment in this enterprise would be close to $1 million, and with luck it could be launched by late summer or early fall of 1929.

M. J. Spiegel had shrewdly anticipated the impact such a proposal would have upon the banker-directors, since it obviously touched upon several elements in which they had already indicated they were interested: retail chain stores to move into a market which other mail-order companies were exploiting, a concentration on big-ticket appliances for which demand was growing, and a bow in the direction of cash selling. When the proposal was presented to the board in July 1929 the directors voted to adopt it, authorizing a capital of $1 million but limiting the initial appropriation to $250,000.[13] Although the directors voted to require specific board approval for further appropriations, the records of the company indicate that no further action was taken by the board; apparently Spiegel advanced between $500,000 and $750,000 by one means or another, principally in paying off the leases which had been made in 1929 and in sacrificing inventory.

M. J. Spiegel was given the responsibility for Standard Home Utilities, found a general manager to direct the technical operations, and the organization was launched in late summer with stores in Mansfield, Ohio; Lorraine, Ohio; and Racine, Wisconsin. Within six months there were a total of nine outlets operating, all with new leases, new managers and sales clerks, with moderate stocks of goods and contracts with sources of supply—and with the economy and the demand for consumer durables sliding ever more rapidly into limbo. The newly acquired general manager, despite an excellent reputation, failed to provide the sort of leadership which M. J. Spiegel demanded, and, unlike his father, he had an instinct for recognizing the need to get rid of a manager before the situation came apart at the seams. But there was seemingly nothing which he or his subordinates could do to arrest the rate at which the losses were mounting. Before 1930 was half gone M. J. Spiegel was conceding defeat and was ready to recommend that the company get out as soon as it could cut its losses.

Edward Swikard, however, could not swallow this counsel any more than he could the previous efforts to abandon apparel. He felt that if they hung on the depression would run its course and Standard Home Utilities would be in an excellent position to capitalize on a resurging demand. M. J. Spiegel was delighted to shift the responsibility for the subsidiary to someone else, and there were more than sufficient hearty reassurances emanating from Washington that prosperity was just around the corner and that the worst of the recession had been reached. So Swikard moved from his familiar office in the administration building to the Standard Home Utilities headquarters in the Old Martha Lane Adams building, and, as M. J. Spiegel later described him,

he was like a caged lion over there, pacing the floor of his office until I thought he'd wear a furrow in it. He tried this, he tried that, but nothing worked. Special sales, cuts in prices, cuts in salaries, new sources . . . nothing worked. I don't think I've ever been so sorry for anybody in my life.

For a short while, however, Swikard evidently believed he had found some answers in changes in store managers—the market was getting pretty full of men with retail experience looking for jobs—and in new merchandising and selling plans. At least he gave his opinion to the board in July 1930 that "Standard Home Utilities would sustain no further losses for the last half of the year." Or perhaps he had heard Harry Fish repeat this formula so often that he was mesmerized by it. Slogans and optimistic forecasts worked no better for Swikard (and Fish) than they did for Herbert Hoover, and the corner remained as elusive as ever. The last half of 1930 was worse than the first half, and if 1931 was any better nobody in the corporation was able to discern it. Swikard was pulled out of the agony chair and the Standard Home Utilities chain was turned over to others to carry out the sad and dirty tasks of liquidation. The principal liquidator was George Meinig, who was gaining a lot of unwelcome experience in this line after his duties with Chicago furniture stores, and under his direction the outlets were closed, the personnel discharged and paid off, the inventories sold and transferred to their new owners, and the blank empty faces of the abandoned stores looked out on streets which were becoming shabbier and shabbier.

In retrospect M. J. Spiegel estimated that Standard Home Utilities cost Spiegel, May, Stern $1 million, but that as things turned out it had been worth it. Without this diversion he was convinced that the board would have pressed forward with the plan Innis had recommended to convert to cash, and that the company would have been caught by the depression half in cash and half out of credit. Perhaps this is a valid assessment, for there is no way to prove any contention. The operating records, like the hopes with which the company was launched, have long vanished.

Such failures, of course, cast a pall over the entire Spiegel organization. As depression deepened in 1931 and the optimistic predictions from Washington sounded more and more hollowly across the land, Spiegel's mail-order division began to be hit hard. Not only were there across-the-board wage cuts which affected everyone in the organization with the exception of Innis and Swikard, but the dismissal rate rose sharply. By the end of 1931 layoffs had cut back the labor force to less than half the 1930 figure and had included people who had been with the company for years. By 1932 morale was not just bad, it was practically nonexistent. The Chicago furniture stores collapsed causing the layoff of the entire retail labor force. Within mail order, which was the only effectively surviving division of the corporation, there was almost a paralysis, from the president down to the merest stock boy. The company had been forced to suspend payment of preferred dividends and its stock was steadily falling on the market. The extended warehouse space stood half empty, the footfalls of the occasional employee echoing mockingly the frenzied activity of 1929. George Meinig remembered the uncertainty, the confused babble of conflicting suggestions from the surviving employees, the frantic urging to get into the cash business from men whose jobs and careers would have been part of the transfer cost since they would have been quickly expendable in such a move.

This depressing condition was magnified when employees sensed there was no commanding hand at the helm. It did not help that the president could later argue that the cash position was sound, that nothing was owed the banks, or that the current ratio stood at nineteen. Business was drying up almost as fast as were the springs of hope and confidence. As the months of 1932 slipped by and the pink dismissal slips reduced the labor force to a hard core, Spiegel was like a storm-driven vessel whose crew were awaiting the beginnings of the list that would mark the end. In these circumstances there is little wonder that Meinig could say that the essential need was to restore some sense of purpose, some goal or objective, no matter how humble, which could be taken by the

organization as a symbol of hope. It was almost too much to expect that a rescue would be effected, too much like the last-minute
appearance of the cavalry to drive off the Indians. In cold print and
out of context a revival of faith in credit mail order and the simple
mechanics of offering some price and loss leaders appear shallow
and almost ridiculous. Yet they did not occur out of context, and
they have meaning and drama and heroism because they did break
the spell of inertia and the omnipresence of disaster.

M. J. Spiegel was by this time convinced that almost any positive
effort was preferable to what he regarded as the fatal drift of the
company. Anything, in fact, but shifting to a cash basis. By early
1932 even the mighty Sears and Montgomery were in trouble and
cash selling seemed to young Spiegel as less than a universal panacea. Such a conversion would require a major reorganization within the company, for which its resources, in M. J. Spiegel's opinion,
were insufficient to stand. He had for several years been critical of
management policies, particularly of merchandising, control of
circulation, and pricing. Now, his position in the company secured
by a record of accomplishment as well as being the son of the
chairman and principal stockholder, he began pressing Innis to
offer some concrete plan which would act as a rallying point for
the increasingly demoralized staff, something which would give
the company a purpose and hope of survival.

He had already undertaken several actions independent of Innis, the most important being to bring several men together to
analyze Spiegel's position and to try to develop a set of viable
recommendations for action. This team consisted of H. George
Meinig, Thornton Adams, and Edward Swikard. Meinig had been
brought back into mail order after he had performed a major role
in the liquidation of the retail stores. Adams, when his men's
furnishing store in Florida had gone under, had obtained a job at
Sears, Roebuck in merchandising, and then had been hired by
Spiegel. Swikard was smarting under the failure of Standard Home
Utilities and was desperately looking for some merchandising angle
which he could successfully promote to hold back the tides that
were engulfing the company. Originally, there was no clear pattern
in the mind of M. J. Spiegel. He was convinced, however, that
there were superior ways of doing business to those entailed in
past Spiegel policy, that careful analysis of business data and bet-

ter information could possibly lead to guides for managerial action, and that there was no hope that effective leadership was going to materialize at the top echelon of management.

When Meinig was brought back to mail order an office was found for him on the third floor of the central warehouse, out of the administration building. Here, Meinig recalled, M. J. gave him copies of the "Red Book" which he had developed containing financial statements going back over the past decade, and current and past catalogs. And from the Red Books—records of the number of units of all merchandise featured in catalogs and sale books which had been purchased and sold, final inventory position, and their dollar complements—the financial statements, and other information which he began to acquire, Meinig began to put together the elements of what can best be described as a business philosophy—concrete plans would flow from this. And this was not a one-man act. Within a few weeks after he had begun these studies Meinig found that he, M. J., and Swikard were spending from eight to ten hours a day together for days on end. What was to become the basic reconstruction of business policy at Spiegel began to take on the outline of substance. As Meinig remembered it,

Originally I don't believe any of us had any idea of what he was groping for. We were seeking solutions for what was wrong. I think I crystallized first, probably because I had been outside [of mail order] and wasn't so imbued with the effect of the slide down or the old way of doing things. But perhaps somebody else hit on it first; I'm not sure and it doesn't seem important who was "first." But I recall that my first thought was, "let's cut out this pessimism, quit thinking in terms of firing everybody tomorrow morning to cut down expenses." I felt we had to get into some kind of campaign, not a concrete thing like increasing advertising, but getting our minds in order, agreeing on something in which we could all believe. Let's quit talking "cash business." If we decide to go into cash, let's do it and get it over with, but I had been studying what had been happening at Sears and I found out that they were in such bad shape that their old employees who were on that wonderful retirement and profit-sharing plan were afraid they were going to be retired penniless. What we needed was to fall once again in love with the credit business, our own business, believe in it, get married to it, make the credit idea work like it had worked before. And, gradually, week by week, we began to accept this and began to get enthusiastic about something again—something out of nothing.

But it was one thing to develop enthusiasm among a handful of men who did not make policy for a company and another to implement it in some complete or partial plan which would produce results. Further there was the problem of getting an acceptance of a concerte plan by Modie Spiegel and Innis. By late spring 1932 M. J. Spiegel and Meinig had put together what became the first operating budget for the company, "a poor little two page thing written on yellow paper" which makes some approximations of unit and dollar sales, merchandise costs, operating expenses, promotional efforts, and profits.[14] Only the estimated profits were negative and Innis received the budget with amazement mingled with scorn. M. J. Spiegel defended it and asked the president what he had to offer as a substitute. He received no satisfactory reply.

Taking advantage of the vacuum created by the paralysis in top management, the three men pushed on. Swikard, newly enthused, was seeking some merchandise which he could promote to increase sales and attract some new customers, and indirectly this led to the introduction of a new pricing policy and promotional program. The search through the Red Books had alerted Meinig to the presence of a little two-burner oil stove. His boyhood had been spent in a home where an oil stove had been used because gas and electricity were nonexistent, and in a depression period in the small towns of the south and west it seemed that a cheap oil stove, which had a life expectancy of two to three years before being discarded, should have customer appeal. Swikard was not certain, but in the fall 1932 catalog he gave a few square inches to this stove, and a price was set substantially below the 100 percent markup level. And in a season where whole pages of merchandise failed to produce more than a few hundred dollars of sales, the stoves brought in orders of over $3,000. Then, Meinig recounted,

Swikard really went to work. He got the buyers together and told them to get the manufacturers in here. The buyers told him these stoves cost the company something like five dollars, but Swike brushed that aside. "Quit saying they cost five dollars; they won't cost that much if you buy 10,000 or 50,000 of the damned things from the manufacturers, and they can make them for a hell of a lot less than five dollars." And he began to turn out flyers and special bulletins featuring this stove, sent them to thousands of new names and old names. We priced them low, and they sold—one dollar down and one dollar a month.

This success gave birth to the idea of variable pricing not just for one item, but for categories of items. For what bothered this triumvirate of revolutionaries was the excessive merchandise mark-ups and very high advertising costs. There was no doubt in their minds that even with depression-reduced prices the high-markup policy undermined successful merchandising. Further, aggressive price behavior for certain goods which had an appeal to customers could be exploited if customers could be persuaded to buy goods bearing higher markups. There was no disagreement among them that what was important for a successful operation was to realize an adequate gross profit over the entire range of merchandise and customers during a given time period rather than to have each item and each customer contribute equally to margin. But generalized price and markup reduction was an objective which could not be reached or even broadly attempted in what remained of 1932.

More important in terms of the moment was the program to which Swikard's unceasing questioning led. Swikard was unburdening himself of matters that had troubled him since Arthur Spiegel's death. He recognized the need to stimulate sales by some new merchandising coup, but his past experience had been discouraging. Every time the company got started on a new merchandising idea and began generating sales as a result of its promotion, management failed to follow it up systematically. That is, each special promotion was handled as a one-shot operation instead of a routine procedure for which a promotional budget was established to adequately finance further campaigns. Swikard was arguing for the establishment of a fund which could be fed by setting aside part of the receipts from a successful promotion. In all previous efforts, including the startlingly prosperous coups of 1926 and 1927, management had settled back contentedly to reap the benefits from new business without apparent long-term consideration of the problems of consistent new-customer recruiting through merchandising. Now, without resources available to set up such a fund, what could be done to break the old pattern and begin something different? It seemed particularly pressing in view of the proposal to offer the oil stoves on a test basis as loss leaders. There had to be some way of accounting for what was, in essence, an investment in new customers. And although a solution did not emerge quickly or without considerable self-examination, an answer did emerge which the triumvirate believed was viable.

The solution to this problem entailed setting up a new concept for recruiting, which came to be called "Division 2." And although the bookkeeping problem came to be recognized as merely a way of diverting attention from the main problem—an important diversion in terms of the attitude of top management at the moment —a revised system of internal accounting was eventually adopted wherein the expenses of new-account building could be charged to promotion and advertising. All of this, however, was still in the prototype stage by the end of 1932. It is of importance though, because this first real attempt at aggressive pricing and the development of a program of systematic new-customer recruitment gave a sense of direction to the company and offered a new hope for the future.

The previous description and analysis of the operations of Spiegel, May, Stern Company have indicated that whereas the organization was strong in mail order, particularly with respect to credit merchandising and promotion, it suffered from being forced to carry a Chicago retail furniture chain which came to be increasingly out of step with changes in the local market. In mail order, the company's product selection and merchandising as well as pricing constituted vulnerable points which intensified the task which credit and promotion were forced to carry. The impact of depression proved a terrible trial for Spiegel precisely because of its retail weakness and its merchandising and pricing vulnerability. Yet a review of the sales and earnings record for the years before the depression indicate an impressive growth of the one and a most commendable achievement in the other. Company net sales were $7.36 million in 1922, jumped to a three-year plateau of around $12 million, then leaped again to rise to nearly $24 million in 1929. Thereafter price and patronage contraction, together with the liquidation of retail, reduced volume until it had fallen to $7.1 million in 1932. Total sales for 1922–29 were over $124.8 million, while profits amounted to slightly under $10.6 million, which produced an earnings rate on sales of 8.5 percent. For the three years beginning with 1930 aggregate sales were just over $32 million, while losses of $3.2 million yielded an earning rate of –10 percent. A substantial proportion of this $3.2 million, however, was taken in liquidation expense and loss and is not representative of the actual operation of the going organizations within the firm.

The distribution of sales and earnings between the mail order and the retail divisions of the company are shown in exhibit 5 (see Appendix). It is clear that mail order after 1922 contributed the largest and steadily increasing proportion of sales and profits, while the record in retail was erratic, varying from years of high profit returns to losses, finally ending in complete debacle and liquidation. Probably most impressive in the mail-order data is the rate of increase in sales volume between 1922 and 1929. During this span of years Spiegel mail-order volume rose by 437 percent and profits were up 562 percent. For the eight years ending with 1929, mail-order sales aggregated nearly $94.5 million and profits $9 million for a return of 9.5 percent. For the three depression years sales were only $30.1 million while losses were $948,700, or a loss percentage of 3.2 percent. The increase in mail-order sales experienced between 1922 and 1929 was small compared to the gain registered by Sears, for example, whose mail-order volume rose almost $100 million. But in terms of relative gains it was more impressive, since the Sears gain amounted to only 60.2 percent. Sears, in fact, was limited by the considerable proportion of the market it already commanded in the rural sections, and by the growing difficulties which any large organization experiences in pushing sales into less receptive markets. The experience demonstrated, however, that when intelligent merchandising was combined with first-class promotional effort there were segments of the retail market which could be switched to a particular seller. Awareness of this possibility provided the Spiegel management with a firm ground for optimism even in a period of depression, if the merchandising lethargy could be overcome.

The retail experience even during the prosperous 1920s was a source of discomfort to management. From almost 48 percent of corporate sales in 1922 retail volume fell to only 14 percent in 1929, with the largest single year ($4.63 million) occurring in 1923. In only three years did profits go over $200,000, or the profit rate on sales exceed 9 percent. In 1925 and in 1929 there were losses, and throughout the 1920s the earning rate was only 5.2 percent, a remarkable achievement when markups typically exceeded 50 percent of sales! Under the aegis of Harry Fish and the Burley Company the retail record was particularly dismal, and during the last two years of its existence the retail divisions managed to lose over eighty-three cents of each sales dollar. For the entire eleven years and taking into account actually incurred liquidation losses and costs—not the contingent liability yet remaining on unsettled leases —the retail operations succeeded in losing 2.2 percent of net sales revenue. When account is taken of the success which Joseph Spiegel and his sons had made of retail after 1892, and the successful offshoot into mail order which this made possible, the debacle is all the more curious. The Spiegels had shown themselves to be effective mail-order merchants who had lost touch with the facts of retail competition.

Despite the financial difficulties of the Chicago furniture stores and the outlays necessary due to the inauguration of the Standard Home Utilities chain in 1929, the company paid the highest dividends in its history, and by the end of 1929 had built earned surplus to $1.5 million. Had the right combination of effective merchandising and pricing been integrated with the kind of promotion and new-account building which had consistently been successful for the company, there is little reason to believe that Spiegel could not have continued to expand its share of the mail-order market. Neither is there any particular reason to assume that the merchandising patterns within the Standard Home Utilities chain would not have evolved more along the Sears and Ward lines rather than along strictly appliance lines. Thus, unless one accepts the thesis that a major depression was inevitable and that the collapse of the speculative boom in October 1929 had only a peripheral bearing on its severity—a thesis which is more than a little difficult to document—there was reason to believe that the 1928 reorganization and financing would have greatly benefited the company despite the burden of fixed outlays which it involved.

The onslaught of depression, however, caught the company with the Chicago store problem unresolved and without an effective or tested organization for the Standard Home Utilities chain. The 1930 loss was $2,257,500, which not only wiped out the existing surplus, but required transfer of $297,200 from the contingency reserve to surplus to avoid an impairment of capital. The retail liquidations of 1931 swamped the $50,000 mail-order profit and capital impairment was unavoidable. In November 1931, with the consent of the owners of more than 50 percent of common stock, the stated value of outstanding common was reduced from $5 million to $1,750,000, the difference being credited to capital surplus which received, in addition, credit for the discount earned through the purchase and retirement of preferred stock. The latter amounted to $1,685,200. Against these amounts were charged an aggregate of $2,942,700 of subsidiary operating and liquidation losses and transfers to reserves. Similar operations with preferred stock added almost $297,000 to capital surplus in 1932, but losses, liquidation costs, and reserve strengthening reduced the surplus by an additional $915,900. By the end of 1932 net worth was only $7 million, less than half the level for 1929.

Despite the huge proportions of the losses which had been suffered during the 1930s, the company was in an essentially sound position by the close of 1932. It could lose no more in retail, the contingent liability on outstanding leases did not represent an unbearable burden, and it was in a highly liquid position. A continuation of high-markup policies, dull merchandising, and wasted circulation could have proved catastrophic. On the other hand, any marked improvement in these areas combined with the unquestioned appeal of credit buying offered a reasonable basis for improvement. Despite the reduction of its capital resources the company would have been able to acquire the short-term funds needed to finance a sales expansion and to enable it to meet its preferred stock commitments. Whether or not this happened rested in the hands of thirty-one-year-old M. J. Spiegel.

No Charge for Credit
1933–1937

Chapter 8

During the five years from 1933 to 1937 Spiegel grew from a small company hovering on the brink of collapse to a position of respected force in the American mail-order market. The upsurge was a solid accomplishment, boosting company sales to over $56 million in 1937 and providing the basis in terms of resources, policies, and market position for what was hoped would be even more substantial expansion in future years.

These changes did not, of course, spring full-grown from the organization which had existed prior to 1933; nor did they occur in an era of general economic expansion and business health. Essentially, Spiegel's development emerged from the contribution of M. J. Spiegel. This is not to argue that nobody except M. J. Spiegel could have salvaged the crippled firm whose earning power seemed to be gone in 1932, or that no other individual could have nursed it back to health and guided it to growth and profits. It was simply that at that time there were few American businessmen available who had the nerve and confidence necessary to tear up the book on past policies which were leading nowhere and the fundamental grasp of the main elements in a business situation which made daring and innovation something more than reckless irresponsibility. *Time* magazine observed in 1936 that when Montgomery Ward was in deep trouble and needed "brains" it acquired them in Sewell L. Avery for $100,000 a year. In addition, Ward had to outlay several times this amount to provide Avery with a layer or two of experienced topflight merchandising executives. Spiegel had neither this kind of money nor the reputation needed to attract such talent. Instead the company found it in the Spiegel family.

M. J. Spiegel brought several obvious attributes to the helm of the company: youth (he was not yet thirty-two years old); energy; a strong native intelligence conditioned by a good education; ten years of experience in merchandising and management; training in and comprehension of basic quantitative data as used in business; and a burning curiosity within the scope of the things that interested him most. He possessed also three other characteristics which were of incalculable value at the time, although, like a sword blade, these were capable of cutting both ways. The first was enthusiasm, a bubbling, seemingly inexhaustible fountain of confident enthusiasm, which flowed from him to engulf his colleagues and subordinates. The second was a faith in the capacity of men— or at least of some men—to rise to challenges that to other eyes might have seemed beyond their abilities. The third was an unshakeable belief in the results which sustained hard work could achieve. M. J. Spiegel himself was in love with the business. In a very real sense he expected a similar devotion from his lieutenants and, rather surprisingly, he got it. This commitment from his lieutenants was surprising in that the financial incentives were not noticeably strong. Yet in a vitally important sense the times and the early performance of Spiegel in turning the corner from loss to profit contributed a tremendous motivation for the men and women in all strata of the organization to perform to the peak of their capabilities.

In 1933 the company began to increase its sales sharply and was actively in the labor market, able to hire almost every type of personnel. For men and women out of work, who had fruitlessly explored all avenues of prospective employment, the opportunity to work steadily at fourteen or sixteen dollars a week under hard pressure and for long hours was an unbelievably fortunate circumstance. With expansion came job opportunities requiring higher skills and there was no shortage of college-educated men available to fill them. Further, for an organization which was loosely-knit and not rigidly formalized, and which was experiencing an unprecedented growth in a period of generalized economic stagnation, there were tremendous opportunities for talented and innovative people. Both the times and the organization were fluid. Men with ability and ambition could look forward to rapid advancement and increased compensation; indeed they could hardly avoid having ever more demanding tasks pushed upon them. Thus, M. J. Spiegel's inexhaustible enthusiasm, teamed with the undeniable accomplishments of the company, permeated Spiegel, providing myriad motivations and eliciting responses which tended to offset deficiencies in organization which began to appear in the wake of rapid growth.

Fundamentally this was a period of aggressive merchandising, hard-bitten buying, and getting prices down to competitive levels by reducing mark-ons. Credit was merchandised even harder under the banner of "No Charge for Credit." The installment feature provided the means whereby consumers on small incomes could obtain goods conveniently, and better merchandise bargains provided the basic appeal. In addition to improved merchandising and more aggressive pricing, there were important new efforts in the recruiting and upgrading of new customers. A relatively high, but profitable, rate of credit loss was accepted as a necessary condition of an expanded market share. Financial resources were accumulated from ploughed-back earnings, from the issue of new preferred and common shares, and from extended lines of commercial bankbook and note credit which became increasingly available as the company prospered. Within management this period was marked by the total eclipse of the influence of investment bankers upon policy, and by a drawing together of three or four men around M. J. Spiegel, each of whom contributed something unique to the company and who were best able to express themselves and realize their own ambitions and talents through him. In a very real sense, therefore, M. J. Spiegel constituted the catalyst for what was his first upper echelon team.

It will be recalled that M. J. Spiegel had proposed what amounted to the first formal operating budget in Spiegel history in mid-year 1932 and it had been scornfully received, based as it was on a sales volume which predicated an operating loss. But it was based also on another element, the introduction of price and loss leaders in company merchandising practice, that is, setting the markup on articles sufficiently low as to result in a lower merchandising net margin or even an operating loss. M. J. Spiegel was not advocating—not yet—a general reduction of markups such that the gross merchandising margin for the entire fall sales volume be discernibly reduced. Rather it was to offer certain promotable items of merchandise, all household articles, at sharply cut prices to a list of potential buyers as carefully selected as available lists, money, and known techniques would permit, on a dollar-down and a dollar-per-month terms.

M. J. also told Frederick Innis that in view of both general business circumstances and the forecasted loss for the fall an across-the-board cut in compensation was necessary, and that he believed Innis should voluntarily set his own salary reduction in the interest of general employee morale. The suggestion had the effect of disheartening the already despairing president. Thus, when M. J. inquired as to what course of action he would set for the company, Innis replied that if M. J. believed he could do any better he should run it. There was, of course, nothing official to this, and it is certain that Innis never meant it to be followed literally. Later, when some of his confidence had been restored, he sought to exercise the customary presidential prerogatives, but by then it was too late. M. J. Spiegel had reported the incident to his father with the recommendation that he either get rid of Innis as general manager and appoint some substitute or sell out his equity for what price he could get. Modie Spiegel, however, was no more ready for this kind of immediate action than he was in the mid-1920s to move determinedly to correct the deteriorating retail situation. He did nothing about Innis but permitted his son to assume much broader responsibilities and to report directly to him, by-passing the president. This was first-order procrastination and could only postpone an inevitable decision, but while it relieved Modie Spiegel of an unpleasant task for the moment it did nothing to simplify the confused managerial condition.

The degree of confusion can be appreciated by consideration of the following factors. First, the board of directors contained two bankers' representatives, J. N. Darrow and Charles H. Jones, neither of whom were able to exercise any influence on management. To this low ebb had the prestige and power of investment bankers sunk by 1932. The balance of the board, including Modie Spiegel himself, were men involved in the company or related to the Spiegels, and all of them except M. J. Spiegel were anxiously seeking someone to follow. Innis was titular president and general manager to whom line officers were responsible, but all matters concerning the actual formulation of new policies were emanating from a small group headed by M. J. Spiegel, who held only the title of treasurer and secretary. Budgets, sales estimates, merchandising, credit, pricing, and circulation policies were being evolved by the triumvirate composed of M. J., Swikard, and Meinig. These, in turn, were made operational by M. J., who managed to get his father's approval for those matters which he brought to his attention, and this by no means included everything which the three were working on.

The situation was not one which M. J. wanted perpetuated, for the small budget which Meinig and M. J. had developed proved all too accurate. Fourth-quarter sales had amounted to under $2.5 million, the poorest the company had experienced since 1922, and were followed by an equally poor January record. Then, under the impact of new low-markup promotions, M. J.'s ruthless culling of the old mailing lists, and a more shrewdly directed circulation program to build new accounts and reactivate certain paid-up customers, sales began to pick up and first-quarter results had exceeded those of the previous year and were almost equal to the 1931 record. Innis protested that the no-profit sales in fall 1932 had been of little use, that the poor results for the year had been the result of bad selling and merchandising, and that proper solicitation of the mailing lists with effective catalogs would have produced better results than leader pricing.[1] But Innis had already lost. His resignation was accepted as of June 16, 1933 although it did not officially take effect on the company's records until the end of the year.[2] M. J. Spiegel became *de jure* general manager.

Organizationally, a more sensible managerial alignment was effected in 1933 and at the stockholders' and directors' meeting in early 1934. J. N. Darrow, who had been reelected a director in 1933, resigned from Otis & Company in November and promptly submitted his resignation from the Spiegel board, since he believed that Otis should continue its direct contact with Spiegel and he wanted to leave this seat available to them. M. J. Spiegel did not agree with him. Darrow's resignation was accepted but no Otis representative was elected to this vacancy in 1934, nor, in fact, was Charles Jones reelected. Instead the board consisted of Modie Spiegel and his two sons, Folger, Swikard, Meinig, John Cheshire, Reuben Don, and Walter Gatzert, all members of management. This board remained intact throughout this five-year period except for Cheshire's resignation in 1936 and his replacement the following year with Howard J. Sachs, a partner of Goldman, Sachs & Company, which had organized the underwriting of the company's $4.50 preferred stock issue during that year.[3]

From the point of view of formal rankings and conventional management-structure orthodoxy the resignation of Frederick L. Innis opened the way for the appointment of M. J. Spiegel as president and general manager, a move which would have formalized the actual power relationships within the company. Instead, the board elected Frederick W. Spiegel president in February 1934, while his brother became executive vice president and treasurer.[4] There were family reasons for this which included Frederick's role as older brother and pressures exerted by his father-in-law. Frederick Spiegel was himself not self-asserting. He possessed certain attributes valuable to a business organization, but these were concentrated almost purely in the area which is today called "human relations." As president it was to such problems as employee relations, contacts with suppliers, publicity, and stockholder relations, that he restricted his attention. M. J. Spiegel was the *de jure* operating executive in every actual sense, a condition recognized by all Spiegel personnel and accepted by the brothers and their father.

The other formal officers of the company as of 1934 included Edward Swikard as sales vice president, Walter Gatzert as secretary, John Cheshire as assistant secretary-treasurer, and Modie Spiegel as chairman of the board. Gatzert had been appointed secretary in October 1933 when he joined Spiegel, May, Stern following the collapse of his own enterprise, Gatzert Company. Walter Gatzert was thirty-one years old when he came to Spiegel. A graduate of the University of Chicago, he was an able man with extensive contacts in the investment and commercial banking and brokerage fields. His sister, Clara, had married Frederick Spiegel in 1923 and Modie Spiegel had heavily underwritten the Gatzert Company. It was inevitable that his experience, training, and natural interest in banking and financial matters should be exploited by the company, and by 1937 he had been delegated M. J. Spiegel's responsibilities as treasurer.[5]

In terms of actual influence and relative importance to the rapidly evolving company, however, this formal organization told only part of the story. For Edward Swikard performed over a broad range of activities which exceeded the narrower implications of his official title, while George Meinig was functioning as M.J.'s key lieutenant with respect to developing a competent staff, in establishing the fundamental quantitative controls in selling and distribution of literature, and in budgeting, with heavy responsibilities for the coordination of warehouse and office service functions. His role was more formally recognized in 1935 when he was elected a vice president and assistant general manager, although his status had been clarified somewhat by his election as director the previous year.

From 1933 through 1937, M. J. Spiegel, Edward Swikard, and George Meinig unquestionably constituted the effective upper echelon of Spiegel management, although Modie Spiegel was the titular head of the firm who had to approve of the planning and programs initiated by the triumvirate. During these years, although sales were pushing consistently up and the labor and administrative force was continually being expanded, the executive management group remained small. M. J., in addition to the broad leadership and administrative roles demanded of a general manager, also performed the duties of general merchandise manager. To him reported not only Swikard and Meinig, but also the heads of the warehouse service and office service groups, the secretary, the various merchandise executives and buyers, a special merchandise-sales coordinator, and a variety of men charged with staff and research responsibilities.

It was inevitable that M. J. Spiegel found himself making decisions continually, big and small, for a dozen or so men; it was equally inevitable that a great deal of confusion had to result from such a condition. A quick decision rendered for one group on Monday was subject to revision a few days or a few weeks later for an entirely different group. Without clean coordination and a smooth flow of information to all individuals and groups involved, distortion, failure of effective execution, and functional traffic jams could not be avoided. During the first two years these were probably of modest proportions and readily adjusted, but as the division of administrative labor grew and the lines of communication lengthened with increasing staff, the situation demanded correction and reorganization.

In spite of the basic weaknesses of the organizational structure, M. J., Swikard, and Meinig were committed to continue the merchandising-selling plan which they had evolved during the second half of 1932. Their confidence was well founded. Whereas the company had ended 1932 with net sales of only $7.1 million and a loss of over $300,000, by 1937 the results were $56,117,700 in sales and over $2.5 million in net profits. Although sales in January 1933 were disappointingly below those of the same month in 1932, from that point on for the next sixty months sales rose continuously.

The sales growth recorded during these five years amounted to 790 percent of the 1932 figure, an astonishing achievement when measured against a relatively small increase in national mail-order sales. But perhaps an even more significant bench mark of success was the rate at which Spiegel gained, relative to its most important rivals. For the period 1932–37, for example, Sears' mail-order sales rose 73.5 percent, from $116.7 million to $202.5 million.[6] Therefore, while in 1932 Spiegel sales amounted to just 6.1 percent of those of Sears; as of 1934 the ratio was 19.7 percent, and by 1937 it was 27.7 percent. Sears, of course, was in the process of drastically altering its distribution structure during these years, with retail sales rising from roughly 58 percent to over 64 percent of the corporate total. The mail-order sales for Montgomery Ward are not known for these years, but according to an industry study done by Dean Langmuir for Wertheim & Company in 1935, Ward's mail-order business revived more quickly than did Sears and was pushed more aggressively. By the end of 1934 Ward claimed catalog sales of $160 million, or $30 million more than Sears, even though its total combined volume still lagged well behind its rival.[7] Despite this gain, however, Ward's relative improvement was less impressive than Spiegel's.

The marketing program that led to this rapid progress was based on imaginative credit merchandising. The theme, "No Charge for

Credit," was pushed as never before. Also, a major drive was made to recruit new customers and to upgrade the customer list with people having somewhat better incomes than the traditional Spiegel customer. In order to attract these new customers, the company stressed offering better merchandise bargains. That is, goods of known quality were featured in the promotional campaigns at very competitive prices.

This program was not, of course, carried out in a vacuum. A number of factors completely external to Spiegel influenced the upward sweep in sales. Most important were increased industrial production, substantial improvements in disposable personal income, federal assistance to agriculture, reduction in unemployment, and federal assistance to the unemployed through the Works Progress Administration and other agencies. Unquestionably the New Deal programs directly affected precisely the income groups which Spiegel serviced. Of course, without a plan of action and effective leaderships this opportunity could well have passed the company by.

Fundamental to the success of the new Spiegel strategy was the attraction of new customers to replace those lost through depression conditions. The Division 2 idea, establishing a special list of new, unproven customers for analysis before showing them on the regular customer list (Division 1), served this purpose nicely. The house had available to it mailing lists of former customers, plus postmaster lists of R.F.D. names, plus varieties of other lists which could be purchased at relatively low cost. To such names were mailed circulars advertising standard household goods such as oil stoves, blankets and bedding, or cheap furniture. At times from two to four separate offers were included on a single circular. Prices were set deliberately low, sometimes below cost, so that the offer constituted a value which a low-income family could not afford to ignore. For example, in 1935 Division 2 circulars offered a combination room heater and cooking range for $11.98, a twelve-piece bedroom suit including a bed, mattress, pillows, blankets, sheets, pillowcases, and spread for $14.95, and a three-burner oil stove and oven combination at $5.98. A coupon was included which, when filled out and returned with one dollar, became the basis for delivery of the goods. These dollar-down terms were good up to a maximum of $15 and the company gener-

ally restricted a Division 2 buyer to that amount. Monthly installments were for two dollars or more so that the obligation would
be paid out within seven months. The coupon provided for a minimum of information, insufficient in itself to provide the basis for
a sound credit evaluation. In addition to direct-mail circulars the
company also used a magazine, *Rural Progress*, for advertising
Division 2 merchandise in those areas reached by the periodical.
During the first two years of the program Division 2 merchandise
was limited to household goods; after this, the merchandise offerings were broadened to include apparel, automobile tires, and
other goods not strictly of a household furnishings type.

Upon receipt of Division 2 coupon orders, ledgers were opened
for these customers and strictly segregated from the regular accounts. For a period of three months following the date the accounts were opened no contact was made with the new customers.
Then the ledgers were reviewed and handled according to status.
Those which were in arrears were given routine collection handling, beginning with the dun letter series. Accounts which were
in up-to-date collection condition, or on which the customer could
be given the benefit of a doubt—for example, if there was one full
installment paid and part of another—the company would break
its silence. The customer would receive a catalog or sales book
which included a table of terms and explained house policy, and
an order blank containing the standard credit-information questions.

The principle upon which management operated at this point
was that the Division 2 customer had qualified himself for classification as a live-account customer by his payment performance and
was ready for the opportunity to buy more from Spiegel. The credit
information provided was useful in building up a general house
criteria for credit passing and for setting limits on the credit to be
extended. Those customers who had demonstrated ability and willingness to pay their accounts, as well as their intention to trade
with the company, could be sent further sales literature in the expectation that it would be productive. On the basis of these assumptions it was further assumed that selling costs per unit of
sale or per dollar of sale would be reduced, and that purchases
from regular sales efforts (Division 1 merchandise) would be
made at higher average gross margins. This trading up from Divi-

sion 2 to Division 1 merchandise, stimulated by catalogs and follow-up loose-leaf promotions, would produce more frequent orders of an amount substantially above the Division 2 average. Combined with lower selling costs this upgrading would produce profitable customers within a year after the original contact.

The campaigns produced some admirable results. For one thing, the estimated number of individual mail-order customers rose almost threefold between 1932 and 1936, from 360,000 to over 1.2 million. For another, average balance per customer at year's end improved from $13.28 in 1932 to $15.12 in 1935.[8] The average order received by the house had reached its nadir in 1932 when it was $12; in 1934 it had risen to $13.54; and by 1936 was close to $15. And this had been accomplished in spite of what M. J. Spiegel called the deliberate policy of keeping the average order small so as to spread risks and minimize the chance for credit loss. The company was enjoying an average order size which amounted to several times that received by mail-order houses which enjoyed heavy cash sales. The Wertheim study in early 1935 had ascertained that the average Ward sales in 1934 was approximately one-third that of Spiegel,[9] and it was probable that Sears had the same experience. Furthermore, the program had been effective in upgrading customers from Division 2 to regular status and obtaining sales from the catalogs. By the end of 1934, 63 percent of sales volume was being produced from catalogs, the balance from sales books, regular loose-leaf efforts, and Division 2 literature.

A modification in treatment of customers originated by Division 2 promotions began in early 1937. One step in the revised program was the introduction of credit control cards; a second was the creation of an intermediate customer classification, Division 1½. The credit control card was a complete credit questionnaire form, containing the questions which had been rigorously tested by experiment and research since 1933 and which seemed to be particularly pertinent in evaluating a credit prospect. Such cards were originally dispatched with the first serious solicitation sent to Division 2 customers, and were sent to customers originally solicited via the Friends' campaigns and other so-called Goodwill credit applicants. At this stage the credit control cards were not a departure from the previous plan, but were regarded rather as (1) a disciplinary technique to encourage respect for the company and to urge conformance with its payment rules, and (2) to weed out persons who were afraid they could not obtain credit. The latter was particularly important from the point of view of circulation control and solicitation expense, since a continuation of the old system would have resulted in a catalog being sent to such persons.

The Division 1½ section was to be composed of all new customer live accounts that had not yet been upgraded to preferred status. The literature sent to this group included the credit control card, and was oriented to the theme that this group was in a transitional period which, if successfully completed, would result in an upgrading to a preferred status with no-money-down privileges, a credit bank account, and the opportunity of buying all needs from Spiegel.[10] Customers in this group had to be in good standing, with at least three installments paid, two of which had to be in succession, and also not to have required more than one letter in any dun sequence. Management sought by this technique to sell a second order on dollar-down terms as quickly as possible, offering somewhat more liberal terms, for example, dollar-down up to a maximum of $25 instead of $15, but limiting both the size and number of these repeat orders. The merchandise to be dangled in front of such customers was to be closer to Division 2 than to regular catalog stock in price and nature. Catalogs were not issued to Division 1½ patrons until after the second testing period was underway and additional experience on payment habits had been gained. Only then, and only with those who qualified, did elevation to preferred customer status follow.

While the Division 2 technique was vital to the improvement in Spiegel's sales position, the use of leader-pricing and solid values for Division 2 merchandise was the necessary condition for attracting the new customers. In order to provide real substance to the company's promotion of the "no charge for credit" theme, and to erase the competitive price-quality edge enjoyed by Sears and Ward, the company had to get its prices down across the board. Therefore, the company hardened its buying practices. Since M. J. Spiegel was, during these years, the general merchandise manager as well as general manager, he was in a position to supervise the activities of company buyers and to enforce the tougher policy. It became very tough indeed. Buyers had to drive the hardest bargain possible with sources, whether they were manufacturers or jobbers, broaden their contacts with the markets, and show no hesitancy in abandoning any source if a better deal or contract could be obtained from others. In a period of economic stagnation when plant capacity was being under-utilized and manufacturers and jobbers were hungry for orders, this was not too difficult a feat. Spiegel was expanding sales and purchases, was willing to order in relatively large volume, and placed fewer demands upon sources than did either Ward or Sears in terms of bookkeeping, deliveries to different plants and retail units, and specifications.

Even though Spiegel generally demanded fewer services from suppliers than Ward and Sears did, this hard-nosed policy could not always be applied. In its relations with apparel manufacturers, many textile firms, and furniture producers, situations in which Spiegel held a superior bargaining position, the company could grind manufacturer margins very close to zero. However, when dealing with producers of nationally branded goods, particularly in the bigger ticket lines, the company could exercise much less advantage. Furthermore, the company made few concessions to manufacturers other than paying cash within the discount period. It rarely advanced money to sources as the goods progressed through the production stages. In addition to vigorous bargaining and the use of competitive advantage during the first few years of this period, management provided a relatively sound argument for persuading manufacturers to supply merchandise at lower prices: that such business utilized otherwise idle capacity, that it paid for direct and variable expenses, and that it made some contribution to overhead costs which otherwise would go uncovered.[11]

Such practices, however, horrified Dean Langmuir, investigating the company and the mail-order industry for Wertheim & Company in 1935. He contrasted the Spiegel procurement position with that of Sears, repeating the claim of Sears' executives that General Wood insisted that suppliers were entitled to a reasonable margin of profit and that Sears' purchase prices insured that they got it. Spiegel, in Langmuir's opinion, was ruthless. Since the company acquired so much of its needs from small manufacturers who "are in such desperate condition that they must sell at any price to avoid bankruptcy," Spiegel was indifferent to the fate of suppliers.[12] Langmuir was concerned lest such practices build a wall of enmity against the company which, when economic conditions changed, would result in manufacturers refusing to trade with Spiegel. With the exception of the little Goodman Clothing Company, which was purchased in 1933 for $13,000,[13] Spiegel held no financial interest in suppliers; therefore, it was quite vulnerable to boycotts by suppliers. Langmuir argued that the bankruptcy of National Bellas Hess was caused in no small degree by the inability to obtain suppliers.

In a letter to Maurice Wertheim written March 20, 1935, M. J. Spiegel defended his company's buying practices and stated his philosophy and what he believed were the real conditions of mercantile life:

I do not believe that individuals win the respect of their fellowmen by being soft and what is commonly called "easy marks." I know of many suppliers who admit that their prices to us must be right or they will not get the business; still, these same suppliers would rather do business with us than the larger firms who theoretically insist upon seeing the manufacturer make a profit, because they claim that those same firms are very apt to change buyers, and when that happens, the new buyers' friends will get the orders, even though they are not earned.

He insisted that Bellas Hess failed not because of buying policy but as a result of its inability to get selling costs below 25 percent of sales, and insisted that while Spiegel tended to concentrate on small manufacturers, it did business with some of the "largest manufacturers in the country" who thought highly of the firm. The truth lay somewhere in between these points of view. Certain Spiegel buyers were, particularly in that period, rough and ruthless. There was no question that they alienated sources and created a real degree of ill will for the company. This had to be made good during the years after 1937, but, as Robert Engelman, a buyer during that period, expressed it:

People's memories are short, particularly when you are buying goods. When you are buying goods and you have an open-to-buy and are going to spend money with a source, he is going to do business with you even if he hates you. If you can put together an open-to-buy and a pleasant, fair personality, it doesn't take long to re-establish a reputation. And we had some good people around here.

The period of reestablishment, however, was not then in sight, and M. J. Spiegel's philosophy antagonized many manufacturers. A few, in fact, refused to deal with the company ever again as a result of that experience. This policy, incidentally, was not in harmony with the philosophy held by Modie Spiegel. According to M. J. Spiegel, his father remonstrated, warning that ruthless behavior with sources was bad business and bad human relations.

Whatever it boded for the future, the procurement policies of 1933–36 unquestionably helped management take down the general price level of the company. At the same time, the relative level of gross profit declined. In 1933, for example, gross profit amounted to 46.8 percent of net sales; from here it went steadily down to 43 percent in 1934, 40 percent in 1936, and 37.2 percent in 1937. Operating expenses also were reduced relative to sales, but not at the same rate as gross profit. Total operating and selling costs in 1933 were 36.9 percent. They dropped to 30 percent in 1934, then varied during 1935–36 and were 32 percent in 1937. The Spiegel management was determined to move prices of merchandise down to levels where they would be directly competitive with those of Sears and Ward mail-order prices.

While hard bargaining with sources and the passing of lower merchandise costs along to consumers in the form of lower prices were fundamental elements in making the company more competitive with its "Big Brothers," they were by no means the only devices used. There had to be quality comparability as well, and even before the firm set up a testing laboratory and developed the first rudiments of rigorous quality control there were some active souls in management alert to the problem. Principal among them was the iconoclastic Thornton Adams. During 1933–34, the company was relying upon national branded merchandise to bolster the claim of no charge for credit, marking up certain nonbranded goods to absorb the loss on margins of the former goods. Adams, who had become M. J. Spiegel's merchandise and selling coordinator as well as a conscience and somewhat impish goad, set up his own informal tests. He bought from Sears and Ward merchandise of the type which Spiegel sold, assembled these with their catalog descriptions and prices, displayed them with competing items from the Spiegel inventory, and invited M. J. Spiegel and department merchandise managers to the exhibit. He reported that M. J. stalked around the displays, occasionally stopping to wrench a Spiegel article from its place and tear it up or slam it to the floor, then he abruptly left the room. Later he observed that Adams was right, and careful merchandise-quality studies were inaugurated, tougher requirements imposed on sources, and the drive to achieve qualitative comparability gained momentum.[14]

Spiegel also protected its price and merchandise position by very tight inventory controls, by careful studies of its Red Books, and by shifting its sales emphasis toward hard line products and men's apparel, on both of which margins were larger and flexibility of price adjustments easier. There were, in addition, extensive studies involving the timing of certain merchandise sales, which permitted the distribution of literature slightly in advance of peak purchase periods with consequent improvement in merchandise turnover. Spiegel's inventory practice was to contract for one-half or less of estimated catalog sales at the time the catalogs were issued. Then, as the season advanced, reorders were sent to manufacturers as comparisons of actual to budgeted sales indicated. The practice at Sears, on the other hand, was to contract for from 60 to 75 percent of estimated sales at the date of catalog issuance.[15] Among the reasons why Spiegel applied such a conservative inventory policy was, as M. J. Spiegel later pointed out,[16]

We have less in dollars available to service customers; therefore, there must be a keen understanding of the saleability of items and a well-oiled machine to expedite the delivery of orders to sources of supply once an order is desirable.

In addition, the company's use of its old National Cash Register posting equipment prevented a detailed breakdown by classes of merchandise. Since the company had to be able to distinguish promptly between profitable and unprofitable merchandise in adjusting its merchandising practices, M. J. considered it vital that "somebody with a merchandise feel" be responsible for merchandise controls. This he had begun in 1930, then had greatly expanded the Red Book controls during the years when he had taken over responsibility as merchandise general manager after mid-1932. The Red Books contained all important data with respect to the buying and selling operation, by classes of goods, and by item, such as the unit and dollar information on purchases, gross profits, sales, prices, returns, and merchandise on hand at the end of a season. That they were an invaluable merchandising guide is undeniable, if only with respect to company experience and the classes of goods which had been bought in the past. Much of the early research in merchandising, discontinued after 1934 under the pressure of other and more demanding requirements, was possible because of Red Book data, and some of the greatest successes, such as with the sale of combinations in apparel, in bedroom sets, and other house furnishings, were achieved as a result of such studies. The Red Books, in fact, were excellent guides to merchandising and selling action, and were amenable to a broad spectrum of handling.

Inventory controls and merchandise budgeting policy made use of the Red Books in a limited and essentially restricted fashion. As a result of sustained study, a mechanical formula was developed for each merchandise department which, when the arithmetic was correct and the merchant's judgment good, provided the number of units of any particular item in the catalog which had to be ordered for any specific time period in order to efficiently service anticipated demand. With a little experience and normal intelligence, both the arithmetic and the judgment tended to be good, and the estimated need accurate. But then buyers ran into M. J. Spiegel's merchandise controller, Miss Esther Coleman, who guarded the concept of minimum inventory with unparalleled vigilance. Miss Coleman, according to men who were active in the buying divisions during this era, was sensitive to all factors affecting the differences between gross profit and initial profit, that is, losses on merchandise which could not be sold in regular or extraordinary sales efforts, depreciation of the value of inventory, freight on purchases, and losses or gains on markups. Control over gross profit tended to be realized by control over unit inventory, and during the early years of this period in particular, Miss Coleman and her assistants had personally to approve each individual buy. Re-buyers brought to her their computed requests for purchases and invariably were told to reduce them. This arbitrary cutting of the buys was based on judgment as to expected demand or guesses as to the capacity of a source to deliver goods more rapidly in the future if the reduced estimates of sales proved wrong. Miss Coleman had much experience in the company and was capable to some shrewd judgments; further, she shared M. J. Spiegel's philosophy with respect to inventory sizes. But the very fact that buyers had to submit every reorder and wait hours before an approval, even begging for a smaller reduction, seems somewhat immature in a corporation selling tens of millions of dollars of merchandise a season.

The end results of this policy soon appeared. Spiegel maintained rigid control over inventory, it had a merchandise turnover rate which was astonishingly high for a company doing its volume of business, and the ratios of year-end inventory to net sales were equally surprising (see table 10).

10. Inventory ratios and merchandise turnover, 1933 through 1937

Year	Inventory to Sales	Stock turnover Rate
1933	22.8%	4.04
1934	4.9	6.82
1935	6.4	11.61
1936	9.8	8.21
1937	9.8	7.13

Source: Corporate records, 1933–37.

Despite the obvious efficiency of use of working capital which the high turnover rates implied, and the equally obvious safeguards against rapid changes in market demand entailed in the low inventory-to-sales ratios, conservative inventory policy imposed some serious costs to the company in terms of consumer service. Most obvious among these were the back order and substitution problems imposed by the short-of-stock condition. Back ordering, a perennial problem unless the seller maintained large on-hand inventories, could be handled with minimum customer dissatisfaction by imposing a fixed limit on the time within which the out-of-stock article could be ordered in from a source and delivered to the customer. If it could not be delivered within that interval, the customer could be immediately notified and the order for that article canceled. But Spiegel did not follow such a policy, particularly in the years 1933–37. Instead the back order was put in, the customer charged for the sale, and the goods shipped when finally received, even though weeks could, and did, elapse. This situation was aggravated by customers having deliveries from a single order staggered over an indefinite time span, not infrequently paying installments for merchandise which they had not yet received. Further, an out-of-stock condition tempted the company to substitute available goods on orders, a circumstance which both tended to heighten customer irritation and increase the return of merchandise. Returns and allowances during this period ranged between 9 and 12.5 percent of net sales. At Sears, by contrast, returned goods amounted to only 40 percent of the Spiegel percentages.[17]

Even more damaging was the loss of patronage from people who had been carefully recruited and conditioned to buy more of their needs from Spiegel. In a rapidly expanding company undergoing a series of *ad hoc* organizational changes which were not always particularly well coordinated, some of this was unavoidable. At Spiegel, however, especially in the warehouse service division, there was a general assumption that the customers were people who would not be able to buy consumer goods at all if they could not get credit, and that since Spiegel extended them credit they would put up with very poor service to get the goods. While inventory policy did not initiate this attitude, it certainly did nothing to mitigate it.

Among the factors helping to offset the ill will created by poor customer service were new approaches taken in merchandising. Already mentioned was the strong tendency to become competitive on a price basis, with the liberal utilization of leader prices in Division 2 and the use of spot pricing for mailing efforts used as catalog follow-ups and in special sales books. A corollary of this was the development of odd pricing as the company probed for variations in demand response. There was nothing new in this, in terms of general retailing practice, but by use of the Red Book records management began to utilize it more scientifically. This development, of course, was expedited by the ability of a mail-order firm to test different price combinations in different regional, community-size, and economic-class situations. A further corollary of the effort to obtain general price competitiveness while still providing for relatively proportional improvements in sales volume and net income was the effort to alter the structure of the product line, that is, by increasing the proportion of goods with higher margins. During these years, when resale price maintenance was being rapidly extended by state and Federal legislation, and before the advent of discount houses, excellent margins were available in appliances and hard lines. However, the general economic and locational characteristics of the Spiegel market precluded any sudden shift into the so-called "big ticket" appliances and rendered uneconomic the introduction of a greatly improved quality of furniture.

Yet throughout this period the company did shift emphasis toward higher margin goods. In 1933 the number of catalog pages devoted to hard lines amounted to little more than 25 percent of the spring and fall books; by fall 1934 this was up to 35 percent, rising to an average of 40 percent during 1935 and 1936, and jumped to 46 percent in 1937. Furthermore, since the number of catalog pages increased from under 230 in 1933 to nearly 360 in 1937, the importance of hard lines to the company tends to be understated by a mere recital of catalog proportions. The relationships between the contributions to sales and to net merchandising profit made by hard lines can be more clearly appreciated by examining the data in table 11. It can be seen from these data

11. Relative performance of hard lines

Year	Gross Sales	Net Sales	Gross Margin	Gross Merchandising Margin	Gross Merchandising Profit
1933	. . .	. . .	. . .	. . .	. . .
1934	22.0%	22.8%	22.9%	22.8%	21.3%
1935	22.9	23.4	22.9	22.5	22.1
1936	28.3	28.8	28.2	28.5	30.8
1937	30.5	31.0	32.3	32.0	42.7

Source: Corporate records, 1933–37.

that hard lines enjoyed a slightly better gross margin, a consistently better gross merchandising margin, and during 1936 and 1937 a notably better net merchandising profit.

Although documentation from company records is virtually impossible, the behavior of rival mail-order sellers had a major influence on the Spiegel product line. Sears' influence can be inferred by the steady shift toward hard goods in the product line, and is reflected by the relatively uninspired merchandising of standard goods by Spiegel throughout this period. Sears stressed dependability in both price and quality at any given price. Under Rosenwald, Sears had evolved the policy of absolute integrity with respect to its customer relationships, and a necessary foundation for this policy—and reputation—had been the development of elaborate studies of merchandise specifications, spread of specification buying, and rigorous standards of acceptability.[18] With few exceptions they showed little concern with fashion, styling, and taste, at least in mail order, and a comparison of their women's apparel pages with those of Bellas Hess in the 1920s, or Ward in the 1930s, reflects this indifference. Prior to the Avery era, Montgomery Ward had shown no desire to modify the traditional view of the mail-order house as being the server of rural needs, specializing in overalls, work shoes, aprons, farm tools, and mail-order suits and dresses. But when Avery took over command of Ward, this atmosphere began to change, a new image was created and, as Avery was later to observe, "the only 'rubes' in the country are now found on Michigan Avenue."[19]

The situation which Avery inherited at Ward closely resembled that which existed at Spiegel in 1932: a chaotic operation condition aggravated by extreme pessimism, particularly with respect to the future of mail-order selling. Once his firm had been reorganized and the management sold on the future of mail order, Avery began to revolutionize the mail-order image. Avery believed it necessary to break the traditional pattern of competing for customers through the appeal of lower prices, that is, devoting the overwhelming proportion of catalog pages to the cheapest articles. By the spring season 1935, according to Dean Langmuir, Avery was able to prove that the Ward catalog emphasized higher priced goods more than cheaper articles, and that on the basis of past results this had paid off in improved sales and profits. During this entire period, therefore, Ward stressed quality goods, gave a free hand to its women's wear merchandise manager, and succeeded in becoming the foremost fashion house in the mail-order field, with merchandised styling in products and in presentation.

There was little question that M. J. Spiegel was excited by the Avery success and influenced by Avery personally. But he was a different type of merchant and Spiegel's merchandising policies tended to fall somewhere between the Ward and Sears examples. At least into 1935, the company was handicapped in the merchandising of higher priced articles by a credit policy which was geared to apparel terms, such that orders for $30 and up were discouraged. Spiegel's principal problem, one which remained unsolved through these years, was in trying to develop a niche of its own based upon something other than—or in addition to—the credit theme.

The early merchandising was frankly geared to exploit the "no charge" claim, although credit terms were not liberal. The "national brands" campaign which had been introduced toward the end of the previous era was continued into 1934, with the catalogs heavily emphasizing the branded goods. This practice was underscored by the introduction of house brands, names such as Argyle and Gateway in tires, tubes, and even washing machines; Columbia, Big Chief, and Air Castle for kitchen ranges, car batteries, and radios. There were also tie-in brands, with house brands superimposed on the names of manufacturers such as Simmons. But the shift toward the objective of merchandise merit could be seen as early as 1933. During these years through 1935 the total merchandise impression was improved also by a greater use of color pages in the catalog, obvious improvement having been made in the rotogravure process. While paper stock was still below the standards used by Ward and Sears, the net impression of the catalogs was distinctly favorable.

While new product introductions were at a minimum during the first two years of the period, there was a noticeable trend toward more modern variations of products in the line. Particularly evident were the substitutions of more modern undergarments in the women's line, with lighter corsets and girdles and uplift brassieres replacing heavier styles. There was also some diminution of heavy, overstuffed living room furniture which was replaced by that of lighter construction, a tendency which extended to dining room furniture. In kitchen cabinets, cooking ranges, and tables the tendency toward cleaner and more functional lines continued. On the other hand men's suits continued to reflect the prevailing lower-middle-class styles, particularly the wide flapping trousers and extreme lapels. The firm was still strongly committed to kerosene, wood, and coal burning heating stoves and cooking ranges, offering only a very few gas models. Refrigerators were exclusively of steel construction but like cooking ranges, no electric models were offered. The first electrical refrigerator entered the line with the spring 1936 catalog, the company offering three sizes of box, from 5½ to 8 cubic feet, at $119.50, $129.50, and $149.50. Credit terms were set at approximately 13 percent down and eight-month maturities. Other new products adopted in 1936 included fencing, wallpaper, electrical fixtures, home power plants, and amplifying systems. Total sales of such products for the year amounted to nearly $100,000, roughly 0.2 percent of total sales. The catalogs also reflected the growing importance of automobile supplies and hardware, plumbing, decorating materials, tool lines, upholstery materials, small appliances, hygienic goods, washing and cleaning equipment, bicycles, sporting goods, and luggage.

Further and more significant changes occurred in 1937. The spring catalog introduced farm equipment to the product line, devoting four pages to harrows, plows, cultivators, corn planters, harnesses and collars, saddles, and the like. The whole tire-battery-accessories line was expanded, several new pages were devoted to household tools, and chicken-raising equipment, bathroom fixtures and installation items, plumbing and outdoor cisterns, garage and housedoor hardware, doors and sashes were increased in number and variety. The company also introduced steel rowboats, outboard motors, and auto-trailers to the line, and for the first time offered a limited optical service for repairing broken or damaged lenses. This direction of merchandising reflected the importance of the rural market for the company, reflected as well the locations of these markets, for in the richer agricultural belts of Illinois and Iowa, for example, even in the middle 1930s there was a strong substitution effect underway of powered equipment for animal drawn vehicles. In terms of merchandising philosophy, these products were closer to the Sears policy than to that of Ward.

The ambiguous nature of Spiegel policy was evident the same year with the introduction of a new element of style merchandising in women's wear. This was the Saindon Models in dresses, a premium-priced line described in the spring catalog as "an added surprise—a real style treat—a complete showing of the famous Saindon Models . . . a distinct achievement by Spiegel." Although she had some influence on the designs, Bernadette Saindon was not "a famous designer," but rather M. J. Spiegel's private secretary and secretary of the company. Her identity and the harmless charade itself, were unimportant. The event heralded the beginnings of the new company policy which would crystallize into the "quality concept" in 1938–39, an orientation closer to the Avery philosophy of mail-order merchandising.

Given such factors as merchandise variation, quality, pricing, and general economic conditions, any attempt to increase sales volume depended largely upon the exploitation of credit merchandising techniques, including terms of sale and standards of acceptance. These techniques, in turn, were dependent upon the financial condition of the company and the availability of money for short- and long-term investment and for meeting current operating expenses. Profit-maximizing goals, of course, imposed the condition that expenses be restricted from rising as rapidly as gross income and the further condition that capital be employed in those uses which increased sales over expenses more rapidly than alternative uses. The firm seeking to increase sales and profits simultaneously must, therefore, reconcile sets of policies and establish priorities for both the execution of decision and the utilization of available resources. For example, cheap and easily obtainable credit with easy terms and long maturities will produce sales; it will also produce bad debts and heavy collection expense and tie up funds in slowly liquidating assets. Tight credit policy, on the other hand, will limit credit losses and collection expense, and turn over the investment in receivables rapidly; it will also discourage sales. Thus, if the principal goal of management is to encourage sales, a priority is given to an easy credit policy. This priority of policy, effectively exploited with available selling techniques and sufficient resources, will affect the rate at which new accounts can be added and the amounts which will be sold the average account.

Furthermore, policy formulation with respect to credit is affected by the availability of financial resources and the relative weights of conflicting claims for money within the organization. When working capital to be employed in financing receivables must be obtained from financial institutions, its quantity and the terms of borrowing are strongly influenced by the credit practices of the organization. Easy credit terms with heavy loss and expense prospects are not, unless offset by substantial net earnings on the receivables, warmly viewed by commercial bankers. Thus, an easy credit policy requires a substantial self-financing by the firm, the funds for which must be obtained from retained earnings or the sale of equity securities; and the availability of retained earnings and/or equity capital depends upon profitability and dividend practices.

As of 1933 Spiegel was confronted by serious financing problems. Three years of sustained losses and the failure to maintain preferred dividends had robbed the company of any reserves of working capital sufficient to exploit quickly whatever new sales opportunities developed as a result of the techniques of Division 2 and lower prices. If funds were to be made available for long-term development of markets it was necessary to get volume and profits up. A better earnings position would provide some opportunity for selling stock, increasing the quantity of short-term debt financing, and reinvesting profits; and if this goal could be achieved the company would be in a position to undertake those strategies which would gain for it a strong market position and sustained prospects for growth.

In light of the company's long-run experience with credit, top management in 1933 was relatively certain that sales could be increased by a strong policy of liberalizing terms, relaxing the existing standards of risk acceptance, and strongly merchandising the advantages of credit buying. Simultaneously management was confronted by pressing claims for, and a shortage of, working capital, plus the heavy losses on receivables which had been going on since 1930. As previously shown, M. J. Spiegel was determined to shift from a position in which the company relied principally upon credit to attract business, with merchandise quality and prices a secondary consideration (the view of the company as a loan office with a little general store attached), to one in which merchandise was sold on merit at competitive prices and credit was one, but only one, of the supplemental appeals.

To achieve the objectives of rapidly increasing sales and spreading and reducing the credit loss risk, the standards of acceptance for new customers were reduced. During the era prior to 1923, the company's goal had been a 5 percent credit loss to net sales, under Landis this had been liberalized to 6 percent, under the new regime it was set at 8 percent. This was not achieved all at once; rather it was a result of a massive test of customer accounts—the Green Star Test—which began in 1933. The test indicated that a substantial proportion of delinquencies had produced credit losses, but, somewhat surprisingly, that a high proportion had still yielded a profitable business to the company. As a result, management accepted the possibility of a higher rate of credit loss, particularly on new customers, on the premise that the lower acceptance standards would encourage a substantial increment in patronage, most of which would produce profitable sales. The 8 percent figure was accepted as an average for the whole body of customers. For new customers a higher rate was set, over 10 percent; while for live accounts a loss rate closer to 4 percent was considered profitable, provided it resulted in sales gains from regular customers. It was, of course, axiomatic that as the rate of growth of new accounts accelerated, the average credit loss would increase, and particularly so if longer qualifying periods were not set for new customers before they were upgraded to a status which provided for no-money-down terms and the opportunity to order from the catalogs. During the first few years of this period, in an effort to capitalize on the body of new customers, the company was overly liberal in shifting customers from the restricted classification to preferred customer status and granting them special privileges and the full package of sales opportunities. For the irresponsible and dishonest, this presented a golden opportunity to pyramid purchases at Spiegel's expense.

During 1933–34 the company also made a serious effort both to stimulate purchases from customers to whom live account status was accorded and to impress upon them the responsibilities of credit buying. One device, a forerunner of a later and more successful effort, was the use of the "Credit Bank Account." When a new customer had been seasoned and accepted as a regular customer, he was sent a letter of welcome and an imitation bankbook which he was invited to keep current by using it as a record of his purchases, charges, remittances, and balance outstanding. No indication was provided, however, of how much credit was available to draw upon. When an order followed and was accepted, the customer knew he was good for at least that amount, but for subsequent purchases of greater amounts he was forced to put his credit to the test. In fact, for Division 2 recruits, not even management knew what the maximum would be until an order was received and the credit questions on the order blank were answered and verified. In the event the applicant proved unacceptable the order was refused.

The most important change in credit policy during this period occurred in 1934: the reintroduction of the add-on. Curiously, this was not proposed by Swikard who had innovated the scheme seventeen years earlier, but by George Meinig. Meinig had been concerned with two problems: one, a way of increasing the frequency of use of the catalog by regular customers, encouraging more orders; the second, reducing some of the operating problems associated with customers having more than one outstanding account in the ledger. With respect to the first problem, he believed that the amount of monthly installment payments directly affected purchases, that if a way could be found by which a customer could order needed merchandise while an account was still not paid up and yet not have to raise greatly the monthly obligation, the company would obtain more repeat business in a given year. Restricted to regular customers who had proved their intention to pay, the plan did not appear to contain excessive credit risks; further, up to some limit of credit, subsequent orders from good credit risks was exactly how the company hoped to increase both sales and profits.[20]

Swikard, to whom Meinig showed his plan, was discouraging, not because he did not believe in it, but rather because of the reception given his own plan seventeen years earlier. However, M. J. Spiegel quickly grasped its potential and persuaded his father to endorse it. Offered first in the fall catalog 1934, the add-on plan contained some restrictive features as well as obvious advantages; it discriminated between preferred and nonpreferred customers with respect to the amount of the add-on without a down payment. Preferred customers could order up to $25 without a cash payment, whereas other customers had to send $2.50 with the new order for amounts between $15.01 and $20, and more with larger orders. Further, the maximum order size was raised for preferreds from $200 to $300. For the nonpreferred customers eligible for the privilege, the down payments in the order size ranged from $15 through $40.

There was no question but that the add-on had a stimulating effect on business in 1934 and for subsequent years. If a customer had an outstanding balance on an existing account of $9 and an installment of $4 per month, a new order of $15 would have, in spring 1934 and earlier, required an installment of $2; thus, with $24 outstanding in two separate accounts, the customer would have been required to pay $6 per month for two months, $3 for the third month, and then $2 per month for five months. Under the add-on plan, however, assuming no down payment on the new order, the installment on the combined balance would have been $3. Further, if the customer was accustomed to paying Spiegel $4 per month, she probably had little difficulty convincing herself that she could continue to do so and find other goods to buy so that her combined balance did not exceed the amount which could be liquidated at a $4 rate.

Under the forced-draft impetus of M. J. Spiegel's driving will and the unforced enthusiasm of his lieutenants, the 1934 policies succeeded beyond expectations. Sales again almost doubled to over $26 million, and the rate of profit increase was even greater, with after-tax earnings reaching nearly $2.75 million. The total experience for the period, including the changes in average year-end receivables balances, average sales, and number of accounts, is shown in table 12.

12. Results of the 1933 through 1937 add-on policies

Year	Estimated Number of Customers	Year-end Accounts Receivable	Average Year-end Balance	Sales per Customer	Percentage Increase in Sales	Percentage Increase in Customers
1933	582,000	$ 8,339,968	$14.33	$23.20	90.4%	61.6%
1934	931,000	14,327,615	15.39	28.00	93.8	60.0
1935	1,200,000	18,148,691	15.12	28.30	29.6	28.9
1936	1,459,000	23,781,820	16.30	30.01	31.4	21.6
1937	1,549,000	30,713,022	19.82	36.20	25.5	6.2

Source: Corporate records, 1933–37.

While strenuous efforts were being expended to build new accounts and increase sales to established customers in good standing through the add-on feature, management sought to cut its credit loss and collection costs and to initiate a policy of improving the quality of customer. The bulk of new customers in 1936 and 1937 resided in northern states where, despite the regional differences in living costs and incomes, educational levels and living conditions tended to be higher than in the south at that period. In view of regular attrition and turnover of the whole body of customers, this action had the effect of upgrading the total group in terms of absolute income levels and a probable effect upon group attitudes toward debt responsibility. Further, it was bound to have an effect upon the incidence of delinquency, and both directly and indirectly upon collections. Losses on bad accounts varied with customer classification, with the heaviest charge-offs associated with new customers (10 percent and higher), the lowest on preferreds who remained active for several years (2 percent or less). In the south, however, the loss ratio was at least as great as in northern states generally. Therefore, as the proportion of new to total customers increased in response to recruiting campaigns, a factor particularly acute in periods when for many reasons, internal and external, attrition rates were high, the charge-off rate tended toward the upper planned limit of 8 percent. With a reduction of new southern accounts the charge-off rate fell.

The results for 1936 and 1937—not all of which, of course, were attributable to the functioning of credit and new customer policies —were generally excellent. Sales increased by over $10.4 million in 1936 and after-tax earnings rose to over $3.4 million, making it the most prosperous twelve months in the company's history to that date. There was a net gain of almost 260,000 customers and a gratifying improvement in average sale and average year-end balance. Even more significant for the future, these results pushed the market value of Spiegel common to a new high and permitted the company to obtain new capital through the sale of preferred stock, the increment amounting to almost $6 million. Even after liberal common dividends the retained earnings, plus the new outside capital, provided management with the resources which M. J. Spiegel considered essential to finance his plans for the future. The effort to reduce gross margins, improve merchandise and service quality, and accelerate the transition to a better type of customer could be intensified. The results for 1937 were also excellent with respect to sales, but disappointing in terms of profit. The spring season was much superior to the record of the previous year, and the fall campaign produced the company's highest volume to date. In all, sales for 1937 exceeded $56 million, up 25.5 percent from 1936, while sales per customer rose 20 percent to $36.20; and the year-end average balance outstanding went up 21 percent. Profits after taxes, however, amounted to only $3 million, down 33 percent from 1936, and while management's price and margin policies had reduced gross merchandising margin by 7 percent, operating and selling expenses rose 6.6 percent. Yet in spite of this, in spite, in fact, of the obvious onset of an economic contraction during the final quarter of 1937, M. J. Spiegel was sufficiently gratified by the overall result to push forward during the following years with the policies of upgrading customer quality and matching this with continued pressures to get margins lower and merchandise quality higher. A continued retreat from the south and a general improvement in credit controls were basic elements of this program, as was the determination to improve customer service.

The achievements of the company between 1933 and 1937 gave M. J. Spiegel every reason to believe that a period of even greater success was just ahead. The company's drive for new customers, and its experiments with credit policies, pricing, product lines, and other merchandising tactics had given Spiegel a new thrust and momentum. In spite of the economic decline in 1937, the general economy held promise of continued expansion. It seemed that the company's management need only plot its course and anticipate great success.

However, the madness on the European continent that was shortly to lead to the Second World War was to have a dramatic effect on the fast-rising Chicago mail-order house. Initially, the growth and spread of the virus of anti-Semitism which boiled out of Hitler's Germany caused management to worry about its effect upon company sales. An opinion survey conducted by the sales department in 1936 indicated that neither the actual firm title nor the name "Spiegel" seemed to arouse any significant antagonism among customers or noncustomers. Therefore, the name Spiegel was retained, but the names May, Stern, which had lost all meaning, were dropped. In 1937 the title on the certificate of incorporation was to "Spiegel, Incorporated."[21] The other challenges growing out of the world conflict would not be so easily met, however.

Modi Operandi
and the
Quality Concept
1938–1943

Chapter 9

Essentially, the activities of Spiegel, Incorporated, associated with the years 1938–43, followed from a fundamental change in the management's point of view with respect to the market it served or, more precisely, *should* serve. As was noted earlier, the success of the business during the years 1933–37 emerged from policies designed to recruit new customers rapidly and cheaply, to exploit regional and income-class markets where resistance to credit selling was low, and where account-creating and selling expenses per dollar of sales produced a strong multiplier effect. Because of the credit loss factor and because of the improved condition of the economy, management decided in 1937 to undertake a shift in market targets that would characterize the 1938–43 period. Customer studies indicated that even through 1936 the average weekly income of Spiegel customers was close to $16, roughly one-half the disposable income of the average household in 1934, and roughly 40 percent the American average in 1937.[1] Even in a society operating at less than full-employment it seemed clear to M. J. Spiegel and his advisors that the group upon which the company had thus far depended was expanding neither relatively nor absolutely. The logical conclusion seemed to be that a fundamental shift was required in company policy, to concentrate more upon families with a substantially higher level of income than was then being served.

Given the previous experience and lack of information regarding alternative markets, it was much easier to pull out of existing regions than to penetrate new ones, but the company sales and credit research arms were already well developed and there was a seasoned pattern to Division 2 which was adaptable to different market segments. The most difficult problems arose for management in the organizational context—the reversal of directions—and in the development of an image digestible for those people it had decided to court. The germ of the revised philosophy was evident in 1937, but it took the efforts of the next four years for its clarification and execution. In essence the plan called for attaining the goal of higher quality, and it set up its own logic. Higher quality customers meant that not only would the level of average income be higher but that the level of personal responsibility toward debt would similarly be raised. For persons with more disposable income and willingness to assume responsibilities could be trusted with more goods and larger outstanding balances without raising the risks. But if differentiation by socioeconomic groupings meant anything in marketing, it inferred that those in the higher classifications tended to be more selective about what they bought and where they bought it, tended to be better informed about consumer goods, and tended to demand better quality of both merchandise and service. Management, therefore, suspected that people in the higher socioeconomic brackets who would be sought as customers would be less impressed with installment credit than those who were then their customers, tending to regard it as one of the services to which they were entitled.

With the expansion of installment-credit selling, both in retail stores and on the part of the mail-order giants Sears and Ward, credit was merely a means of payment and would not, by itself, be considered a sufficient substitute for quality, price, and physical servicing. Thus, a better type of customer implied better quality goods and better merchandising. These requirements, in turn, demanded higher quality buyers and merchandise managers, better sources of supply, and the development of more continuous relationships with sources capable of providing standardized, quality merchandise and dependable services. To secure better quality customers with the requisite attitudes demanded improved mailing lists, improved methods of selection, verification, and classification of prospects and customers, and a continuous survey of consumer behavior such that optimum sales and profit results could be obtained from them. The customer improvement policy similarly demanded that the better merchandise be more effectively displayed and promoted, that the catalogs be upgraded in appearance and organization. The policy implied also that inventory policy be re-examined and, where necessary, modified in such a way that back orders and substitutions could be reduced, thereby decreasing cancellations, returned goods, and lost customers. It implied in addition that clerical and warehouse services be greatly improved, that orders be promptly filled and delivered, that the work flows be simplified and improved through systematic standardization and efficient supervision. And this, in turn, demanded improvement in the quality of the labor force, or at least the quality of performance. All of which cried aloud for better organization, tighter coordination of functions, improved managerial qualifications, better training, methods, and procedures. Qualified younger men and women had to be encouraged to accept more responsibilities and all executives had to be tied more tightly to the company through effective incentives.

Following a brief vacation in 1938, M. J. Spiegel returned to order a fundamental shake-up in the buying divisions and in clerical service, and to announce the creation of a new apparatus for coordinating operations in general. The new apparatus, called the "Commission Form of Management," was put into effect in March 1938 and consisted of a series of boards, each responsible for one or more operating committees. As explained by M. J. Spiegel, the boards were established as clearing houses for: the creation and crystallization of ideas; making certain that the ideas were executed; proper dissemination of information; and ensuring the constant review of all important company problems. The boards and their supporting subcommittees were composed of so-called commissioned officers, individuals whose work was intimately connected with the types of problems for which the boards were responsible. As a later document pointed out, perhaps somewhat optimistically, "These individuals were thus in a position where they had to work out solutions to the mutual benefit of all concerned. In this way we obtained integration throughout the company, a coordination of activity and effort that led to the start of a smooth-running organization."[2] While a large number of members of management received "commissions," there were additions to this hierarchy including such names as Earl D. Weil, A. W. Kolbert, William H. Garvey, Jr., Thornton Adams, and Miss Bernadette Saindon.

The creation of boards and supporting committees, the apparatus through which executives and subordinate officials would accomplish the goals which M. J. Spiegel was busily conceiving, constituted an interesting if controversial stage in the company's organizational evolution. Miss Saindon, in retrospect, argued that it was a logical and fruitful development.

Spiegel found itself with people in certain positions who were not really any longer technically equipped to handle the scale of business which the company had attained. Many of these men had come in without too much professional or technical training. While the firm was still flexible and growing, they had performed well; but once a certain size was reached some of these people became problems. Also, a number of our junior executives needed help. And, going a little further up, there needed to be better systems, better clearing house, all the way through. The commission system offered us many advantages. For one thing it was an excellent clearing house for information; for a second, it helped develop some of the weaker members in teamwork. Teamwork was very necessary. We had a lot of individual stars who had done exceedingly well individually, but as we became larger we required a better coordinated team effort. Commission management became one of the ways of getting this accomplished.

M. J. Spiegel defended the move in terms which correspond closely to those of Miss Saindon and, in addition, pointed out that it tended to provide for the development of effective assistants in the various departments, and in this way helped provide for the essential follow-up of directives and policy, a follow-up which he was convinced was lacking in management.[3]

The commission system operated through six boards, eleven committees, and an interorganizational council. The two principal boards under the system were the "Campaign Review" and "Operating Review." The functions of the former were "to review and approve plans for campaigns, sales policies, and trends," and it operated through three vital committees: the "advance seasonal planning committee"; the "merchandise-advertising committee";

and the "Spiegel Market Survey Committee." The latter, the "Operating Review" board's functions were "to review and approve plans for service operation, and for employee relations." Under this board were formed the "base committee" and the "Employee Relationship Committee."

Behind these in importance came the "Board of Merchandise Review," the "Board of Budget Control," the "Board of Collection Control," and the "Board of Credit Control." The duties of the first included the review of merchandise buying programs, continuous examination of general merchandising problems, and the establishment of merchandising budgets. The Board of Budget Control was responsible for the review and approval of plans for expense budgets. The Board of Collection Control and the Board of Credit Control were charged with the responsibilities of reviewing and approving plans for collection policies, credit approval, as well as for solicitation policies.

The composition of the boards and committees provides insight into both the prestige-status relationship of the individuals concerned, and the nature of their functional contributions. Both M. J. and Frederick W. Spiegel were members of all boards. Meinig was the other most active member of management in this respect, sitting on all boards and six committees. This was due not only to the technical nature of his responsibilities but because by temperament and disposition he was an excellent counsellor. Swikard served on four boards and six committees, Gatzert on six boards and three committees. Adams, Garvey, and Rose, because of their combined staff and administrative functions, were involved with from six to eight boards and committees. On the other hand, Weil, originally a member of only two boards and three committees, was rising in the hierarchy, destined for a vice presidency in 1940 and membership on the board of directors in 1943, while Don and Folger, both directors in 1938, were relatively uninvolved in the commission arrangement and due to go off the board of directors in 1940 and 1942, respectively. Kolbert's rise in status during this middle period is reflected by his five memberships on boards and committees, which, in turn, were tributes to the growing regard for his technical competency.

In spite of the heavy demands made upon the time of executives by the commission system, there was ample evidence that when it was introduced the innovation fitted into the rationale of the gradually changing organization. Until well into 1937 the organizational structure of the company had developed without hard-and-fast rules, meeting spot problems with spot solutions whether in merchandising or operating. There was an adherence to managerial techniques which had performed well in the past, particularly a dependence upon small groups to solve problems and formulate ideas. But growth itself, particularly when it occurred beyond the frontiers of previous experience and knowledge, produced decentralization within the executive structure. Thus, there had to be improvisation which enabled a centralized authority to exist while permitting some of the creative spontaneity of decentralization.[4]

It was particularly disheartening to have the introduction of a new system coincide with the business recession of 1937, but intensive effort and individual capacity began to yield substantive results within the year. Meinig and Swikard, with the help of the other members of the Advance Seasonal Planning Committee, produced a paper which they called "Modi Operandi," in October 1938; this document not only clearly reviewed past developments, objectively evaluated current operations, and called attention to fundamental weaknesses and inconsistencies of policy, but also provided a clear basic program for future development. "Modi Operandi" coupled with additional analysis of the company and its market potential led to a further specific plan, "The Five Year Plan," which was enunciated in January 1939. Modi Operandi was principally concerned with providing a blueprint for sound policies with respect to credit and circulation policies; the Five Year Plan was more far-reaching, particularly with respect to merchandising, but of necessity was developed upon the foundation of Modi Operandi.

Fundamentally, Modi Operandi accepted the technique which had been evolved from years of experimenting with and testing classes of new customers. A point-rating system had been adopted, based upon a tested credit questionnaire called a "credit control card." Points were assigned to the answers to questions which had been weighted by company experience with customers. Few points were given for good responses; many points for poor responses. Depending upon the final score applicants fell into three categories: those who could be accepted immediately, those who could be promptly rejected for credit, and the intermediate group—the largest—which required further investigation. Except for the development of the control cards and the standardization of the weighting system, there was nothing completely novel in this; it had been evolving since 1933. What was new was the treatment to be accorded those who were accepted. In the past, following the trial period in which three payments were being made on a Division 2 purchase, the customer was validated as "good pay," and immediately became eligible for preferred customer treatment, including no-money-down terms, and the full battery of promotional mailings. No effective attempt had been made to provide an intermediate stage of seasoning, particularly with respect to providing clear limits on the amounts which could be purchased in terms that were understood by customers.

According to Modi Operandi, the company would continue to use Division 2 methods of recruiting new customers, since it had proven itself as the most efficient, low-cost method of building new accounts. But, instead of instituting full-scale solicitation when the second installment was received from a Division 2 customer, the new practice would be to send the credit control card and refrain from stimulating another order until it had been returned and evaluated. The evaluation would then place the customer in the appropriate classification generally, and this would be further implemented by assignment to any of several specific sub-categories, each of which had an upper credit limit. The revolutionary feature, however, lay in then announcing to the individual customer what his limit was, and in setting up the mechanics for a regular review of individual behavior so that on the basis of experience customers could be upgraded, downgraded, or eliminated. Sales literature would then be geared to customers' rated behavior. High quality patrons, that is, those whose incomes, assets, amounts spent with Spiegel, and frequency of purchase qualified them as such, would receive the optimum solicitation treatment; those acceptable for credit but rated, say, for a maximum obligation of $25, would receive more restrained treatment. It was believed that the interpositioning of the credit control card, with its more comprehensive questionnaire, after Division 2 treatment and before full-scale solicitation, would tend to reduce the formation of fraud rings and cut substantially into the losses which these had caused in the past. But the critical variable was whether announcing the credit limit to customers would improve or reduce sales. A company as research-oriented as Spiegel would not rush into such a step as a broad policy unless it had been satisfied through tests on sample customer categories that the harm would be offset by or neutralized by the internal benefits to be enjoyed. However, as late as 1941 the case had not been unquestionably demonstrated.

Modi Operandi was integrated with a much more rigorous policy of collecting overdue and written-off accounts. The "Nep-men," under the leadership of William Garvey, Jr., tested, experimented, recommended, and had adopted a tightly organized body of field collectors which was systemized in a newly established firm which bore the title, In-state Collection Corporation. Most of the techniques employed by this method were time and experience proven, if not by Spiegel, certainly by other creditors.

However, the company's overzealousness at times caught the attention of the Federal Trade Commission. Early in the war Spiegel undertook, apparently at the urging of collection personnel, to employ the talents of two agencies specializing in providing collection and tracing services for retailers. Among the techniques popular with these firms, National Administrators of Winona, Minnesota, and International Trustees of Des Moines, Iowa, was the counterfeit trust fund. Both these firms printed and serviced letters and questionnaires purporting to be searching for addressees for whom "money is being held in trust," and that "in order to deliver this money quickly, we must have the enclosed Trustee Question Form filled out and returned to us at once."[5] The questionnaire provided for a listing of the individual's occupation, employment, income, personal property, previous address, and other information pertinent to a creditor. The mechanics of the technique involved the purchase by the creditor (Spiegel in this case) of the form letters, envelopes, and questionnaires, and payment of standard fees for servicing. These materials were then sent to Chicago where the company's last address for the debtor was typed on the envelopes and letters and postage added; they were then returned to the headquarters of the respective firms for mailing. When a response was received, the respondent received in return one cent, his "trust fund," and the information he had provided was forwarded to Spiegel for appropriate follow-up procedure. Spiegel found itself rather promptly in trouble.

The Federal Trade Commission complaints were filed in November 1942 on the grounds that the described practices constituted "unfair and deceptive acts and practices in violation of the Federal Trade Commission Act," and that the International Trustees had misrepresented itself as a "fiduciary agent" offering a beneficial interest of more than a trivial amount. Spiegel had no defense and admitted the material allegations in both complaints. Cease-and-desist orders were issued against all defendants,[6] and the details of the violations and identity of the parties at interest released to the newspapers. However, the F.T.C. actions apparently were not widely enough broadcast to do substantial harm to the public image, and the total effect of war hit Spiegel sufficiently hard so as to prevent any valid assessment of the new collection practices upon existing customers or new prospects. What is perhaps most surprising is that company attorneys were unable to advise management regarding the dubious legal grounds for this enterprise, since this was by no means the first instance of this kind and Federal Trade Commission rulings were available for examination.[7]

In spite of these legal problems, the company proceeded with the implementation of the Five Year Plan. As was mentioned earlier, the plan was basically merchandising oriented, applying the quality concept and the fundamental tenets of Modi Operandi philosophy to the development of an improved selling organization based on the concept of a "complete store." In the simplest form, the Complete Store concept demanded that all phases of merchandising be tied to the central schemes of quality business, modi operandi, and the revised collection policy, with the plan evolving around the company's "main store," the catalog. The emphasis was placed on quality merchandise for quality customers—the quality of customer, of course, being somewhat below the upper-middle-class in terms of income and social characteristics. Basic criteria for the complete store included the "enlargement" of the store, required because of the necessity of offering complete lines, while not cheapening the appearance of the catalog. Successful implementation of the plan demanded that the catalog be reorganized, as well as enlarged and upgraded, in such a way that items and groups of merchandise were arranged to suit the convenience of customers rather than of the operators or bookkeepers—what M. J. Spiegel termed, "not making the customer run from floor to floor to find items of a kindred nature."[8]

Enlarging, upgrading, and/or organization of catalogs, together with better quality merchandise, were merely starting points. The new merchandising plan called for the development of an atmosphere for the encouragement of sales. While certain lines required a bargain atmosphere, others demanded a more sophisticated presentation emphasizing style, color, and accessories. Those responsible for deciding the nature of these sales "arguments" would have to distinguish between the psychological advantages each offered, and they would also have to display the lines to their best advantage in the proper atmosphere. While variety of line and selectivity were to be emphasized in such a way that the customer could not obtain a better selection from any other store which she would patronize, the planners and expediters could not afford to lose sight of the rigorous controls over buying and inventory which Miss Coleman and the Red Books continuously represented. If these tasks were not sufficiently demanding, the merchandisers were informed that they were to design for the "shrewd shopper of Middle-class America . . . a store where she knows the price is always right." That is, the complete store was to carry the base items carried by competitors, at a price as low or lower on those items than competitors, and *"right on all items."* Not only must every division contain one or more items obviously lower priced than competition, but throughout the lines must be "outstanding values that are so obvious to all customers that they incite them to talk about the store to friends and relatives."

All of these goals had to be achieved within the framework of higher quality merchandise. The Five Year Plan demanded the development of methods for establishing quality standards as yardsticks, and insisted that these be continuously improved over time. Lamenting that in the past "too little effort has been made to improve standards of quality and too little thought has been given to it," the new blueprint called for having the highest quality merchandise for any given price and for never permitting the customer to forget it. An indication of the direction to follow in attaining the goal, the plan pointed out that trade names were helpful and directed that programming must "provide trade names on all articles." The merchandisers responsible for evolving methods of making the Complete Store viable were also enjoined to include all usable contributions of modern merchandising and retailing. "The Complete Store must always have the latest merchandise: if not, it does not deserve to command the patronage of the customer." This injunction, together with the trade-name concept, was bound to have enduring effects upon the merchandise divisions. Not only was the development of a successful brand name a long-term and expensive investment for a mercantile house, but mail-order firms had notoriously been followers, not innovators, with respect to the introduction of new products. Spiegel was proposing to develop a brand name for a substantial proportion of an expanded line.

The Complete Store blueprint demanded some other accomplishments. One was that orders be filled promptly, completely, and without fail, including an ironclad return guarantee and the provision of prompt payment of transportation both ways for such goods. Second, to reduce customer complaints that something purchased in one sales effort was later offered for a lower price in the same season merchandisers were to see that customers should not be permitted to find that they could buy any article cheaper from one effort than from another within the season, and that when a price was cut the action had to apply on "all current offerings, irrespective of classes of customers, and . . . of operating problems." Furthermore, in addition to the price, quality, and service goals set for the merchandisers, customers had to be offered "the heaping measure . . . the baker's dozen," such extra values ranging from as small as extra buttons, thread, or a "large patch sent out with a suit of clothes," to as large a value as an extra drawer in a chest "which is offered without such feature by competition."

The extremes to which Spiegel went in implementation of the "heaping measure" and the ironclad return policies are amusingly reflected in this personal letter from a customer in Florida addressed to M. J. Spiegel:

About a year ago I ordered a —— from your catalog. When it came there was a small ornament missing. It worked fine without it, and I was pleased, but I wrote to your company and told them what hap-

234

pened and said if they found the little ornament part lying around would they please send it. They shipped me another whole ——. So I wrote again and told them I didn't want another ——, I just needed the little part. Next thing I knew I received another ——. So I wrote again, told them about the first letter and the second letter and explained all over again—and a little later along came another ——. This went on and on, Mr. Spiegel, and I now have seven ——. Now, Mr. Spiegel, I know that this isn't the way you want to run your business, and I feel sorry for the way your employees are wasting your money. I won't tell you what it was I ordered, for I have a feeling someone would send me another ——. But if you will call me by telephone, I'll tell you, so you can tell me what to do with seven ——.[9]

The importance of the Five Year Plan is difficult to overemphasize, although not all of the elements would be executed, and much of the plan was to be carried out over staged intervals. The impact of war and of wartime restrictions would accelerate the implementation of certain parts and retard the adoption of others. But, in effect, the Five Year Plan and the Complete Store concept assured management that the Spiegel of 1944 was going to be a fundamentally different company than that of 1938. Strongly implied was the promise that features of good department stores would be used, such as telephone shopping service. Further, although the matter was not hinted at in the blueprint, the Complete Store concept was obviously amenable to another departure, invasion of retail-store fields. Long the symbol of installment selling in the industry, Spiegel was preparing to abandon that position in favor of utilizing *all* methods of purchase. And, although no member of management would then admit it, let alone advocate it, when the door swung open for cash and limited charge accounts, it was going to be neat conjuring indeed that could continue to maintain the "no charge for credit" policy.

In part the program promised by the Five Year Plan had its antecedents in the successful innovation which Sewell Avery had introduced into Ward during the decade, and which had enabled that firm to narrow the gap which separated it from Sears and the industry. Avery's triumphs had effects which spread out over the mail-order industry like ripples on a pond. The competition with Sears intensified, regardless of the sphere of activity, price, style, quality, depth of line, catalog presentation and distribution, service, and credit terms. Only in terms of balance of lines, with Sears more heavily committed to durables, did they sharply differ in mail order, although in retail the heavier Sears' concentration of department stores in large communities and in major shopping areas tended to provide an edge which Ward was unable to narrow appreciably. And, just as Sears felt the competition Avery policies offered, so also did the middle-sized companies in mail order.

Before 1938, M. J. Spiegel had demonstrated his own competence in the industry, innovating, improvising, meeting problems with an excellence of timing; he was his own man and no blind follower of anything. But he, too, was acutely aware of what Avery was doing, and even more importantly, why. It was impossible for him not to have been significantly influenced by the Ward achievements, nor did he ever deny Avery's influence. The quality upgrading, the growing emphasis upon merchandising, the search for greater flexibility of approach, the significance of the larger town and different income group as mail-order patrons, these were Spiegel decisions taken in light of the Ward lessons. But M. J. Spiegel was always able to add his own particular twists, one of these being the hiring of the great Maholy-Nagy as a consultant on design and styling, after this member of the Bauhaus had fled Germany following the triumph of the Nazis.[10]

There was no question that with respect to merchandise quality and improvement in the organization and the appearance of the catalogs the company upgraded itself significantly between 1937 and 1942, nor that with respect to pricing they became competitive with their major rivals on many more articles. It was much more difficult to improve customer service, since a more satisfactory performance here entailed the completion of major reorganizations of the service divisions. The drive to get orders out of the house more promptly, the "24 hour service" campaign, was only partially successful, while heavy receipt of orders and correspondence outran the capacity of the changing organization to handle, with the result that some mail was destroyed, some customers were infuriated, and the officers of the company spent some unpleasant hours with the Chicago postmaster and Federal Judge Michael L. Igoe.[11] But there was no essential modification in the company's terms of credit; here they fell behind Sears and Ward with respect to the length of maturities, continuing to sell durable goods on what E. L. Swikard called "wearing apparel terms." Nor were the tight controls over buying and inventory noticeably relaxed in such a way that the back-order and no-substitutions policies could be brought in line with the quality-service ideal. In fact, even in the Five Year Plan document it was admitted that while these goals should be stressed "in consumer education and sale book propaganda," they were not recommended as a set policy, and that the added costs of heavier inventory, losses on jobbed merchandise, and increased depreciation were not worth reduction of the back-order load. On the other hand, the consistent application of the efforts of credit and sales research did result in a major shift in sales territories and in a significant change in the attributes of the average Spiegel customer; by the end of 1940 M. J. Spiegel could announce to stockholders that the average weekly income of new customers in 1940 had been $28.29 compared with $16 in 1937, and that the management was prepared to sacrifice larger immediate volume in favor of developing the substantial, long-range profits which had been assumed in the adoption of the new policies in 1938.[12]

Spiegel had done some other important things in line with the new quality goal policy, particularly with respect to strengthening the management and integrating the interests of executives with those of the company. One set of decisions pertained to what could be called the company's image, and the attitudes of suppliers and customers toward the firm. A second set can be described as an attempt to break the "ingrown" character of the board of directors by seasoning it with outside directors.

During the earlier years of the period management had not been entirely unconcerned about its customer relations; M. J. Spiegel had himself gone into the field to talk with Spiegel patrons and had obtained a firsthand impression of their opinion of the company. But with the shifts in policy toward different income groups and different communities and regions, more information was considered desirable. Furthermore, the tough attitudes adopted toward sources during the 1933–36 era had resulted in a brisk turnover of sources and an end to continuity of relations with firms which had served the company for a decade or more. With increased production absorbing more and more of idle capacity, with the growing tendencies toward restrictive resale price maintenance agreements between manufacturers and retailers, and with the pressures born of the changed quality goals, the company, rightfully, became concerned with manufacturer attitudes. This concern was increased by a growing fear after 1939 that United States involvement in the war was inevitable, and that manufacturers would then be in a much stronger bargaining position and able to shut off merchandise to certain customers in favor of others.

Thus, in 1940, management contracted with Elmo Roper to conduct through his organization surveys of the opinions of customers and suppliers toward Spiegel. The results of such polls indicated that a majority of manufacturers found the company's buyers able and helpful, and considered the company itself a customer whose patronage they valued. A surprising number of customers sampled professed to believe there was no charge for credit at Spiegel, and indicated a general satisfaction with their experience. There were, of course, significant exceptions in both cases: manufacturers, particularly of durable goods, not infrequently expressed contempt for most mail-order houses, and were suspicious of the ethics of the larger, integrated, distributors; many customers considered Spiegel services poor and merchandising incomplete. A significant number of durable goods producers reflected anti-Semitic attitudes in expressing their criticisms of Spiegel and mail-order firms in general.[13] Just as importantly, the evaluated results of these surveys were integrated into house policies and influenced the direction of change within operating divisions and departments.

Although generally pleased with the results of the Roper survey, M. J. was less satisfied with the composition of the Spiegel board. Following the elimination of banker-directors in 1933, the board had been composed exclusively of Spiegel officers. While such an arrangement had obvious advantages under the conditions which prevailed during the resurgent years through 1936, the radical shifts in policy that followed 1937 required a board which was not so insular or parochial in outlook and experience, not tied so tightly to short-term goals and operating results. Further, despite their qualifications as operating officers, some of the inside directors could contribute only limitedly to the functions which a responsible board of directors was designed to perform for a large organization operating over a broad landscape. Therefore in 1937, after a second underwriting, Howard Sachs, partner in Goldman, Sachs & Company, was elected to the board, and in April 1941

Elmo Roper became the second outside director. Sachs evidently provided only conventional services to the company as a director, but Roper's contributions were broad-ranging and his influence upon Spiegel proportionate to his wide knowledge and experience in sophisticated consumer research and in developments in other areas of American business management. There were, of course, other changes in the composition of the board, during the remaining years of the period. Frederick W. Spiegel was on leave of absence with the Army Air Force during 1942–44, and Modie J. Spiegel died on January 8, 1943. Earl Weil was elected a director, filling the latter vacancy, and through the rest of this period Swikard, Meinig, Folger, Gatzert, and M. J. Spiegel constituted the balance of the directorate.

Further changes, of course, were made among the executive ranks as well. It was only logical that as the new program of upgraded quality became more firmly integrated into the Spiegel organization policy that some of the informal structure which had been tolerable in previous years had to be abandoned. Also, despite M. J. Spiegel's philosophy that it made little difference what a man's title was so long as his functions were known and his authority and responsibility recognized, it became necessary to provide titles for more of the upper echelon executives and provide more of the ritual of a formal table of organization. The most obvious change was that of publicly acknowledging M. J. Spiegel as the chief executive officer under the chairman of the board by naming him president. This was accomplished in April 1939; M. J. Spiegel was elected president and Frederick W. Spiegel joined Swikard and Meinig as vice presidents.[14] The following year Weil was elected a vice president. In terms of the responsibilities of the top echelon it was immediately apparent that even as late as 1941 operating executives, while unquestionably growing in importance within the company, were not considered as belonging to the same elite as men charged with the merchandising, selling, and credit management functions.

The full implications of the changed policy goals inaugurated in 1938 were a long time in revealing themselves to the hardworking management, and the failure to attain more quickly a position of greater profitability obviously preyed upon managerial morale. M. J. and his lieutenants had not expected the shifts associated with developing a "higher quality" customer to be accomplished painlessly, and had anticipated that one of the prices which would be exacted would be a slowdown, even a temporary reversal, in the rate of sales growth. But this would be, according to the estimates of the Modi Operandi and Five Year Plans, compensated for by the reduction in credit losses, stepped-up collections, and diminution of the rate of customer mortality associated with improved service, merchandise quality, and increased size of the average order received. Thus profits should have risen by 1939 or 1940, and while net earnings had improved in both these years over the low level of 1938 they were still over $750,000 less than the 1937 level, and $1.5 million below 1936 profits.

It was becoming increasingly obvious that the stock market was turning a somewhat colder and more critical eye upon Spiegel's performance, and that this, together with the reduced earnings and dividend performance, was having a disturbing effect upon stockholders. Common dividends, which had averaged $1.27 million during 1936–37, fell to under $400,000 for each of the next two years, and although pushed up to $765,395 for 1940–41, was still 4 percent below the mid-1930s peak. From the 1937 high of $29 per share (following the stock split) the market price of Spiegel common fell to a high of $16 for 1938–39, fell by another $5 in 1940, and never exceeded $7 in 1941. When the new policies had been adopted management had anticipated the direction of the market adjustment as reflected in stock prices, and the need to strengthen a relationship with stockholders which the solid earnings and dividend accomplishments of the first few years had alone been able to carry.

In May 1939, the Finance Committee reported that M. J. Spiegel "for some time" had been concerned with the problem of establishing and maintaining better relationships with stockholders, and announced a policy that would provide for more frequent contacts, such as more numerous news releases of matters which would interest shareholders, distribution of mid-year earnings statements, and the dispatch of welcoming letters when an individual became a Spiegel stockholder.[15] While these presumably had some positive effect, a more significant contribution to the goal of closer relations with shareholders was the extent to which the company's annual statement provided detailed explanation of company policy, objectives, and the steps being taken to attain the specified goals. In 1940, for example, the entire editorial section of the statement was devoted to this purpose, its nine-plus pages providing a candid account of progress, and a convincing argument for the continuation of purely mail-order and installment-selling policies within the context of the higher quality objectives.

The 1940 statement was notable for something else, although the stockholders could not have been aware of it. This was that the strong faith expressed in traditional basic policies—reliance purely on mail-order distribution, the installment plan, and "no charge for credit"—only partially existed. The stalwarts of 1933, Swikard and Meinig, together with a host of other executives of more or less exalted stature, tenaciously believed in the validity of these policies. But M. J. Spiegel was already looking beyond this as a careful interpolation of the Five Year Plan showed. Further, as the events in 1941 unfolded, with ever-stronger rumors of a Federal crack down on credit—rumors which gained in credibility as a result of some rather broad hints from at least one member of the Federal Reserve Board—his loss of ardor for "no charge for credit" was perceptible.[16]

The spring season 1941 had been somewhat informally set as the critical point for the company, the time when the internal indicators of sales, credit losses, and profits would validate or deny the assumptions which underlay the policies adopted in 1938. Hopefully Spiegel executives watched the critical gauges, did what they could to stoke the fires, and, disheartened, counted the results. These were: net sales and profits down from the spring season 1940, improvement in collections, some diminution in credit losses, a small increment in the size of the average order. There had been a careful reappraisal of the decision to cut back selling in southern territories during 1940, and, based on a credit analysis of southern business, a modified reentry on a selective basis. This should have helped, and unquestionably the sum results would have been even less impressive in the absence of this action. But the aggregate performance had been substantially below expectations and there was an understandable gloom hovering over management.

At this point M. J. Spiegel undertook a novel, even bizarre, step: he organized a seminar to which were invited seven men prominent in merchandising, advertising, public relations, and investment.[17] This group was bolstered by eleven members of the Spiegel management, plus Elmo Roper. The purposes of this seminar, which was confined to one day in August 1941, were:[18]

1. To determine if Spiegel policies were correct; if so, whether greater volume and profit should have developed during the first half of the year.

2. To determine whether the small upper management group had sufficient breadth of vision, including external contacts which enabled a broad view; if not, to suggest means of correcting the deficiency.

It is also probable that, since he was well acquainted with the outside members of the seminar and with their views, M. J. Spiegel was using this method to prepare his own lieutenants for one or more steps which would bend company policy in the direction of his own growing convictions. The nature of the agenda and the ability of the chairman to direct discussion provided him with the tools with which to emphasize those aspects of policy which he desired to highlight or, conversely, to discourage unwelcome recommendations. Yet in no sense was the seminar rigged; M. J. was genuinely interested in the opinions of the participants, sincere in his desire to test his own and his colleagues thinking against the criteria of able professionals who possessed a wealth of pertinent experience and broad business knowledge.

And if M. J. Spiegel sought objective criticism, as well as considered recommendations, he got it. First, on the level of Spiegel's merchandising of credit and the policies associated with the management of credit; second, on the company's general merchandising and selling practices; third, on the development of the new quality image and the policy of upgrading the customer level. In addition, and this was particularly important for the future, there were some interesting commentaries on the point of view of the Spiegel board of directors, and observations concerning the trend of integrated mercantile organizations in the United States, with implications regarding the direction Spiegel might take.

In general, the outside group favored a modification of selling policy to de-emphasize credit and provide the flexibility of multiple terms of sales; the inside group, with some exceptions, were in favor of continuing the current policy. The latter, while generally sympathetic to criticisms which bore upon problems of how effectively programs were executed, were concerned with the many difficulties which a more flexible program would technically entail, such as the criteria for distribution of catalogs, the effects of cash selling upon size of average order, and shifts in per capita selling and servicing costs.

The outside members of the seminar were more circumspect with regard to merchandising and selling policy and practice than they were with credit. In terms of credit several of these men acknowledged that Spiegel had the satisfaction of knowing that Sears and Ward had "come to them" rather than it being the other way round, but with respect to general merchandising this had not been so. Interestingly, those at the seminar closest to the mercantile fields believed that Spiegel prices, assuming equal quality, were competitive with those of its big rivals over the ranges of those goods which all sold in common, and that this implied validity for the "no charge for credit" theme. But there were many criticisms concerning the organization of goods in the catalog, failures to merchandise effectively articles on which the company had a significant competitive advantage, and, in particular, the failure to merchandise the advantages of mail-order buying over conventional retail buying as effectively to customers as to company stockholders. There was also some skepticism shown about the pace of the program for upgrading customer and merchandise quality, because, as one man put it, "you can't go from being a borax house to a Marshall Field in four or five years."[19] That is, while the new customer class to which Spiegel was trying to appeal was more affluent than the former average customer, the members of this market segment were still not sufficiently well-off to be able to handle some of the goods which Spiegel now tended to stock, regardless of the value these represented. Even more criticism was leveled at the company's action of abandoning its southern territories, particularly since the beginnings of the defense boom, the construction of new military and air bases, and the effects of the Fair Labor Standards and Walsh-Healy Acts upon the south. It was pointed out that the Sears Atlanta mail-order location was probably the most active in that corporation's entire mail-order operation, and that giving up a geographic region whose economic condition was changing so rapidly for the better was something less than wise. This opinion was only partially mitigated by the explanations of company executives that Spiegel had begun re-entry into such areas on a selective basis.

As to the image the company was engaged in developing, and the techniques that were being employed to activate it, the seminar had some conflicting opinions. A very successful American merchant, who was unable to attend the seminar, had counseled the company to undertake a program of personalizing the role of the Spiegel family in the sales literature, emphasizing the successive generations that had led the firm. It was hardly surprising that the advertising-public relations—public opinion members of the seminar should have subscribed to this, or embroidered it with places for personalizing the whole house, its management, its problems, in all phases of its selling effort. But another member was frankly contemptuous of anything that hinted at glamorizing the family—that would not sell merchandise; it was more important to personalize the company through the people who answered customer's questions, or those who merchandised the products. Nor was there any coincidence in the grouping of the advertising-public opinion fraternity in support of the thesis that, as one of them expressed it, "the Spiegel and its customer of 1935 was outmoded; that it was necessary to rebuild the reputation and appeal of the company to prevent an actual decline, a decline which only the improved economic conditions of 1939–1941 had offset." [20]

While a passionate avowal of a point of view, the statement was hardly germane. First, the company *had* been engrossed in improving quality and service and making price competitive, in upgrading credit standards, and in selecting higher income customers since 1937. Second, this had not improved sales or profits. Third, there was no proof that had the old policies continued, including concentration on the old sales territories, but with some improvement in service, the firm would have been less profitable than it had been up to 1937. Obviously, several members of the Spiegel team present were skeptical of this doctrine; equally obviously, their views were not being encouraged by M. J., and this was particularly evident when recommendations for future policy were being solicited from the floor.

With respect to the Spiegel management, there was little overt comment. Only one observer commented that the tightness of the

Spiegel executive group, and the fact that many of them were also directors, tended to make them "somewhat ingrown . . . disinclined . . . to disagree with one another."[21] This was obviously a safe statement to make, since the unconventional step of exposing an entire management group and corporate policies to the open criticism of a group of outsiders was fairly good evidence that M. J. Spiegel had reached a similar conclusion.

An objective evaluation of the seminar would conclude that insofar as it permitted executives and directors to discuss policy and procedure with successful men able to view the company in a detached frame of mind it was probably beneficial. Certainly the suggestions of outsiders with respect to merchandising and selling, market concentrations, and characteristics of mail-order markets was graciously received by the Spiegel officers. Just as tenaciously, however, all Spiegel executives clung to their belief in the viability of continued credit selling, and their rejection of recommendations to encourage more cash business. All of them believed that the tides were flowing in the direction of greater use of credit by the public, while none of them overtly objected to rounding out the company's credit plan by introducing a nominal, thirty-day charge account feature. On the other hand, at least at that moment, the recommendation to enter retail had, to the Spiegel group, all the appeal of an empty hook to a hungry trout. All, that is, except M. J. Spiegel, and at the time he was keeping his own counsel. As to the basic purposes of the seminar, there can be no valid general conclusion. The outsiders were by no means unanimous in their opinions as to whether the company had or did not have the right to expect an upsurge in volume and profits at this stage of development of new policy, or that much better results should have been realized in view of improved economic conditions.

As the fall season progressed in 1941 the company's fortunes improved, with net sales exceeding $32 million, highest in the company's history, and profits sufficient to wipe out the unhappy spring results. For the entire year sales amounted to $56.7 million, 1 percent above those for 1937, the previous peak, but profits, before strengthening contingency reserves, lagged 28 percent behind the 1937 level, although amounting to $1.8 million. The reasons for the fall upsurge were not easy to sort out, but perhaps the safest explanation would be that improving national income and reemployment, the strengthened governmental measures to control certain materials which would stimulate some consumer buying in anticipation of shortages, and the net cumulative effects of company selling efforts combined to produce the effect. Certainly, the company's decision in October 1941 to freeze catalog prices for the rest of the year, and its public announcement of this decision through the distribution of over two million circulars must have helped increase volume. Earlier in the month the company felt inclined to increase catalog prices because of the sharp increases in manufacturers' prices, but as it became clear that Sears and Ward were raising prices there appeared some advantage to holding the line.

This advantage was supported by the changes the Federal Reserve Board's Regulation W, announced as of September 1, 1941, was effecting in consumer purchase behavior. Regulation W provided that for selected items costing fifty dollars or more, specific down payments and maximum maturities were required. For articles which required large amounts of metals, such as refrigerators, washing machines, cooking and heating equipment, sewing machines, radio receivers, phonographs and combination radio-phonographs, and certain musical instruments, 20 percent; sanitary fixtures, considered more necessary for healthy household maintenance, 15 percent was demanded; and for new furniture, bedsprings, and mattresses, 10 percent down was ordered. The curtailment of maturities, a device directed at improving the quality of the credit extended rather than just its reduction, affected Spiegel much less than it did Sears and Ward, both of which had permitted comparatively longer maturities on durables and other big-ticket merchandise than did Spiegel.

All large distributors had anticipated that the shift to defense and war production would curtail the availability of certain goods, particularly appliances, furniture, and hard line articles, and the mail-order firms had drastically switched their buying patterns. Instead of keeping inventories on hand down to the amounts which they anticipated would be sold in a short period and relying on sources to replace these in subsequent months as sales developed, they were accepting delivery on orders as soon as they could get their hands on goods.[22] One result of this was that the mail-order giants enjoyed huge increases of sales in September, but that most of the sales were on a cash basis; credit sales actually declined over those of the previous year.[23] *Business Week* maintained that this was the result of two consumer beliefs: that in the face of Federal Reserve Board publicity it was unpatriotic to buy on credit; and that it was virtually impossible to buy goods on installment.[24] To offset these fears among its own customers (and in the hope of attracting customers from rivals) Spiegel issued its combined announcement that it would hold prices constant and explained the operation of Regulation W.

Although it would have been possible for the company to have maintained its "no charge for credit" policy even under these conditions—a simple catalog explanation that on specifically identified goods the *government* required a down payment would have sufficed, although considerable technical readjustment of terms tables and consumer accounting would have been required—M. J. Spiegel utilized the opportunity which the emergency situation presented to throw out the whole policy. Three weeks after Pearl Harbor the company announced that effective January 18, 1942, it would require a carrying charge on credit orders. This, of course, was a very painful blow for Spiegel. While the change in policy could be defended, it had the effect of robbing the house of its fundamental distinctiveness without providing any immediately offsetting advantage other than helping provide a somewhat larger service-charge income against which to balance credit losses and collection costs.

M. J. Spiegel was convinced, after December 7, 1941, that the company was going to take a serious beating financially relative to its competition; it would be preferable, therefore, to absorb it within a short period of time and in the interval to perfect the plans and organization and provide for the capital which would be necessary to strike for new goals when the war's end provided the opportunity. He realized that abandonment of "no charge for credit" would reduce the value of Swikard and Meinig to the company, but he had prepared for that in advance. The solution: they, together with others in the old guard who had outlived their usefulness to the organization he visualized, would have to be separated from the company. But not immediately, not until he was ready for the step. And this would not be until 1943.

It is difficult to judge whether or not M. J. Spiegel anticipated just how bad a beating the company would take before the new organization had been prepared, the operating deficiencies made good, and American military fortunes improved sufficiently to increase the flow of civilian goods. It proved to be very bad indeed. Sales fell to under $41 million in 1942 (down 28 percent from 1941), then plummeted to $27.8 million in 1943 (see table 13). But even this net decline of over 50 percent was more than matched by a downward spiral in profits. The 1942 loss was almost $1.4 million (a net swing from 1941 of nearly $3 million), while the 1943 loss totaled just under $2.4 million. Customer receivables diminished from $30.6 million in 1941 to $7.7 million in 1943, and the only encouraging aspect of these years was the growth of cash assets from $2.9 million to $5.8 million.

To catch whatever business was available the company tried every known means, such as including in catalogs merchandise which management knew could not be obtained from sources in more than token quantities, offering scarce cigarettes as bait, partially absorbing freight for customers through a system of multiple reshipment points, and substituting available goods for precious and nonexistent durables in the sales literature. National conservation needs entailed cutbacks in paper stocks and hence in the number of catalogs and other mailing pieces which could be distributed, while rationing, with its complexities, introduced special handlings and further operating difficulties for a work force which was reduced both quantitatively and qualitatively. Because of these circumstances, plus the problems and new procedures associated with cash, C.O.D., and thirty-day charge account terms, plus grouping with the problems that arose out of the typed-sales-slip and complete-order handling which were introduced in the operating divisions at the end of 1941, costs stubbornly resisted reduction, and returns, cancellations, and not-taken merchandise just as obstinately refused to stay down.

The labor situation was such that during late 1942 and 1943 executive officers, not excluding M. J. Spiegel, were frequently to be found in the warehouse performing long-forgotten jobs as stockmen, order fillers, and packers. The only exceptions were those who had gone off to the war in military or bureaucratic capacities. Included in the latter group were Frederick W. Spiegel,

13. Spiegel, Inc., corporate income statement, in thousands of dollars, 1933–1943

	1933	1934	1935	1936	1937	1938	1939	1940	1941	1942	1943
Net Sales (1)	$13,541	$26,243	$34,012	$44,696	$56,118	$49,733	$52,861	$53,477	$56,739	$40,915	$27,828
Cost of Goods Sold (2)	7,209	14,952	20,093	26,816	35,220	30,225	32,360	32,454	34,741	25,540	17,834
Gross Operating Profit (3)	$ 6,332	$11,291	$13,919	$17,880	$20,898	$19,508	$20,501	$21,023	$21,998	$15,375	$ 9,994
Selling, Operating, and Administrative Expense (4)	4,863	7,879	11,229	13,475	17,965	17,544	18,261	18,561	19,088	16,858	12,547
Net Operating Income (5)	$ 1,469	$ 3,412	$ 2,690	$ 4,405	$ 2,933	$ 1,964	$ 2,240	$ 2,462	$ 2,910	$(1,483)	$(2,553)
Other Income (6)	86	50	25	51	76	54	90	157	193	107	177
Other Expense (7)	26							208‡	256‡		
Net Profit, before taxes (8)	$ 1,529	$ 3,462	$ 2,715	$ 4,456	$ 3,009	$ 2,017	$ 2,330	$ 2,411	$ 2,847	$(1,376)	$(2,376)
Contribution to reserves (9)		250*					179§		242‖		
Federal Income Taxes (10)	213	463	373	1,021†	437	404	400	620	1,000		
Net profit, before distribution (11)	$ 1,316	$ 2,749	$ 2,342	$ 3,435	$ 2,572	$ 1,613	$ 1,751	$ 1,791	$ 1,605	$(1,376)	$(2,376)

* Contribution to contingency reserve.
† Includes Federal Undistributed Profits Tax.
‡ Company contribution to officer's and employee's incentive salary plans.
§ Provision for employee's profit sharing plan.
‖ Added to contingency reserve to provide for possible future inventory price decline.
Sources: *Annual Reports*, 1933–43.

commissioned a captain in the Army Air Force, and many of the middle management cadre.

M. J. Spiegel, however, was not so occupied with counting the declining sales, pulling orders, or feeling sorry for himself that he could not develop plans for the years after the war and for the organization that had to carry on in the war period before a more extensive reorganization could be undertaken. The interim reorganization was designed to help accomplish the transition by:[25]

1. Holding down current expenses and maintaining a continuity of operations while providing due consideration for
2. Mastering the problems of operating under the multiple-term sales plans with optimum efficiency and profit, and
3. Contributing to the development of the type of distributional organization and structure that would be adopted when the war emergency was past.

It also formalized the *de facto* power and prestige relationships within the company, particularly the emergence of Earl Weil and the decline and incipient exodus of Meinig and Swikard. Further, it reflected the new importance of the operating departments both in meeting the immediate needs of the company and in preparing the way for a future in which merchandise and customer service would have to be unexcelled if Spiegel was to progress. Finally, it formally tore up the Commission Plan which had already been largely emasculated in an effort to conserve executive time and expedite action, but substituted a new and simplified set of committees. Under the new organization, the number of executives reporting directly to M. J. Spiegel were greatly reduced; in spite of this, he commented, "I have no intention of losing personal contacts with those individuals. As a matter of fact, I hope to enlarge the scope of my contacts with executives."[26] The functioning of the new committees, he believed, provided this opportunity, while control was assured by the fact of his chairmanship of all of them.

Under the 1943 reorganization plan there were three major divisions established, Buying and Selling, Operating, and Treasury. In addition, a Staff Sales Director and a Controller were named, the former, in the person of Edward Swikard, was commissioned to act as "special assistant to the Buying and Selling Manager for the creation and execution of certain sales work which will be assigned to him from time to time"; the latter, in the person of

H. R. MacKenzie, was responsible to the president. Chief of the Buying and Selling Division was Earl D. Weil; Walter Gatzert remained as treasurer; and Charles J. Folger was named manager of the Operations Division. Miss Saindon continued as secretary of the company and was named labor relations director as well. Meinig was completely undercut and isolated from any important responsibility; he had previously performed many of the functions which were assigned to the new controller, but M. J. had tenaciously resisted earlier recommendations for appointing such an executive, apparently on the grounds that Meinig was the logical man for the position and he did not want Meinig any longer. He would be kept around until later in 1943, then neatly dispatched with severance pay commensurate with his final salary. Although there was no equivalent ruthlessness shown in his case, Swikard was effectively diminished in stature by the organizational changes.

The committees which were to serve as means of coordinating policies and divisional activity and to serve, also, as the vehicle whereby M. J. Spiegel was to intensify his personal contacts with the operating offices included the Credit and Collection Committee; the Merchandise Review Committee; the Operating Committee; the Personnel Committee; the Postwar Planning Committee; and the Sales Committee. The Credit and Collection Committee was designed to deal with all credit and collection problems, credit sales, costs, and reserve policy; its membership was limited to Garvey and Gatzert. The Merchandise Review Committee handled reviews of general buying programs and merchandise problems plus the development of merchandise budgets; its members were Adams, Gatzert, Weil, Swikard, and Miss Coleman. The Operating Committee concerned itself with "understanding operating problems and costs" and was composed of Cowan, Folger, and MacKenzie. The Personnel Committee was to deal with the formulation and consideration of broad personnel policies and their execution; Miss Saindon, Miss M. J. Paul, the personnel supervisor, Cowan, Folger, and MacKenzie comprised its membership. The important Postwar Planning Committee was organized to develop the long-range Spiegel plan for the postwar period. Its membership included Gatzert, Swikard, Weil, and Elmo Roper. For a brief time it also included Meinig, but omitted both Folger and

Cowan. The Sales Committee was set up to deal with customer and prospect lists and the problems associated with "broad selling policy," and committeemen included the responsible officers in the Buying and Selling division plus Swikard and MacKenzie. The differences between the new committees and those which had existed under the Commission Plan were made clear by M. J. Spiegel: "Under the old set-up, committees were concerned with too much detail. Under the new set-up, committees will limit their work to reviewing and understanding problems, and deciding broad policies. Details will be assigned to and worked out by individuals."

There was some irony to the company's annual meeting in April 1943 at which Swikard, Meinig, and Folger were reelected directors and the first two again named to their vice presidencies.[27] Within six months all three were effectively out of the organization: Meinig was chopped down first, and Folger and Swikard were formally retired on pension by October, although both were retained on the board during 1944. The gaps left in the executive organization by these departures were, in M. J. Spiegel's opinion, adequately filled, but the forming plans of the Postwar Planning Committee included a program for reentry into retail stores and in this area Spiegel had nobody with experience or detailed knowledge of operations, store planning, location, or investment. An experienced analyst, John W. Miller, was lured away from Montgomery Ward, whose wealth of executive talent was beginning to be dissipated by the same Sewell Avery who had so painstakingly assembled it, and appointed vice president for retail operations. The committee discussed many things, advanced some marginal ideas, even offered criticisms and suggestions for change; but, in essence, the initial concept emerged into the final plan. The principal ingredients of the plan were:[28]

1. Organization of the company into two distinct divisions, retail and mail order. The organization to be carried through in terms of separate operating divisions as well as separate merchandising and selling apparatus and personnel.

2. Retailing would be organized on a specialty store basis, with five distinct chains of stores, each having a separate merchandising manager responsible to the retail general merchandising manager. The individual chains would be: women's fashion; infants' and children's goods; farm-automobile-hardware; men's apparel and sporting goods; and home furnishings and furniture.

3. Development of a catalog shopping system, with desks in retail stores as well as distinctive "stores" devoted exclusively to soliciting catalog sales. This system to be the responsibility of the mail-order division.

4. Reorganization of the mail-order catalog on the same lines as the retail structure, that is, the "five store" plan.

5. Continuation of quality upgrading in merchandise, but with a reorientation toward the establishment of three quality ranges: good, better, best.

6. Reorientation of assortment and price-range selling policies. Only complete assortments to be offered, while only a limited number of selling prices would be set with large selections in each range.

7. Broadening of the market to include from 65 percent to 75 percent of the total population, excluding only the economic group extremes.

8. Reorientation in buying and in source relationships, such that much greater attention be given to consumer acceptance standards and more systematic canvassing of resources to provide what is needed by consumers and to improve knowledge of what was available.

9. Display of merchandise, in stores and in catalogs, to be put on "ready to go" basis. This to be achieved by better packaging and display techniques, improved standards of inspection, and more rigorous demands upon suppliers.

10. Persuading manufacturers who have established private brands to produce comparable quality lines for Spiegel under Spiegel brands to be heavily exploited at slightly lower prices.

11. Improving the quality of and extending the scope of the responsibilities of the company's inspection and standards division.

The soundness of the plan could only be tested against the kind of economic conditions which would exist in the postwar period, but the plan itself reflected M. J. Spiegel's determination not to follow in the path of the company's two large competitors, but to develop a distinctiveness which would permit a further form of insulation from direct and continuous competition of the type which they, not Spiegel, were in a superior position to exploit. Further, there were questions which the 1943 condition did not permit to be fully explored or answered, such as the amount of resources needed to achieve the goals, and the firm's capability to command these. Yet, *prima facie*, there was an internal consistency to the elements of the plan which should have been appealing and was certainly sufficiently demanding to have called for putting aside all other considerations. This, however, was not the case. M. J. Spiegel was a highly curious man, and restlessly insisted upon simultaneously exploring further ways of adding to volume and profits, whether or not these were consistent with the available energies and the time schedules for implementation of the main plans. For example, during early 1942 members of management had been immersed in developing a plan for making more effective the sale of war bonds by the Treasury, an effort which probably contributed some sound promotional ideas to the development of plans for payroll deductions to pay for such bonds.[29]

In spite of these diversions, a tight schedule for building the proposed organization was set. Divisional merchandising managers for each of the five store groups were to be appointed by December 1, 1943. Each such manager was to be responsible for both retail and mail-order merchandising, although initially his responsibilities would be confined to executing the plan for mail order in 1944 and charting the development of the retail sections awaiting store acquisitions or construction. Such managers were to develop their own buying staffs, down to re-buyer levels, select budget assistants, develop guidelines for selections and prepare selling programs, estimate sales and catalog pages required, and estimate selling expense. They were required also to scout for complete source coverage, identify and contact new sources, screen out suppliers of dubious merchandise quality, and develop budgets in line with the limits provided by the general merchandise manager. Further, these managers had to develop personally and in their staffs "an alert customer consciousness" aimed at the elimination of back orders, substitutions, and what were called "other current mail-order deterrents."[30] Organization charts for these divisions were to be finished by January 1, 1944, even if personnel were not available, and the plans had to be ready for implementation in the fall 1944 catalog, which was to be the first catalog organized on the lines of the Five Store Plan.

There were analogies and contrasts between the company's position at the end of this period and what it had been in the beginning. In both cases a new set of plans and concepts was replacing older systems which were regarded as outmoded. In both cases the company had suffered several years of financial reverses; in both, also, the organization had been somewhat skeletonized as a result, and was amenable to staffing by personnel who understood the tasks involved in the new planning and had the energy, ambition, and requisite ruthlessness in carrying these out. But the reduced organization of 1943 was infinitely better prepared to undertake the tasks of the future than was that of 1937. Research, organizational and operational techniques were better understood, seasoned by experience and success, and ready for application. A better balance had been achieved between merchandising and operating functions in the company although the former were still accorded a priority in status and prestige. M. J. Spiegel was still sufficiently young and energetic to provide the continuing leadership of the enterprise, and had enjoyed sufficient success to bolster his own confidence in his ability to find a new direction which would permit the company to realize the kind of initial success in its new ventures which it had attained during 1933–37. By the end of 1943 the regrouping stage was over, and Spiegel was prepared to launch what M. J. Spiegel confidently hoped would be its most prosperous era.

Frustration Decade
Retail Store
Operation
1944–1954

Chapter 10

During the three years between the creation of the program for expansion in January 1944 and the date that the retail store organization was virtually completed, the Spiegel management enjoyed no respite from M. J. Spiegel's drive. The company's president was acutely aware that his decision to reenter retail on a national basis, to adopt strong competitive pricing policies, and to abandon the umbrella of pure installment selling placed the company in direct competition with the two powerful giants of mail order. He was also aware that the success which Sears and Ward had won after 1932 was achieved fundamentally because of their expansion of retail stores. The 1944–54 period in Spiegel's history would be characterized by a move into retail store operations designed to place the company in a position to experience rapid growth in that field without becoming more directly involved in competition with either Sears or Montgomery Ward. To avoid direct competition with the two mass distributors and to take advantage of the growth trend which specialty store chains had experienced in recent years, M. J. Spiegel made the decision to move into this area of retailing rather than open a series of department stores. The specialty stores would be classified by five categories of merchandise: apparel shops for men, for women, and for children; house furnishings; and stores offering a line of auto-farm-hardware merchandise.

In order to achieve the sales objectives set forth in the 1944 postwar merchandising plan within the eight-year time limit then established, the decision was made to purchase existing businesses. M. J. Spiegel was aiming for corporate sales of $250 million by 1953, 46 percent of which were to be through retail stores, and acquisition of established specialty stores was viewed as the fastest route to this goal. Spiegel's decision to broaden its distribution system and to go into retail operation was not based entirely on the successes of Ward and Sears. M. J. Spiegel was acutely aware that the postwar environment would be fundamentally different from that in which Spiegel, Inc., had gained its previous success.

The setting within which Spiegel contended for a new market position and a larger share of the dollars which Americans expended on personal consumption was conditioned by a number of powerful political, economic, and social forces. The United States government had emerged from World War II with the overseas responsibility for reestablishing orderly governments in Europe and Asia and with the responsibility at home of maintaining an orderly transition from a wartime economy to one of peace.

Acceptance of world responsibility, even a recognition that it had been thrust upon them, came neither easily nor uniformly for Americans and their government. The total victory over Germany and Japan was quickly followed by the clamor to "bring home the boys," reconvert the awesome wartime industrial machine, and get down to the serious business of consumption. There were, to be sure, those who viewed the future with trepidation, recalling the large numbers of unemployed that had existed up to 1942. There were those, also, who looked at the backlog of accumulated liquidity which years of full employment, rationing, and goods shortages had accumulated; they saw the shortage of housing which depression, then wartime rationing, had imposed, and called for a continuation of price, wage, and rent controls to dampen the threat of explosive inflation. But these, like the voices calling for only gradual reduction in the armed forces, were drowned in Congress and elsewhere. Controls over the economy were liberalized in 1946, almost completely thrown off in 1947. A Republican victory in the 1948 congressional elections gave that party control of the national legislature for the first time in sixteen years and represented a shift toward a more conservative Congress. Federal purchases of goods and services plunged from $89 billion in 1944 to $15.7 billion three years later, national security expenditures alone accounting for $67 billion of the gross decline.

Compensating for this reduction in governmental purchases of goods and services was the vigorous resurgence of private consumption and domestic and net foreign investment between 1945 and 1949. As a result, gross national product, which fell almost $3 billion to $210.7 billion in 1946, rose to nearly $260 billion in 1948. Price increases kept virtual pace with this gain; but despite sporadic consumer resistance to upward spiraling prices, as price and credit controls were removed, private consumption outlays went up even more rapidly. This powerful shift of emphasis toward the private sector of the economy prevented the specter of massive unemployment from materializing; but even with the rapid demobilization of millions of military personnel the unemployment rate did not exceed 4 percent.

Over the entire period, 1944–54, the basic determinants of consumer demand for goods and services demonstrated a remarkable consistency. Total United States population rose from 138.4 million in 1944 to 162.4 million in 1954, a gain of 17.4 percent, almost double the comparable rate for the preceding eleven years. Total households increased from 37.1 million to 46.9 million, a gain of 26 percent compared to the 18.5 percent growth recorded for 1934–44. The birthrate per 1,000 population had been 19 in 1934, in 1944 it went up to 21.2. In terms of actual numbers of live births, the 1954 figure was 4.08 million compared to 2.94 million in 1944 and 2.40 million in 1934. One reason for the increase in the birthrate was the tendency to marry at an earlier age; a second was rising personal income; a third was the tendency of families to treat increases in the number of children as part of a normal consumption function. There was a continuation of the long-term trend toward urbanization and an accelerated decline in the number of persons living in rural areas and in the number of farm households. The latter, for example, fell from 7.15 million in 1940 to 5.49 million in 1954. By 1950 there were over 96 million persons living in what the Bureau of the Census defined as urban locations; four years

later it was well over 100 million. Among communities with populations of 25,000 or over, the greatest rates of increase were experienced by those in the 500,000 to 1,000,000 and 25,000 to 100,000
population ranges. Cities with populations in excess of 1,000,000
experienced the smallest gain in numbers between the 1940 and
1950 census. Yet this classification, while valuable, fails to account
for the most significant demographic development of the period:
the growth of the suburbs around the big urban centers. As these
settlements expanded around such cities as New York, Chicago,
Los Angeles, Philadelphia, and Detroit, vast complexes of almost
continuous urbanization were created. All of which merely reflected the trend of growing mobility of Americans, for suburban
populations typically expanded as a result of movements from the
central cities, or the transfers of people from one urban complex
to another.[1]

The income determinants of consumer behavior also changed
dramatically between 1944 and 1954. Personal disposable income
and personal consumption expenditures rose at a steady rate over
the period. Earlier marriages and the formation of new households
resulted in rising birthrates and, in turn, stimulated the demand for
new residential housing. Demand for household appliances and
home furnishings followed logically from this development. There
was, in addition, the strong desire to improve the standard of living as income rose, by a shift in preference to better quality goods
and improved services. The migration to the suburbs strongly affected purchase patterns and the choice of goods and services.[2]
There was, for example, an increased demand for casual clothing;
for automobiles to meet the mobility needs of suburbanites; for appliances such as refrigerators, washing machines, television sets;
for paint, wallpaper, seed, lawn mowers, barbecue pits and outdoor furniture; for the host of do-it-yourself tools and equipment.[3]

Although the dollar amounts expended for durable and nondurable goods and services steadily grew on an annual basis, the
relative distribution of such expenditures underwent a significant
shift. With respect to the distribution of consumption outlays by
specific categories of goods, the relative importance of general
merchandise, apparel, and furniture and appliances in the average
budget tended to decline during the 1944–54 period. Spending for
housing and motor vehicles, on the other hand, was rather constant

as a percentage of aggregate consumption expenditures, particularly during the 1950s. The growing popularity of casual apparel, attributable to the advance of suburban living, definitely had an adverse effect upon the sales of apparel, but still only a minority of people resided in suburbs, and there was a growing population of children to be clothed. Expenditures for furniture and home furnishings did not keep pace with other expenditures, as they were no longer major symbols of individual achievement. Also the makers and sellers of home furnishings were unable to develop in consumers the pronounced sense of dissatisfaction with older goods through the techniques of annual model changes and planned obsolescence.

The mechanism through which so much of this new consumption was made possible was installment credit. From 1944 to the end of 1954, the decisive upward thrust of installment credit was one of the fundamental characteristics of American consumption behavior. From $2.2 billion in 1944 total installment credit climbed to $23.6 billion in 1954, a more than tenfold increase. Automobile credit provided the greatest single impetus in this growth, but charge-account credit also experienced a consistent rise after 1944, and by the end of 1954 was almost one-third the amount of non-auto installment credit.

The 1944–54 period also ushered in another social phenomenon—the "new middle class." In earlier generations members of the middle class had been vitally concerned with capital accumulation and with judicious use of money as influenced by the moral values associated with the Protestant Ethic. The new middle class, as C. Wright Mills has argued, was both broader and less homogeneous in character, comprised of people with quite different attitudes and expectations, with wide disparity in occupational, educational, and ideological traits.[4] Thus *middle class* represented a term which possessed little more than economic meaning. As more households increased their earnings, both through wage and salary boosts and by having two or more members employed, the number of people in the middle-income group expanded much more than at either end of the income distribution scale.

Given the nature of the economy and the pace and direction of change within it, Spiegel's principal problems were in selecting the areas in which it would specialize and correctly appraising the opportunities available to it—specifically, the opportunities for chain distribution of mass-produced merchandise, priced to meet the tastes and incomes of the new middle class. Spiegel was to attempt to take advantage of these opportunities through direct-contact mail order and a five-store retail operation. As has been suggested, it would have been impossible to undertake the rapid development of five chains of stores from scratch, given the post-war shortages of construction materials, consumer goods, and experienced retail personnel. Furthermore, by any estimate, the capital outlays involved in starting from the bottom appeared to be greater than those required to purchase established firms. Spiegel, its president believed, could acquire the management of going concerns and their leases, inventories, reputation, and merchandise sources. Spiegel began this effort with the purchase of Sally Chain Stores, Inc., in April 1944.

The purchase price for Sally Chain Stores, a twelve-year-old organization with annual sales of $8.3 million and earnings of $300,000, was $1.73 million. Spiegel acquired, in addition to the forty-six retail outlets which were concentrated principally in the East North Central region, the services of Arthur S. Kahn, who, with his wife, Sally, had conceived and developed the chain, and the services of Abner Parker and Abraham Brownstein. Parker was one of the principal owners of Sally, while Brownstein had been a key merchandise executive.

The Sally stores constituted the backbone of Spiegel's planned fashion chain, but management sought both more outlets and greater geographic dispersion. Earl Weil and Walter Gatzert, along with various business brokers, were kept occupied in the search for another chain throughout 1944. By October, negotiations had begun with the owners of the twenty-six-unit Askin-Beverly chain of women's dress shops. Each unit of the chain was separately incorporated under the laws of the state in which it was located. Ten of the outlets were in the states of Texas, Louisiana, and Arkansas; another ten were strung out over the states of Michigan, Indiana, Missouri, and Wisconsin, with the remainder scattered throughout Florida, North and South Carolina, Mississippi, and Pennsylvania. These stores tended to have high traffic locations in communities with populations of under 150,000 and carried merchandise priced in the low to moderate ranges. The scatter of units in the Atlantic seaboard states presented problems of central warehouse servicing because of the long distances from Chicago, but the grouping in the Southwest provided a good wedge into that territory and the Midwest locations complemented the Sally distribution. The price paid by Spiegel for Beverly amounted to $835,000. No long-term employment contracts were offered to Beverly executives and store managers. They were employed with the company on a month-to-month basis. Beverly sales for the year ending July 29, 1944 were about $4.2 million.[5]

Acquisition of the Sally and Beverly stores provided the company with seventy-two retail locations, including the services of individual unit managers and sales clerks, plus merchandising and operating executives. It also provided sales in the range $13–$15 million even under wartime merchandise shortage conditions. However, the combined purchase price of $2.56 million had been expended on two chains that were largely women's apparel lines, with the exception of those children's goods carried by the Sally units. With more than $3 million in cash still in hand, management sought outlets in the house furnishings and auto-farm-hardware fields, plus whatever likely opening existed in men's apparel. It was surprising, therefore, that the Federal Outfitting Company, Inc., of San Francisco, became the next business to be acquired. For although Federal possessed twenty retail outlets (nineteen in California and one in Nevada), was managed by several lively executives, and enjoyed a substantial profit margin on approximately $4 million of sales,[6] it had several characteristics which required some imagination to fit into the image which Spiegel had planned to develop. The merchandise handled in the Federal stores included apparel, jewelry, and other personal furnishings, together with some furniture, and some domestics, thereby making the stores small-scale, limited department stores. Further, the price and quality of the goods varied widely, bore substantial markups, and the fundamental sales plan was aggressive credit merchandising. It seems evident that Federal was acquired not to fit harmoniously into the corporate concept of the Five Store Plan, but rather to obtain Pacific Coast distribution and, more to the point, because it was highly profitable.

With Federal, Spiegel obtained the services of R. M. Gisser, who was later installed as president and general manager of the chain. In addition, the company enjoyed the output and earnings of the Dortch Stove Company of Franklin, Tennessee, which Federal had purchased at the end of 1943 for $520,100. Dortch had been purchased to strengthen the company's source position, but under wartime metal restrictions and until Spiegel had acquired retail outlets for house furnishings and major appliances, the manufacturer's main contribution to the parent firm lay in the profits generated through sales to other distributors.

By the end of 1944 Spiegel had used $5.5 million of its cash reserves for acquisitions, but during 1945 the company pushed ahead with the multiple chain concept, concentrating almost exclusively on acquiring house furnishing outlets. The first of these purchases was made in February 1945 when, for $986,000, the company obtained from Straus & Schram five neighborhood furniture stores (four in Chicago and one in Joliet, Illinois), and a five-floor warehouse adjoining Spiegel's main plant on 35th Street.[7] The warehouse was the most coveted asset in view of Spiegel's growth plans. Although the retail units, which were typical borax-type, hard-sell, credit stores, did not conform to the image which management was struggling to create, they did constitute a start in Chicago. Management assumed—somewhat too easily as it turned out—that under central Spiegel direction and merchandising, the character of the units could be transformed. The Straus & Schram acquisition possessed some advantages for Spiegel; the units had been centrally serviced from a Chicago warehouse and constituted a fairly homogeneous chain.

This advantage, however, could not be claimed for the other furniture stores acquired that year, which were scattered over such a wide geographic area that centralized warehousing was virtually impossible. Harbour Longmire, the preeminent furniture retailer in Oklahoma City, was purchased in April 1945 for $802,100. Three months later the Dorris Heyman Company in Phoenix, Arizona, was gathered into the company's retail fold for a price of $599,500, and in November the highly reputable Morrison Neese store at Greensboro, North Carolina, was bought for $227,900.[8] In all these purchases Spiegel obtained receivables, valuable inventories, delivery equipment, fixtures, and prepaid assets. In all cases the company took over a going organization, including store personnel;

and in at least one case, the existing top management of the store.

In addition to the breakthrough in house furnishings, the company also launched its program for the boys' and girls' store chain by opening two outlets in 1945; one in Aurora, Illinois, the other on Chicago's northwest side. Because of myriad difficulties subsequent development of children's wear merchandising was confined to opening departments in the company's women's wear stores; thus this element of the Five Store Plan suffered a rapid demise.

In September 1945, Spiegel purchased a Pacific Coast operation which also failed to fit into the Five Store concept, the Whitney Department Store of San Diego, California. Whitney enjoyed a unique position in American retail distribution, having specialized on a low-price, low-expense principle (promotional expenditures had averaged about 0.25 percent of sales compared to a national average for department stores of 3 percent). The company had maintained a profit rate, before taxes, of around 6 percent of sales before 1941, and over 12.5 percent during the war.[9] The purchase price was $746,735.

The Whitney purchase can be rationalized only as a technique for acquiring demonstrated business talent. C. D. "Rox" Ryan had resigned in August 1945 from the presidency of Montgomery Ward to go to Whitney, following the latest in the series of bizarre episodes involving Sewell Avery and his executives, a process which was bleeding that organization of talent at such a rate that by 1953 Ward would have lost four presidents and thirty-one vice presidents.[10] In terms of its commitment to build retail chains, Spiegel could not help benefiting from the counsel of someone with Ryan's experience and ability. Ryan, however, evidently preferred the quasi-autonomy of Whitney to the alternative of accepting a position at the Spiegel headquarters. For the company itself there was the problem of how to adjust the functions and powers of Earl Weil and others to accommodate such an addition. But as head of Whitney, and as a company director, a post to which he would be elected the following year, Ryan could be expected, as *Time* predicted, "to inject big-time know-how into Spiegel policies."

By June 1945, Spiegel, Inc., had seventy-two retail dress stores, two children's stores, and a quasi-chain of house furnishing outlets, all without entirely neglecting its mail-order business. The program for the catalog order units, that is, direct contact mail-order selling, was of more than passing interest. The company planned to have order-desk facilities located in fifty of its planned retail stores by 1948 and double that number in 1952. It expected, however, both greater volume and profits from its combination dress shops and order-desk units, the first of which had been installed in Chicago. Of great significance in the company's expansion plan was the role assigned to direct mail. According to the estimates presented in 1945, Spiegel management believed that by 1952 only 21 percent of all mail-order sales would take place through the order-office units. Of more importance, however, was the assumption that if Spiegel was to retain any reasonable proportion of the patronage developed in the vital states of Pennsylvania, New York, and West Virginia during the no-charge-for-credit era, it would be necessary to establish a branch plant in the east. Further, if the southwestern territory was to be effectively exploited, a branch plant was also vital in that area. A tentative direct-mail sales target of $25 million was forecasted for 1948 in the eastern market, and was to be expanded to $30 million by 1953. The southwestern branch plant, to be established by 1952, was expected to yield an additional $15 million.

Branch plants in both of these regions were considered very important by management if the company was to compete with Sears and Ward, a competition which seemed unavoidable in view of the company's professed determination to emphasize cash sales. To serve the Middle Atlantic region and the border states of the Atlantic seaboard, Sears had a branch in Philadelphia, and Montgomery Ward had one in Baltimore. Spiegel had suffered a reduction of sales in the area since the credit emphasis was abandoned in 1942. By 1945, only 27 percent of the company's sales were produced in its eastern market, a ratio substantially below that which the house had enjoyed in 1941.[11]

As a result of the board's decision to accelerate the implementation of chain building, management pressed ahead with its acquisition of house furnishing stores in 1946 and, through the purchase of an existing chain, entered the auto-farm-hardware field. Such actions were supplemented by aggressive real estate action, as Arthur Kahn toured the retail territories selecting sites, negotiating leases for additional outlets, and assisting in the closing of marginal units.

Between March and July of 1946, Spiegel purchased three additional furniture firms, all possessing the same general characteristics of merchandise quality, patronage, and price as those acquired in 1945 in the out-of-Chicago locations. The first of these, the Stoehr and Fister store in Scranton, Pennsylvania, was purchased for $448,100 and Spiegel, in return, obtained inventories, receivables, furnishings, equipment, and contracts with key personnel. In April, the purchase of the Sydnor and Hundley store, with its unrivaled reputation, in Richmond, Virginia, was consummated for a price of $211,800.[12] In July, Spiegel acquired all of the shares of Robert Keith Furniture and Carpet Company of Kansas City for the price of $1.4 million, which included the land, the building which housed the downtown store, a second and relatively new plaza store, the usual inventories, receivables, equipment, and fixtures.[13]

In October 1946, Spiegel purchased the Miller Brothers furniture store in Chicago for $307,400, a price which included a building valued at $230,000.[14] This acquisition provided a fifth retail furniture outlet in Chicago and completed what became the Chicago Furniture Store Chain. It also completed, although this was not specifically the intention of management at the time, the company's retail acquisition program. For Spiegel had already entered into the auto-farm-hardware distribution field in March with the acquisition of the J & R Motor Supply Company, whose fifty-five retail outlets were concentrated in a seven-state area comprising Illinois, Indiana, Michigan, Iowa, Missouri, Nebraska, Iowa, and Wisconsin.[15] The purchase price was actually $2,955,400, which included 21,241 shares of Spiegel common stock and $2.4 million in cash.

Although J & R Motor Supply did not rank with such giants in this merchandise field as Gamble and Western Auto it had annual sales of $7.5 million and occupied a strategic niche for Spiegel because of its geographic coverage in the Middle West and because of its management. The principal owners, Isadore Jacobson, Carl Ragnitt, and James J. Simon, had developed the chain during the years of depression, and had constituted the key executive group. All accepted contracts with Spiegel.

Although the described transactions completed the basic arrangement of the company's retail chain stores, one further acquisition was undertaken in 1946. This was the purchase of the Joseph Berlinger Manufacturing Company of New York for $960,000.[16] Berlinger manufactured rayon and its value to Spiegel was as a source of supply. The company would assure Spiegel rayon piece goods with which to supply its own sources of manufactured apparel, and to trade with other firms for other materials.

As a result of acquisitions, Spiegel had added a total of 158 retail outlets between April 1944 and September 1946. (A summary of these transactions are provided in exhibit 6 in the Appendix.) Geographically, the retail stores were concentrated in the northern half of the Middle West (see Appendix exhibit 7). The East North Central region had over 57 percent of the outlets (Chicago alone had nearly 18 percent); the West North Central states had over 15 percent; the West South Central, the next most heavily covered area, had less than 10 percent. In terms of the type of chain, however, there was an even more striking concentration. Of the sixty-seven fashion stores operated by the company, nearly 63 percent were in the East North Central region (Chicago had 25 percent); while almost 20 percent were located in the West South Central states. Of the fifty-seven farm-auto-hardware stores 68 percent were in the East North Central region, and the rest were in West North Central states. The Federal stores were overwhelmingly concentrated in California, while Chicago contained nearly one-half of the eleven house furnishings stores.

In terms of the accomplishment of the objectives announced at a 1945 seminar, management had little to be ashamed of with the exception of before tax profits. The company had succeeded in opening more retail units than the plan had originally (and tentatively) called for, and the 1948 net sales for the corporation were $134 million.

Spiegel's entry into direct-contact mail order during this acquisition period lagged behind major competitors, and was marked by uncertainty that was complicated by the company's commitment to aggressively promote the specialty retail chains. During the spring and summer of 1944, the company opened five Chicago "neighborhood catalog order stores." By the end of the year, one of these had been expanded to include a Sally dress shop, a new unit had been opened in Moline, Illinois, and order desks had been installed in the boys' and girls' stores in Chicago and Joliet, Illinois. The original units were modern, well-furnished installations, containing comfortable facilities, a complete assortment of catalogs and other literature, and a staff of trained clerks to assist in making out orders and to suggest merchandise. A forty-eight-hour service was provided for delivery, which could be made to the units for pick up by customers, or directly to the home. Another convenience provided for Spiegel customers was the telephone-order facility. As the company acquired chains of retail stores, these order desks were installed on a selective basis in the larger cities like Chicago, to encourage purchase of goods not contained in the inventories of the stores themselves.

The preference for order desks rather than for the pure catalog offices, which characterized management policy during these beginning years, can be attributed not only to the growth of desk facilities within the company's own stores but to the experiments conducted in the facilities of other proprietors. In April 1944, for example, Spiegel sought to arrange an agreement with the Phillips Petroleum Company whereby forty-five of the latter's oil stations would carry certain of the company's automobile lines and would promote the sale of merchandise from Spiegel catalogs which would be supplied to them. These dealers were to receive a discount equal to 7 percent of catalog prices. In 1945 similar arrangements were worked out with the Deeprock Oil Company and with Food-Fair, an eastern grocery chain with sixty-four supermarket outlets. These efforts, though, proved disappointing to Spiegel for several reasons, which included the difficulty of promoting the Spiegel name to customers of another enterprise; overcoming a pattern of shopping habits; and not having stocks of goods on hand from which customers could select. In addition there was the problem of inadequate space in the retail outlets and the orgnizational and motivational problems of infusing supermarket and filling-station operators and managers with the conviction that forceful and aggressive utilization of the desk facilities was to their own advantage.

Despite the knowledge that competitors had, in times other than in a sellers' market, transacted up to one-third of mail-order volume in catalog-order units and desks, the Spiegel management was most unaggressive in promoting the development of desks and units. By the end of 1947 its field structure consisted of the Chicago teleservice and two catalog-order offices, twenty-nine desks installed in the company's own retail stores, and seventeen on the premises of the outlets of independent retailers. In part this was one of the results of the concentration of attention being devoted to retail-chain organization and the serious problems that were arising in that distribution channel. Also, it partly resulted from the inadequate organization and central planning of the catalog-order department, and from divided responsibility. The men who were charged with this development were hard working, with some experience in order-office operation, but the entire effort lacked cohesiveness and a feeling of occupying an important role in the corporation. By the end of 1946, however, some order had been established in terms of longer-range expectations and organization. Robert Stecker, merchandise manager, had enunciated a basic scheme wherein order desks were to be established in all retail stores except nonintegrated chains, where store size was too small to permit effective operation of a desk, where separate catalog-order offices were being tested, or where neighborhoods were considered adequately serviced by desks in existing units. The program was more completely detailed during the spring of 1947 in a paper presented by Edward Rubin.

The fundamental philosophy of the 1947 plan was that the catalog-order units were to be considered as essentially a Division 2 objective, and would be accounted for and expensed within that framework. In addition to producing additional sales volume by "suggestive selling of substitute items for those out of stock and upgrading items ordered to higher price levels," the purpose of the order units was seen as "increasing mail-order circulation" by direct-contact selling in the territories covered by catalog units.[17] The order-unit concept was regarded as providing a means whereby mail order could cut into some of the competitive advantages possessed by retail merchants in desirable communities. This objective, of course, emphasized the importance of personalized contacts between consumers and the units, and the need to provide effective services in selling, handling returns and complaints, in emphasizing credit, and in accepting payments and performing collection functions.

The structure of units as presented in this plan was to include teleservice for large metropolitan centers, and order desks and "stations" in communities where metropolitan delivery service was not available. The teleservice-units orders would be phoned in (customers would either have received mailed catalogs, or borrowed them from the circulating libraries maintained by the units), processed through Chicago by teletypewriter service, and delivered at the homes of customers by metropolitan delivery facilities. In metropolitan areas outside Chicago arrangements were made for trucking the packages to a central distribution point where they were sorted and ultimately delivered. Order-desk service in retail outlets provided adequate and comfortable facilities, clerical assistance in ordering and arranging for deliveries. Here, obviously, clerks had the opportunity for direct selling as well as for developing a more personal relationship with customers.

Although catalog-order offices were hardly mentioned in the 1944 plan, these became the backbone of the program after 1947. During 1948 six such offices were opened, followed in 1949 by an additional eighteen. The teleservice units increased to three in 1948, and six more were opened the following year. By the end of 1950 (see table 14) the company had nine teleservice, twenty-

14. Distribution by states and metropolitan regions, 1950

State	Offices	Desks		Teleservice Location
Illinois	16	16	1	Chicago
Indiana	2	3	1	Indianapolis
Iowa	3	4		
Michigan	3	8	1	Detroit
Ohio	3	2	3	Cincinnati, Cleveland, Toledo
Wisconsin	1	6	1	Milwaukee
Kentucky			1	Louisville
Missouri		1	1	St. Louis
Total	28	40	9	

Source: Corporate records, 1950.

eight catalog-order offices, and forty order desks in operation, with a significant proportion of the latter concentrated in the farm-auto-hardware stores. Order-unit and desk sales had, over the five-year period between 1946 and 1950, increased at three times the rate at which teleservice units had risen, but teleservice units were proving to be the most productive. In 1950, for example, teleservice sales comprised over 41 percent of all direct-contact volume compared with roughly 11 percent in 1946. On the other hand, catalog desks accounted for only 34 percent of the $15.7 million 1950 direct-contact sales, whereas such desks had produced 78 percent of the 1946 volume of $3.9 million. On a unit basis, productivity indices showed that teleservice offices increased sales from $423,000 in 1946 to $720,000 in 1950, whereas the comparative values for order offices were $216,000 and $138,-700, and for order desks, $89,600 and $129,000.

By 1950 Spiegel had completed its multichannel selling organization composed of 162 retail stores, 68 catalog offices and service desks, and 9 teleservice locations. Total corporate sales for that year were $143 million and the expansion program seemed to be going as scheduled. However, after 1950 environmental changes took place which could not be foreseen in 1944. These changes later led to the failure of Spiegel's retail plan and to its subsequent return to a more aggressive mail-order operation. Consumer buying habits changed radically after 1950. Consumers became more price conscious and the previous sellers' market was reversed. Accompanying this change in buying behavior was a new phenomenon which began upsetting the conventional methods of distributing goods—the discount house.

The essential characteristics of a discount operation were low prices, low margins, fast inventory turnover, few services, low-rent locations, and modest selling expense. Such enterprises typically invested little money in fixtures and most of them remained small. But it was the imaginatively managed, promotionally aggressive discounters who captured the public's imagination and had the most pronounced effects upon conventional retailing. These firms, such as Polk Brothers in Chicago and Korvette in New York, advertised extensively, merchandised brilliantly, bought in large quantities, and judiciously added services such as delivery, repair, and even credit.

More immediate was the impact upon conventional retailing, already staggering under the multiple blows inflicted by the rise of suburban and regional shopping centers, the shifts in population, and the deterioration of older centers. Hundreds of local appliance dealers were bankrupted; many department stores ceased to handle appliances entirely, and still others met the new competition by reducing prices or by resorting to individual bargaining with customers such as was the common practice at many of the major discount houses. The impact would have been dramatic even had it been confined exclusively to consumer durables, but this was not the case as the "discounting revolution" progressed. When packages of consumer services were adopted by the big discounters, the squeeze on profits caused many to seek relief on margins by other lines, soft goods and home furnishings. These items were not characterized by strong brand identifications, but the selling problem was eased by the general discount connotation of the house, a "halo effect," permitting a higher profit return. The net result of this, of course, was to put discount houses into direct and continuous competition with every type of general line retailing, including the mail-order houses.

In spite of the impact of the discounters mail-order buying experienced a postwar resurgence. The renewed demand did not come from the rural areas but from urban communities, a fascinating and challenging reversal of past behavior. One reason for this pick up was the relative convenience for consumers which teleservice and catalog-shopping units in large towns and cities provided. When coupled with metropolitan delivery systems, local sales promotion and servicing of accounts, and the ready extension of installment credit, such distribution systems offered urban populations a further alternative by which to satisfy their consumption needs. The growth of catalog sales from $608 million to $1.22 billion between 1945 and 1955 provides a useful indicator of the growing importance of mail order, for this 101 percent gain was clearly greater than the growth of general merchandise sales and, in fact, all other broad groups of merchandise, with the exception of automotive equipment and motor vehicles.[18] The big catalog houses accounted for a major share of aggregate mail-order sales, of course, but specialized forms of direct-mail selling of books, phonograph records, and novelties enjoyed an expanding market after 1945; and at this time various types of retail institutions, such as department stores, resorted to direct-mail techniques.

In aggregate, then, the rise of the discount house, the spread of branch stores, the development of suburban and regional shopping centers, the intensification of mail-order selling, all tended to result in overlapping patterns of retail distribution. The upshot was a decided blurring in the conventional classifications of retailing, and, more vitally, a sharp intensification of competition among all retailers. The very nature of this competition made more difficult the problems for any seller, particularly with respect to finding and holding some niche and market position which would provide both identity to highly mobile consumers, and a more secure base upon which to build.

Omniscience cannot be considered a normal attribute of an executive group, and the Spiegel management cannot be criticized for failing to anticipate the numerous changes which characterized American distribution after 1950. Certain situations were, in fact, anticipated or discovered early by management, resulting in significant shifts in planning. One of these was the recognition that entry into the men's apparel market was encumbered by the major barriers of the unavailability of stores for purchase, and the amount of capital required for building such a chain. A second was the decision to discontinue development of the children's stores after two units had been opened and to confine the retail distribution of children's goods to sections in selected fashion stores. The reasons for this were the disproportionate investment in inventory that was required, the large preopening expenses, and the small profit margin to be expected even when optimum merchandising and operating efficiency was presumed. These decisions, taken before the expansion program was fully launched, in effect reduced the Spiegel strategy to a "three-store" plan.

A management team did not require omniscience, however, to recognize certain inherent contradictions between formulated strategy and organizational and locational execution. Consider, for example, the relationship between the plan for a branch plant in the east and the acquisition of existing chains. The branch was considered of primary importance in helping Spiegel acquire competitive parity in mail-order distribution in a key market area. Yet, as had been foreseen, the Sears branches, as central warehouses for the concentration of purchased merchandise and control centers for the strategic distribution of goods to retail outlets, had contributed strongly to the success Sears had achieved in retailing. A clear rationale, therefore, argued for the development of retail stores in territories around the central and branch plants, although this was not as important with respect to fashion goods for which there were different demand and supply characteristics than existed for other goods. What was disturbing was the apparent disregard of the possibilities for optimization of corporate rather than either chain or mail-order strategy. Management continued to go through the motions of opening an eastern branch plant while actually acquiring the Federal store chain in California, and a thin scatter of furniture and fashion stores in the Middle and South Atlantic states. A clearer locational logic had already been offered management by the 1945 seminar, where a recommendation to establish a branch plant in the West South Central region was made. The company-acquired fashion stores in this area and the combination of mail-order and retail distribution around a hub strategically within the economically expanding area around the Gulf of Mexico offered greater return on total investment than either a branch mail-order plant with no retail outlets, or a cluster of retail stores with no branch plant located in California, or both.

Nor was infinite intellectual power required to perceive the fundamental contradictions posed by the image Spiegel desired to create and the reputation, organization, and business methods of the stores which were purchased. The Straus & Schram furniture stores, for example, were undisguised borax operations, characterized by the price-emphasized, step-up selling, and fictitious value advertising that was a bench mark of this and hundreds of furniture chains in the United States. The six independent furniture stores which were loosely lumped together in a chain, on the other hand, were at the opposite end of the quality continuum, all enjoying a distinguished reputation in their communities, all serving a significantly different class clientele than that which traded at Straus & Schram.

Excluding the merchandising, selling, and operating problems, management intended to improve the Straus & Schram reputation by substituting the Spiegel name—which still fell well short of a quality connotation. The out-of-town stores, on the other hand, were to be granted a considerable amount of autonomy at the store manager level, and more popularly priced, mass-production merchandise was to be fed into the units so that the basic appeal would be broadened without, it was hoped, surrendering the original reputation of the stores. The Federal stores were pure and simple credit operators, and it is difficult to reconcile M. J. Spiegel's judgment that the day of the pure-credit operator in mail order had closed with his decision to acquire a chain based upon this attribute. Simultaneously, if Federal's success could be attributed to anything except the advantage of the credit accommodation to low-income people for whom the purchase of nondurable goods on installment terms was a necessity, it was probably due to the range of its product line. For these were limited-line department stores rather than specialty shops, and the merchandise range at least provided a broader appeal to the mass of consumers and the opportunity of spreading overhead costs over a larger sales volume. That Federal proved to be the only consistent profit maker among the company's retail chains would seem to argue strongly for the conclusion that (1) autonomy was the better organizational structure for operating disparate chains of stores, (2) a greater emphasis upon time-payment selling in retail and mail order would have been in the corporation's best interest, and (3) that limited department stores were superior to specialty shops in terms of both consumer appeal and operational efficiency.

Because the costs of a branch plant were too high, apparently, to justify the investment which would have to be paid off from the necessary "plus" mail-order volume and because of the drain of capital into retail acquisition, refurbishing, and new store openings, this aspect of the strategy was effaced. This left Spiegel with only limited opportunities to attain the desired market position. The decision to scrap the branch-plant goal forced the company to depend exclusively on the Chicago plant in mail order, and effectively confined the bulk of sales to the territory within a five-hundred-mile radius around Chicago. Only Texas lay wholly beyond this radius. As of 1950, when plans for the branch plant had been finally abandoned, the East North Central states contributed nearly 39 percent of mail-order sales; Iowa and Missouri, the only West North Central states where the company made an appreciable dent, about 6 percent; the Kentucky-Tennessee market was only 4.7 percent; and Pennsylvania, western New York, and West Virginia produced 15.2 percent. The company, by combining a rigorous program of comparative shopping with tight specification buying, rigid quality controls, and comprehensive inspection, had been able to achieve prices and quality comparable to its main mail-order rivals, but only at the catalog level. Branch-plant distribution by Sears and Ward continued to provide them with a net-delivered-price and time-service differential.

The contribution of Spiegel's shrunken set of specialty chains to the establishment of a secured market position was minimal. Because the Federal stores have to be considered mavericks in the original Five Store Plan, the effort to acquire a distinctive styling and fashion position in the market was restricted to the fashion stores, the auto-hardware group, and the home furnishings chains. The unhappy record of retail outlets, from 1944 to 1954, shown in exhibit 8 (see Appendix) reveals that Spiegel's specialty chains fell far short of M. J. Spiegel's goal of $115 million in sales by 1952. Total corporate sales for that year were $146.1 million, only $47.5 million of which were attributed to the retail chains. Of the $98.6 million of mail-order sales, $21.3 million were produced in the catalog-order units, only $77.3 million in direct mail (see Appendix, exhibit 9 for sales by distributive channel and net income after tax, 1945–54). Thus, retail volume, instead of rising, actually declined almost 13 percent. Only order-unit volume provided any balm for management, rising over 280 percent since 1948. Measured by profitability, the accomplishments were still more depressing. Before tax operating profit for the entire retail division was only $427,000 under 1 percent. Even this result was superior to that for any year since 1948, 1952 being the first year since then that the fashion, auto-hardware chains had done anything but lose money; it was but the second year the out-of-town furniture stores had gone over the break-even point (the Chicago furniture group had a perfect record on this score: in no year since having been acquired by Spiegel had these stores ever earned a profit). In fact, had it not been for the company's maverick group—the Federal stores—no retail profit would have been earned from 1945! A review of exhibits 8 and 9 will reveal that only mail order kept Spiegel from operating at a loss from 1945 to 1953. Even this edge was wiped out in 1954 when the company had losses of $2.3 million.

Since the majority of the operating and merchandising executives employed in the retail divisions were experienced, educated men, who had enjoyed success in previous jobs, the explanations for the difficulties which beset retail cannot be found in personnel quality. A major contributory element was the division of responsibility between operating and merchandising-selling. The structure of the merchandising divisions insured that the division and group merchandise managers in the lines carried both in mail order and retail were forced to allocate their time and energies to both, thus spreading themselves too thinly. Whereas the merchandising executives at Lerner, Grayson-Robinson, or Gambles devoted full time to the problems of merchandising those chains, Spiegel merchants of comparable ability were using only part of their time.

A second important factor which contributed to the difficulties in retail was the set of misconceptions regarding scale efficiencies and the magnitude of overhead costs. In terms of the fashion chains, overhead costs had been held down by restricting services, by close negotiation of rentals, and by spreading fixed charges over a large number of units. With the same number of outlets, however, the heavy burden of fixed costs which the Spiegel organizational pattern imposed changed the entire cost structure, and the net income margin was sharply compressed. To reduce unit overhead the pressures mounted to open more stores. Competition became more ferocious as large existing chains, experiencing similar problems, struggled for locations and expanded outlets. Whatever volume increases Spiegel won were quickly offset by rising expenses. In the out-of-town furniture stores, there were no scale advantages. Because of the heterogeneity of patronage, consumer tastes, and business style of these units, central buying was impossible and there was no possibility of exerting mass purchasing power upon sources. The broad geographical spread of the units rendered central warehousing and regular meetings with unit managers equally uneconomical.

The Chicago stores for home furnishings, on the other hand, provided some opportunities for scale economies. They could be centrally warehoused, merchandise could be centrally purchased since the units were standardized, and such services as credit and collection could be combined for the Chicago outlets of the other chains, thus permitting a cycle-billing operation to be performed for a large block of customers. Such advantages, however, served principally to reduce the losses which the chains suffered. For if the out-of-town home furnishing stores were plagued by such phenomena as customer resentment of a foreign corporation taking over a symbol of local autonomy and pride, the Chicago stores suffered from the pure borax image and merchandising quality long associated with Straus & Schram, L. Fish, and other local furniture chains. With the improvement in incomes, upgrading in tastes, and the breakout from the foreign-born enclaves by succeeding generations, the market opportunities for this type of store were sharply compressed.

There was a further factor involved in retail decline—switching the chains to the Spiegel image and identification too quickly. The Sally and Beverly units disappeared and became Spiegel units, a name which had far less impact upon consumer consciousness in the retail market. The same was true of the Chicago furniture stores, but not the auto-farm-hardware chain where the J & R name was retained. Added to the consumer acceptance difficulty were the problems associated with having different teams of auditors, and a multiplicity of merchandising and operating personnel touring the retail locations, conferring with managers, seeking solutions to problem situations, issuing directives, and involving store and home office people in mutually recriminatory controversy.

Management sought a solution to these tribulations in 1948 by making Garvey responsible to Robert Stecker, general merchandise manager, and by making Erich Moos, a former store manager and supervisor for Sally, chief of the fashion stores. When this failed to solve the problems efficiently, the entire retail operating division was turned over to W. E. Cowan to be integrated with his mail-order operation functions. Cowan was made vice-president and general manager of the company.

Cowan had not sought the responsibility for retail operations and quickly became aware that under the divided organizational structure he had inherited there were few opportunities for making a significant improvement. Within the given limits, however, some gains were made. First, he folded up the retail headquarters and transferred all retained operating personnel back to 35th Street, amid some grumbling and a not inconsiderable apprehension on the part of the people affected. Garvey had been demanding, as the turnover records demonstrated, but Cowan had a much more frightening reputation in the company as an iron-willed, driving taskmaster. Second, he made all retail staff with the exception of sales promotion and advertising responsible to Budd Sills, his chief staff assistant. Sills also was made accountable for general credit and collection activities, mail order and retail, with the exception of the Chicago operation which was assigned to the Chicago furniture chain manager. Sales promotion functions were assigned to the individual chains and general staff promotional activity was terminated. Merchandising continued to be handled in Stecker's division, and the basic problems were not noticeably reduced. Tension continued between the merchants and store operating personnel, the former convinced that the store managers did not know how to display and promote; the latter certain that the buyers and merchandise managers were incompetent to provide merchandise that could be promoted.[19] Although there was some reshuffling, this essentially was the organization for retail operations before 1950.

The optimism which consolidation of retail operating functions under Cowan had generated proved illusory. Since so much of the bright expectations for the retail chains had already proved illusory, this should have come as no great surprise. The Five Store organization for merchandising, both retail and catalog, had broken down under its own weight by 1950. Now, despite the characteristic energy and tight planning with which he handled assignments, Cowan learned that retail was a different phenomenon from mail order. With several other company executives, he was in favor of abandoning retail entirely, but there was still too much of a vested interest involved—pride, prestige, the reluctance to abandon a dream, as well as the hard issues of the marketability of retail stores with an indifferent record of performance. Also there were the contractual lease obligations to be considered. Instead, the decision was taken to make the chains autonomous. In 1951 this reorganization was undertaken, and general managers for the five chains (fashion, auto-hardware, Chicago furniture, and out-of-town home furnishings stores, plus Federal stores) were appointed, and made directly responsible to M. J. Spiegel. Under this new system, the general managers were held responsible for total merchandising and selling as well as operating and housekeeping functions. Tom Lance, general manager for Dortch Stove, also reported to the president, as he had since 1946, in addition to five line and key staff executives. Thus, as Spiegel's situation worsened, the president found himself bearing a greater burden of administrative responsibility.

The implications of these strategical miscarriages were grave. The principal burden for whatever success the company attained had to be borne by the mail-order division, and within this context the primary load had to be shouldered by merchandising—particularly in apparel and soft goods—and by effective new customer recruiting. A sharply conceived and well-merchandised program of time-payment selling could have provided a strong market appeal; the emergence of such a program from the Spiegel heritage of credit selling was almost a foregone conclusion, particularly in an era of steadily expanding installment buying. The company's terms of sale, however, were actually more conservative than those of competitors, a condition imposed by the desire to rid the house of its former credit image and by the need to turn working capital. The company simply did not have the means of financing a larger body of receivables over the longer period which more liberal terms required. Efforts to make the credit plan more attractive to consumers after 1949 were continuously aborted by this immutable fact.

More aggressive mail-order selling would have added significantly to sales and profits and offset somewhat the disappointing showing in retail. Mail-order sales volume, however, depended upon many variables, particularly upon such factors as the number and location of catalog-order units, the price-quality-styling characteristics of the merchandise being advertised, the size and quality of the catalogs, sale flyers, and other promotional literature employed, the number and timing of the latter, the size of the mailing list, and the copy and graphic arts skills employed. Also significant were inventory position and the quality of operating services rendered, for a short stock position which resulted in heavy cancellations or excessive back orders could defeat a promotional campaign which was otherwise effectively conducted. A similar result would follow if services were slowly and inefficiently performed. In general, Spiegel selling campaigns were beset by a few significant shortcomings. The catalogs, at least during Stecker's tenure as general merchandise manager, were larger than those of the preceding decade, used more color, and were more costly to produce and distribute.

Distribution costs of literature were obviously influenced by factors other than decisions to print more copies or use more color pages. Rising printing costs were one cause, and during this decade the United States Post Office succeeded in raising postage and parcel post charges substantially above their prewar levels. Because of its dependence upon mail order, Spiegel fought the postal increases harder than any other member of the industry, but won only partial successes. After Stecker's departure, the catalogs suffered a reduction of pages and some of what one executive called "the pretty pictures" disappeared, but they tended to become more efficient selling instruments. That they still left something to be desired was demonstrated in 1952 when the company employed the head of the Associated American Artists as a consultant to help the company improve the selling appeal of the catalogs, particularly their graphic art content. There were also some deficiencies with respect to the number and timing of sales flyers. The chief difficulty of the mail-order operation, however, and one which was tightly related to the problem of new customer recruiting, was the area of circulation control. Both of these problems were directly traceable to the failure to acquire the desired market position.

By 1953 it was evident that mail order was being seriously neglected. The retail organizations had been uninhibited in draining off executive talent, and the ranking Spiegel executives and some directors had given up all hope for retail; pressure on M. J. Spiegel to divest was intense. The president was not yet willing to confess total defeat. Between April 1953 and the end of the year, however, a series of events made the decision inevitable. McKinsey & Company, a prominent management consulting firm was engaged to survey the organization; their counsel indicated Spiegel would benefit from divesting at least some of the retail chains. Then, Sir Isaac Wolfson, head of Great Universal Stores, Ltd., the dynamic British merchandising group, began his campaign to acquire a major American enterprise and initiated discussions with the Spiegel directorate. With the value of Spiegel stock scraping bottom and confronted by a future which appeared bleak unless the mail order could be freed from the constraints which retail imposed upon corporate resources, M. J. Spiegel opted for divestment.

A major reorganization followed this decision. Charles W. Helser, from Macy's San Francisco store and a former colonel in the army's supply service during World War II, was appointed head of mail-order sales and Sam Turner, another experienced merchandising executive, took over the Chicago stores. With the assistance of these men, and Jim Burd, M. J. Spiegel proceeded with the divestment program. The Chicago home stores were liquidated, since the leases had terminal dates ending in 1954 and 1955 and it was simpler to dispose of the inventory and collect the receivables than to obtain a buyer. The out-of-town stores required individual disposition, involving a few troublesome lease problems—particularly in Kansas City—and divestment stretched out through 1955 and 1956. The fashion store chain went as a block, sold to Darling Stores, Inc., in 1954, and the auto-hardware chain was sold to a syndicate formed by Richard Knowles, its previous manager.

The essence of the 1954 reorganization move was that M. J. Spiegel moved up to the re-created position as chairman of the board and chief executive officer of the corporation, his presidency going to Robert Engelman. Directly responsible to Mr. Spiegel were: Engelman; the treasurer-controller, Jim Burd; Frederick W. Spiegel. Responsible directly to Engelman were the general merchandise managers, the mail-order sales manager, and the general operating manager. In addition, the personnel manager, who had traditionally been responsible to the general operating manager, and the catalog-order unit manager, were also repositioned and made responsible to the president directly. In the process of this change Bill Cowan left the company voluntarily. Replacing Cowan was Budd Sills, who, like Jim Burd and Cowan, could be called a graduate of the "Al Kolbert Technical Institute," since he had received his fundamental training in administration and organization from Kolbert in the late 1930s. Since returning to the company as an assistant to Cowan, following almost five years in military service, Sills had easily demonstrated that he was Cowan's logical successor.

The organizational changes in 1954 were an integral part of the broadly conceived program adopted at the beginning of the year to liquidate its retail divisions. Despite the losses believed to be inescapable in such a liquidation, the directors had agreed that the move would release the capital frozen into the chains, permitting its reinvestment in catalog-order office expansion and new promotional plans. Mail order, despite the handicaps of inadequate financing, had been profitable. In 1954, management finally acted to cut its losses and concentrate on the kind of operation which it knew best, bolstered by the character of the changes which were sweeping American distribution, principally the rising popularity of mail-order buying by an ever-expanding metropolitan population.

The 1944 to 1954 period in Spiegel history was most traumatic. The company had attempted to emulate the successes of Sears and Montgomery Ward by establishing a series of retail store chains. The goals of management had been to purchase five categories of specialty store chains and to build corporate sales to the $250 million mark by 1952. Neither goal was accomplished; only three specialty store chains—women's apparel, house furnishings, and automotive—were purchased, and total corporate sales never exceeded $146 million in any year during the period. This venture ended with another reorganization similar to the many that had dotted Spiegel history. This latest reorganization centered around the demise of the retail store operation and the building of an organization geared to credit-merchandising by mail.

The End
of an Era

Chapter 11

M. J. Spiegel must have felt a sense of déjà vu as he found his company surrounded by the ruins of a grand venture in retailing, with mail order the only sound structure in the corporation. One writer in *Fortune* subsequently reviewed this near disaster and concluded that "Spiegel is free to concentrate on the two things it understands well—credit and catalogs—and is no longer distracted by operating stores, which, on the record, it doesn't understand very well."[1] The company's record between 1944 and 1954 left little doubt of the soundness of this conclusion. The next decade was to be one of rededication to mail order, but it was also to mark the end of an era, for the period would end with Spiegel being merged into the corporate structure of the Beneficial Finance Company.[2]

Spiegel's rededication to mail order took several forms: returning to the company's greatest strength, mail-order installment credit; building new automated warehousing facilities and computerizing the order-handling and credit-checking process; and modernizing the Spiegel main store—the catalog.

In 1955 Spiegel established the Budget Power Plan which might be described as a very liberalized charge account. The plan assigned a customer a line of credit, the limit of which was normally

284

$550, but which in some instances went as high as $1,000. The terms called for payments as low as $5 per month with up to thirty months to pay. Thus, a down payment of $5 could bring the customer $150 worth of merchandise. Budget Power had one major purpose and that was to generate sales and service changes by making it as easy as possible for customers to be added to the Spiegel rolls.

Spiegel's basic premise, according to M. J. Spiegel, that credit customers spent more money than cash customers was supported by the fact that the average order was $13 from the company's cash customers, while the average order from a credit customer was $31.[3] Exhibits 10 and 11 (see Appendix) demonstrate the stability of credit sales as a percentage of total sales and the growth of the average credit balance from 1960 through 1964.

In the five years shown, credit sales ranged from a low of 84 percent of total sales to a high of 86.7 percent, while the average credit balance grew from $141 for 1,752 accounts to $180 for 2,086 accounts. Because of the strong emphasis again on credit sales the company's accounts receivable created an almost insatiable need for money—long-term money. Also because of an estimated 20 percent attrition rate among customers, the system had to generate a steady stream of new customers. M. J. Spiegel must have questioned almost daily the wisdom of his decision to retire Edward Swikard, the master of this art.

To keep the credit machine going, Spiegel sent out over thirty million direct-mail solicitations annually. Regular customers were encouraged not to "waste their trust fund." Bright orange letters on each statement reminded the customers of how much more they could buy. The idea was to make them feel they were losing out on the good things in life when they failed to "use their Spiegel trust fund to the hilt."[4] The primary target of the Budget Power Plan was families in the $3,000-to-$7,500-a-year class. The return to this segment of the market reflected the confidence the company's management must have felt in its highly successful courtship of the lower-middle income group during Spiegel's golden era of "no charge for credit" in the depression years.

The financial feeding of what the *Fortune* article called "the credit monster" presented a rather unusual problem. The amount of debt required to make the liberal credit policy profitable pushed the company close to insolvency. The $20 million Spiegel received from the sale of its retail outlets was invested in receivables and yet it had to keep applications flowing in from many thousands of potential customers, most of whom would only further increase the company's need for debt.[5] Spiegel's mail-solicitation program produced 2,500,000 applicants a year. The company used the point system developed through years of experience to evaluate these applicants: family status, home ownership, income, employment record, and the like, but no longer relied explicitly on information concerning race. The firm found that a person who was married, owned his own home, was in the $3,000-to-$7,500 income bracket, and had a good employment record was likely to be a good credit customer.[6]

After 1955, the Budget Power Plan was modified twice in an effort to differentiate Spiegel's credit policies from competitors. These changes also were designed to erase once and for all taboos against indebtedness, a continuation of the assault on the Protestant Ethic long spearheaded by Spiegel. The first was free insurance coverage for customers to cover any posthumous debt to Spiegel up to $1,000. The second improvement in the plan was introduced in 1958 and it provided every credit customer with a thirty-day statement detailing all transactions affecting his account.[7]

Although M. J. Spiegel told the *Fortune* writer that "if you put too much in brick and mortar, you won't have the liquid assets you need to finance receivables,"[8] he also knew that a major credit program demands effective internal systems. Therefore, between 1958 and 1962 Spiegel invested over $5 million in brick and mortar, or, more precisely, plant modernization and computerization.[9] The program consisted of a $1 million computer, a $1.5 million automatic order-writing system, and a twelve-story warehouse with a $500,000 merchandise-processing system. The three-part program, with an expected payoff of four years, in fact did save the company $800,000 in annual distribution cost in addition to the all-important intangible benefits derived from better customer service.

The first step in the modernization program was the acquisition of an IBM 7070 computer. The computer was considered necessary to maintain an adequate inventory control system and to provide better customer service. In the late 1950s high clerical costs were viewed as the major factor accounting for reduced net income in spite of rapidly increasing sales. The computer seemed to be a panacea, not only processing orders but also in cutting costs by answering such questions as "who should get the catalog; when they should get the catalog; when they should be mailed; and when other promotional materials should be mailed."[10] The computer also generated savings in the routine function of billing charges and calculating sales tax.

The second part of the program, a Ferranti-Packard Order Writing System, in the process of development for the prior eight years, was installed in 1961. Up to this time a clerk had sent sales slips to the proper warehouse, where they were distributed to order-pickers to select the items out of a storage bin. Under the new system the sales clerk selected a coded card and pushed a button, whereupon an electronic scanner "read" the card, typed up a sales slip, and recorded the transaction on an inventory control tape. One relatively unskilled person was thus able to perform five separate clerical functions at the same time, while assuring that merchandise inventory would be perpetually maintained.[11]

An automated twelve-story warehouse, also completed in 1961, comprised the third part of the modernization program. It was considered by *Business Week* to be "the first fundamental change in mail-order warehousing in 50 years."[12] The new warehouse had over five million square feet of floor space, stocked about 120,000 items, and was operated by one of the most efficient order-handling and processing systems in the world. The heart of the merchandise-handling system was a twelve-story elevator and conveyor known as the "Ferris Wheel," which allowed one man sitting at an electronic console to control the flow of merchandise in and out of the plant. Since all goods stored in the new warehouse were in modular cartons and were palletized, they served as their own storage bins, thus allowing the conveyor to handle up to 240 pallets per hour or some 55,000 items.[13]

The merchandise-handling system began not at the warehouse but at the vendor's plant where merchandise was packed to Spiegel's specification in coded modular cartons. When the cartons arrived at the Spiegel warehouse, they were put on pallets and were automatically routed by the Ferris Wheel to an inspection area and subsequently to the proper floor to await customer orders. The order-writing system and the electronic merchandise-handling system cut handling costs by 25 percent, saved 20 percent in storage space, and reduced delivery-time by one-half. However, these modern facilities were available only for soft goods.

Along with an updated credit plan and a more efficient merchandise-handling system, Spiegel created a better catalog. The effect of Spiegel's return to a single-minded emphasis on mail order was perhaps most visible in its catalog. As will be recalled, during the years from 1937 to 1944, the "Quality Concept" era, higher quality-name-brand merchandise began to appear in the Spiegel biannual catalogs. The catalogs themselves were upgraded by the use of the latest in photographic techniques to display their products. But the 1944 decision to reenter retail led to the distraction or complete removal of much of the company's merchandising talent away from mail order. Consequently, between 1944 and 1954 catalogs were economically printed and the merchandise advertised in them was fashionable; but the "first with the latest" motto of the early 1940s was no longer applicable. The company's emphasis according to the Spiegel *Annual Report* in 1951, was on the "fastest selling lines in price ranges to fit the wage earners that make up the American 'mass' market."[14]

While Spiegel continued to emphasize the mass market after 1954, its methods were in sharp contrast to those used in the early 1950s. Efforts after 1954 were aimed at making the Spiegel catalog not only a "profile of the American way of life" but also a "wish book" which the consuming public could use as a fashion guide.[15] To be a profile of the American way of life, the company had to respond to changing consumer-buying patterns. These trends were met with new emphasis on children's wear for the growing juvenile market, more garden equipment and do-it-yourself tools for the demands of suburban living, casual clothes, and travel goods for the millions enjoying more leisure time.

The goal of making the Spiegel catalog a wish book meant that the company had to offer the latest in fashion and design in wearing apparel and home furnishings, as well as merchandise in other areas that were either unusual or difficult to obtain elsewhere. To increase the fashion distinctiveness of its apparel line, Spiegel hired prominent designers to create fashions specifically for them.

288

In 1957, for example, the catalog featured fashions by Charles Le-Mavie, designer for Twentieth Century Fox. Subsequent catalogs looked like the offerings of a series of specialty shops or a department store by mail. The effort to be "first with the latest" theme inspired the company not only to buy Paris originals and consult with top American fashion designers, but also to offer many items that in the past were not considered suitable for mail order: live pets, pharmaceuticals, stock animals for farmers, life insurance, and aluminum fishing boats.

Although Spiegel purchased 15,000 different items, ranging from spark plugs to spider monkeys, from over 3,000 suppliers by the early 1960s, the great majority of its sales derived from apparel or house furnishings. Exhibit 12 (see Appendix) reveals that by 1964 the sale of apparel accounted for about 53 percent of sales, house furnishings 15 percent, and other merchandise 32 percent. The apparel lines were made up of clothing for men, women, and children; and household furnishings included furniture, draperies, and carpets. The "other" merchandise category was comprised of radios, television sets, automobile tires and equipment, sporting goods, jewelry, hardware, plumbing fixtures, tools, and appliances.[16]

Not only the contents, but also the physical characteristics of the catalog underwent considerable change after 1954. The catalog was no longer "economically printed"; it cost $1.50 per copy to produce and distribute. In 1965 its nearly seven hundred pages definitely reflected a fashion distinctiveness and innovative spirit, both in merchandise and in graphic arts. As a predominantly direct-mail merchandiser, Spiegel had to depend almost exclusively on its catalog not only to be a distinctive store, but also a salesman. Thus, the catalog, in addition to being attractive and containing the latest merchandise in a wide range of categories, also had to anticipate and answer all customer questions about the products displayed within its covers: "How does it work? Will it wash? What are its dimensions?" The pages of the Spiegel catalog apparently answered these questions, and its "iron clad" guarantee policy, competitive prices, size standardization, wide selection, and available credit enabled the company to regain an important position in mail order. Because of the lack of access to internal sources after the 1954 period, it is impossible to identify which elements of the program were most responsible for the phenomenal growth in Spiegel sales. Perhaps it is enough to know that M. J. Spiegel and his associates had returned the company to its area of strength.

Spiegel's 1954 decision to divest itself of its retail-store outlets did not completely dull M. J. Spiegel's appetite for retail-level activities, however. The new Spiegel expansion program centered around one aspect of the 1944–54 ventures which had proven successful, catalog shopping centers. The centers allowed customers to ask questions about the products they saw pictured in the catalog, have some personal contact with the company from whom they were buying, and have their orders teletyped to the company's main office. After the elimination of its retail outlets, Spiegel still retained 117 catalog shopping centers. By 1965, it had 250 such centers and their popularity is suggested by the fact that they accounted for 27 percent of total corporate sales in that year.[17] The catalog stores were originally concentrated in the Midwest, mainly within a five-hundred-mile radius of Chicago. In 1960, Spiegel established a mid-Atlantic test to establish the feasibility of creating order centers on the East Coast. The expansion plan called for the creation of a branch plant to be located in Philadelphia, as well as numerous catalog shopping centers in the New England area.

The "plant" was a clerical office which channeled Atlantic coast orders by teletype to the home office in Chicago. This eastern office handled all orders and all customer solicitation in its area. Personnel at the office solicited new customers with an extensive mail and telephone campaign. Respondents were mailed Spiegel catalogs, and their telephone orders were accepted from anywhere in the area on a "collect" basis. The promotional campaign, coupled with the telephone and teletype service, made the mid-Atlantic test a success and a model for future expansion.

After the successful mid-Atlantic test in 1961, Spiegel did initiate two exploratory market tests, one with the expectation of possibly setting up a mail-order company in Germany, the other to test the possibility of establishing a small loan company to offer personal loans by mail.[18] That Spiegel, in fact, got involved in both ventures in at least a minor way is of interest not because of the details of these enterprises and their operations, but because of what these activities suggest about M. J. Spiegel. On the one hand, they signaled the survival of M. J.'s thirst for diversity in his business. And yet, on the other hand, the fact that they were kept within bounds suggests that he had, unlike a confirmed alcoholic, learned how to have a few drinks without going on a bender!

As might be expected, M. J. Spiegel's concentration on mail order and his resistance to other temptations led to a generally good corporate performance between 1954 and 1964. The company's profit performance was sporadic, but sales grew dramatically over the period. Sales in 1954 were $129,201,000 with earnings of $3,-138,462, excluding losses on the sale of the retail division. By 1964, the company had sales of $298,670,000 and earnings of $9,042,403. Sales increases were negligible until 1959 (see Appendix, exhibit 13), but during the recession in 1959 the granting of easy-credit terms proved sufficiently attractive to increase sales 60 percent over 1958 figures. From 1959 to 1963 sales rose to a high of $300,-341,000. This sales growth apparently can be attributed not only to an improved economy but also to increased public awareness of the Spiegel name, to the convenience offered by the catalog stores, and to the liberalization of credit terms.

With a liberalization of credit terms came more accounts to screen and greater credit losses. Therefore, even though sales increased rather significantly for this period, net income did not show so marked an increase. Net income increased from $3 million in 1954 to $11.5 million in 1960 but dropped off to $7 million the following year. The drop in net income suffered by the company in 1961 was attributed to a number of possible causes other than increased credit losses. M. J. Spiegel believed that the economy had not fully recovered, and even though sales had increased, credit sales had not. The increases in sales Spiegel enjoyed, he believed, was not enough to offset a "higher level of advertising expenditure and a higher level of expense associated with transitioning from a manual to an automated process" and still produce net income as high as the previous year.[19]

Although net income rose to $9 million in 1964, with the company again demonstrating that it could produce at a substantial growth rate, there was another problem worthy of closer management attention. Spiegel's capital structure had also changed significantly over this period. In 1954 the company had an outstanding debt of $31 million and common stock equity of $29 million, yielding a debt-to-equity ratio of 1.07 to 1. By 1964 the outstanding debt had increased to $281 million and common stock equity to $82 million, yielding a ratio of 3.43 to 1.

This change was brought about by the continual financial "feeding" of the credit monster as credit terms became more liberal. To get additional funds, more stock was sold; but debt, especially short-term, became the predominant means of raising money for the company. In 1954 Spiegel owed $31 million in the form of short-term debt; in 1964 it owed $160 million. The company's financial position was not critical, but it was not healthy. Ironically though, in 1964 *Financial World* reported that the Spiegel common stock issue was "suitable for addition to a businessman's diversified portfolio."[20] Apparently the management of Beneficial Finance Company agreed that Spiegel was a good buy—they acquired the company in 1965.

In October 1965, Spiegel, Inc., merged with a wholly owned subsidiary of Beneficial Finance Company—Midwest Mail-Order Company. The inside reasons for the merger are not known, but high on any speculative list would be Spiegel's constant need for capital. Beneficial Finance doubtlessly not only saw Spiegel as a vehicle for greatly expanding its role in mail order, but also saw opportunities to expand sales volume of another of its subsidiaries, Western Auto Stores, by the installation of Spiegel catalog desks in its retail outlets throughout the country. The merger was accomplished through an exchange of stock. M. J. Spiegel was retained as president of Spiegel, Inc., and was elected to a position on the Beneficial board.

Although M. J. remained as president and there were the usual announcements assuring continuation of past policies and freedom to the management of the newly acquired subsidiary, the merger marked the end of four generations of Spiegel owned and managed enterprises. But much more than a legal, professional classification was passing away. It was another example among thousands of the rise of professional or technocratic management in the place of a purer form of entrepreneurship. Because it is so widespread, the significance of this phenomenon is by no means limited to the Spiegel experience.

The roots of the largest purely mail-order business in the world could be traced, of course, to the retail furniture ventures initiated by Joseph Spiegel in Chicago following the Civil War. Joseph Spiegel and his enterprises experienced the disaster of the Chicago Fire of 1871, the depression of 1873, and, ultimately, brankruptcy in 1893. It was Joseph's son Modie who bolstered the spirits of his father and launched an entirely new kind of furniture business which completely reversed the family's traditional commitment to quality. The future of the family business, as Modie saw it, was tied to lower-quality merchandise, sales gimmicks, and installment credit which would position the company to tap the large market in Chicago composed of recent immigrants and workers. In retrospect, one may question the methods, but there is little doubt that it took courage and imagination to chart such a dramatically different course for a financially and spiritually bankrupt business.

An even more important change in the family business came when Joseph's youngest son, Arthur, entered the business in 1904. Simply put, Arthur was bored with the traditional business of Spiegel House Furnishings. Therefore, he proposed a modest venture in installment selling by mail. This restless and highly impatient young man felt that the company could secure a special niche in the mail-order market, so far not penetrated by Sears and Montgomery Ward since both of these large houses operated on a cash basis. Within two years Arthur's small venture had reached a sales level of nearly $1 million and was contributing a handsome profit. Before his family relinquished control in 1965, that enterprise had reached an annual sales volume of nearly $300 million.

The company's experience between 1906 and 1965, was an incredibly exciting one. In many respects it resembled a roller-coaster ride, both in terms of excitement and performance. At times the company's sales and earnings would soar to new heights only to plummet to disappointing lows. Environmental dynamics explain much of this record. Spiegel had to meet the threat of economic downturns; of institutional revolutions such as the chain store, supermarket, discount houses; of remarkable changes in consumer preferences; of other changes in the legal, social, and technological spheres. In many cases Spiegel responded creatively. In others its management's performance was marked by missed opportunities and the failure to act decisively or consistently. On balance, the occasional flashes of brilliance were too often dulled by inadequate follow-through or were offset by unsound diversions from the company's basic business.

Regardless of the unevenness of their performance, one element which remained constant was the fact that it was their business and the Spiegels were dedicated to it. From a personal financial standpoint it was critical that the business do at least moderately well. The family members of the Spiegel management could not afford to be complacent or lethargic for too great a time or the marketplace would reject the company's offerings and, in turn, threaten their personal fortunes. When one member of the family or one generation seemed to lose a sense of purpose and commitment, another would respond. Thus, when Modie Spiegel, who had saved his father and the family business from economic disaster in his youth, lost his courage and resolve in the face of the Great Depression, it was his son M. J. who took charge and produced a period of imaginative leadership and prosperity. Apparently, M. J. had it within his capability to pull the company from the edge a second time, given the remarkable growth Spiegel experienced under his leadership following the postwar retailing debacle.

It may sound like rank sentimentality, but what gave Spiegel the resilience to withstand the ups and downs which the company experienced was the fact that men like M. J. Spiegel were in love with the business. At times it was a neglected love, as when racehorses, summer homes, or the stock market served as mistresses to lure away the management. But at other times there was a passionate attention to the well-being and fulfillment of the enterprise. The business was capable of causing bitter and painful divisions in the family, as when Sidney Spiegel and his son found they could not share the management role with Modie and his sons. At other times, as in the golden era of "no charge for credit" when the company thwarted the depression and experienced a phenomonal period of growth, Spiegel brought the owners and managers unbounded joy. When the young M. J. Spiegel told Edward Swikard and George Meinig in the dark days of 1932 that the owners, managers, and workers had to fall in love again with mail order, he was giving testimony to the vital importance of profound commitment to the enterprise.

It may be argued that professional managers and technocrats

are equally capable of profound commitment to an enterprise. Indeed, it could be said that a creative genius like Swikard would have been given greater freedom in a large, professionally-managed company and this would have produced much greater success. Furthermore, one need only point to the superior performance of Sears and Montgomery Ward as evidence that public ownership and professional management offer more consistent and higher quality leadership. In fact, it is clear that many professional managers do fall in love with their businesses. Such affection, however, must be difficult to preserve when the business is absorbed by a larger enterprise. Its identity is altered, its priorities ultimately revised, and certainly its sense of uniqueness must decline. The subsidiary's economic performance is often hidden from the public as only the parent's aggregate data are revealed. Parent company officials must pass on plans for new capital expenditures, important changes in marketing strategies, and the like. Suffice it to say that it may be more difficult to fall in love when being chaperoned. Indeed, this may help to explain why intercorporate movement by executives is so common and why loyalty to the company and its purposes seems so limited.

In spite of the organization's sporadic performance and missed opportunities it is somewhat sad to see Spiegel lose its special relationship with the founding family, only to become another acquisition in an era of conglomerated enterprises. And given what is known of its performance since 1965, there is little reason to believe that the merger with Beneficial Finance Company instilled any special qualities or magic into the enterprise. What was from time to time one of the most innovative marketing institutions in the United States seems now to be a relatively colorless subsidiary of a large financial company.

Appendix   Notes   Index

Appendix

EXHIBIT 1: SPIEGEL, MAY, STERN COMPANY

Net Worth, Net Income, and Return on Investment
1907–1921 *(In Thousands)*

Year	Capital Stock	Contingency Reserve	Unapportioned Surplus	Net Worth	Net Income	Net Income as percentage of Net Worth	
						Year-end	Av.
1907[a]	$ 500.0		$ 92.2	$ 592.2	. . .	. . .	. . .
1907	500.0	$ 14.7	222.2	736.9	$ 144.7	19.6%	21.8%
1908	500.0	31.2	307.2	838.4	133.7	15.9	17.0
1909	500.0	71.6	580.0	1,151.6	373.3	32.4	37.5
1910	1,000.0	110.9	440.0	1,550.9	402.4	25.9	29.8
1911	1,000.0	118.8	470.0	1,588.8	107.5	6.7	6.8
1912	1,000.0	122.6	970.0	2,092.6	504.7	24.1	27.4
1913	1,000.0	154.1	1,610.0	2,764.1	742.9	26.9	30.6
1914	1,000.0	154.1	778.9	1,933.0	(851.1)	(44.0)	(36.2)
1915	1,000.0	154.1	943.5	2,097.6	164.6	7.8	8.2
1916	1,000.0	154.1	1,616.7	2,770.8	799.1	28.8	32.8
1917	1,000.0	154.1	1,622.6	2.776.8	425.6	15.3	15.3
1918	1,000.0	154.1	1,656.4[e]	2,810.5	732.6	26.1	26.2
1919	1,000.0	154.1	2,441.2[e]	3,595.3	1,205.7	33.5	37.6
1920	1,000.0	154.1	2,736.5	3,915.6	659.1	16.8	17.6
1921	1,000.0	154.1	2,395.8	3,549.8	(341.1)	(9.6)	(9.1)

[a] As of date of organization of the company; all other years as of December 31.
[e] Estimate.
SOURCE: Data from Spiegel, May, Stern unaudited balance sheets and income statements, *Directors Minutes*, except 1914 Price, Waterhouse audited statements of financial condition.

EXHIBIT 2: SPIEGEL, MAY, STERN AND MARTHA LANE ADAMS

Net Sales and Before Tax Net Earnings
1907–1921 *(In Thousands)*

Year	S.M.S.	Sales M.L.A.	Total	S.M.S.	Earnings M.L.A.	Total
1907	$1,517.2		$1,517.2	$ 144.7		$ 144.7
1908	1,933.9		1,933.9	133.7		133.7
1909	2,452.1		2,452.1	373.2		373.2
1910	3,008.1		3,008.1	402.4		402.4
1911	2,779.7		2,779.7	107.5		107.5
1912	3,300.9		3,300.9	504.7		504.7
1913	6,849.1		6,849.1	742.9		742.9
1914	2,592.4	$ 385.0	2,977.4	(831.0)	$(20)[e]	(851.1)
1915	2,717.8	875.0	3,592.8	79.0	86.0	165.0
1916	3,235.8	1,206.0	4,441.8	588.0	211.0	799.0
1917	2,799.5	1,978.0	4,777.5	83.0	343.0	426.0
1918	3,359.2	2,143.0	5,502.2	670.0	63.0	733.0
1919	4,215.7	2,579.0	6,794.7	1,037.0	169.0	1,206.0
1920	4,173.4	3,129.0	7,302.4	725.0	(66.0)	659.0
1921	2,758.7	1,932.0	4,690.7	(46.0)	(295.0)	(341.0)

[e] Estimate.

SOURCES: Spiegel, May, Stern company records; Spiegel, May, Stern operating statements, 1912, 1913, 1917, 1920, 1921.
Martha Lane Adams: trial balance ledger from which data were reconstructed.

EXHIBIT 3: SPIEGEL, MAY, STERN AND MARTHA LANE ADAMS

Consolidated Balance Sheet
1922

New financing and its effects in the liquidation of the Waldheim interest and the organization of a new corporation integrating Spiegel, May, Stern and the Spiegel House Furnishings Company.

	Before New Financing	After New Financing
Assets		
Cash[a]	$ 115,538	$ 141,623
U.S. Bonds & cash value of insurance	3,121	3,121
Accounts receivable (net of reserve)	3,531,292	3,531,292
Inventories	1,009,933	1,009,933
World Film Corp (6% notes)[b]	41,850	
Westminster Building[c]	165,113	398,097
Clement Company[d]	90,000	
Amounts owned by officers and owners	168,635	168,635
Land, plant & equipment (less reserve)[e]	510,160	1,152,674
Deferred assets[f]	115,162	365,162
Total Assets	$5,750,776	$6,770,537
Liabilities & Net Worth		
Accounts payable	$ 394,430	$ 394,430
Notes payable[g]	560,000	
Accrued payroll	90,304	90,304
Accrued taxes	19,747	19,747
Debenture bonds (6.5%, sinking fund)[h]		2,500,000
Purchase money mortgage[i]	89,915	
Total Liabilities	$1,154,396	$3,004,481
Net Worth		
Capital stocks[j]	$1,500,000	$3,000,000
Contingency reserve	154,130	154,130
Unapportioned surplus[k]	2,942,250	611,927
Total Net Worth	$4,516,380	$3,766,037
Total Liabilities and Net Worth	$5,750,776	$6,770,537

Explanations of net changes:
[a] Proceeds left after settlement of Waldheim payment, other payments.
[b] Charged off to Surplus as without value.
[c] Appreciation resulting from introduction of appraisal value of property.
[d] Written off to Surplus.
[e] Appreciation resulting from introduction of appraisal value of plant.
[f] Bond discount of 10%, $250,000 (to be amortized).
[g] Liquidated from proceeds of bond sale.
[h] Par value of new debentures.
[i] Liquidated from proceeds of bond sale.
[j] Issue of new shares in Spiegel, May, Stern Co. of Illinois.
[k] $131,850 charged off the investment accounts for World Film and Clement; $1,174,000 payment of Waldheim's share of Surplus; balance accounted for by other indicated adjustments. Total difference: $2,330,323.
SOURCE: Corporate records.

EXHIBIT 4: SPIEGEL, MAY, STERN COMPANY

Sales, Receivables, Legal Expenses, Bad Debts, and Net Credit Charge-offs
1922–1932 *(Total In Thousands and per Dollar Basis)*

Year	Sales	Customer Receivables	Reference & Legal	Bad Debts	Net Charge-offs[a]
1922	$ 7,358.7	$ 4,580.0	$132.5	$ 236.8	. . .
1923	12,384.0	6,728.0	174.2	548.3	. . .
1924	12,561.3	7,261.0	228.8	723.4	. . .
1925	11,717.0	6,882.0	223.1	683.1	$ 564.7[e]
1926	16,860.9	9,170.0	258.5	753.6	735.1[e]
1927	19,431.7	11,439.0	306.6	978.6	1,033.8[e]
1928	20,571.8	12,274.0	332.5	1,104.4	1,310.4[e]
1929	23,921.9	14,317.0	438.1	1,373.6	2,705.6[e]
1930	14,997.6	9,948.0	435.6	1,502.6	1,775.7[e]
1931	9,923.7	6,896.0	306.3	1,005.2	838.6[e]
1932	7,114.7	5,532.0	. . .	. . .	530.8[e]

[a] Charge-offs are made to the year in which a minimum of 51% of sales were made, and are on basis of year of sale, not year charged off.
[e] Estimate.

Items per Dollar of Sales

Year	Receivables	Legal	Bad Debts	Charge-offs
1922	$0.622	$0.018	$0.032	. . .
1923	0.543	0.014	0.044	. . .
1924	0.578	0.018	0.058	. . .
1925	0.587	0.019	0.058	$0.0482
1926	0.544	0.015	0.045	0.0436
1927	0.589	0.016	0.050	0.0532
1928	0.596	0.016	0.054	0.0637
1929	0.599	0.018	0.057	0.1131
1930	0.663	0.029	0.100	0.1184
1931	0.695	0.031	0.101	0.0845
1932	0.778	. . .	. . .	0.0746

SOURCES: Price, Waterhouse & Company reports 1922–31. Credit charge-off data in relative form from company credit research office.

EXHIBIT 5: SPIEGEL, MAY, STERN COMPANY

Distribution of Sales and Earnings Between Mail Order
and Retail Divisions
1922–1932

I. Sales *(In Thousands)*

Year	Mail Order	Mail Order as a Percent of Total Sales	Retail	Total
1922	$ 3,830.9	52.1%	$3,527.8	$ 7,358.7
1923	7,753.4	62.6	4,630.6	12,384.0
1924	8,605.3	68.4	3,956.0	12,561.3
1925	8,343.4	71.2	3,373.6	11,717.0
1926	13,069.9	77.5	3,791.0	16,860.9
1927	15,909.5	81.9	3,522.2	19,431.7
1928	16,400.4	79.7	4,171.4	20,571.8
1929	20,581.2	86.0	3,340.7	23,921.9
1930	13,054.9	87.0	1,942.7	14,997.6
1931	9,923.7	92.4	820.3	10,744.0
1932	7,142.4	100.0		7,142.4

II. Profits: after Federal taxes *(In Thousands)*

Year	Mail Order Amount	Rate	Retail Amount	Rate	Total Amount	Rate
1922	$ 286.3	7.5%	$ 368.2	10.4%	$ 654.5	8.9%
1923	687.6	8.9	425.3	9.2	1,112.9	9.0
1924	552.6	6.4	180.9	4.6	733.5	5.8
1925	717.7	8.6	(77.1)	(2.3)	640.6	5.5
1926	1,477.0	11.3	491.5	13.0	1,968.5	11.7
1927	1,823.0	11.5	180.0	5.1	2,003.0	10.3
1928	1,561.8	9.5	194.5	4.7	1,756.3	8.5
1929	1,893.5	9.2	(175.7)	(5.3)	1,717.8	7.2
1930	(625.3)	(4.8)	(1,632.2)	(84.0)	(2,257.5)	(15.1)
1931	42.6	0.4	(672.6)	(82.0)	(630.0)	(6.4)
1932	(366.0)	(5.1)			(318.0)	(4.5)

SOURCES: Price, Waterhouse & Company records, 1922–31; Spiegel, May, Stern Company, *Annual Report*, 1928–32.

EXHIBIT 6: SPIEGEL

Acquisition of Retail Outlets
1944–1946

Date of Acquisition	Number of Outlets	Acquisition[a] Price	Title of Acquisition	Type
April 1944	46	$1,732,700	Sally Stores, Inc.	Apparel
Dec. 1944	26	835,000	Beverly Chain Stores	Apparel
July 1944	20	2,347,300	Federal Stores	General[b]
Feb. 1945	4	986,100	Straus & Schram	Home
April 1945	1	802,100	Harbour Longmire	Home
July 1945	1	599,500	Dorris Heyman	Home
Nov. 1945	1	227,900	Morrison Neese	Home
March 1946	1	448,100	Stoehr & Fister	Home
April 1946	1	211,800	Sydnor & Hundley	Home
July 1946	1	1,400,000	Robert Keith	Home
Sept. 1946	1	307,400	Miller Brothers	Home
Aug. 1945	1	746,700	Whitney	Department Store
March 1946	55	2,955,400	J & R Motor Supply	Auto-Farm-Hardware

Recapitulation: Spiegel Retail Chains, by cost and number of outlets, following acquisition.[c]

Title	Number of Outlets	Acquisition Price
Fashion Chain	72	$2,567,700
Chicago Home Stores	5	1,293,500
Out-of-Town Home Stores	6	3,689,400
Federal	20	2,347,300
Auto-Farm-Hardware	55	2,955,400
Total	158	$12,853,300

[a] Cash and Spiegel common stock.
[b] Included apparel, jewelry, small appliances, and personal furnishings.
[c] Whitney is not included in the Spiegel chain group.

EXHIBIT 7: SPIEGEL

Geographical Distribution of Retail Stores, by Type
1948

Region and State	Ladies' Fashion		Boys & Girl's[a]		Home Furnishings		Farm-Auto-Hardware		Other[b]	
	Units	Towns	Units	Towns	Units	Towns	Units	Towns	Units	Towns
Middle Atlantic	(2)	(2)			(1)	(1)				
New York	1	1			1					
Pennsylvania	1	1			1	1				
South Atlantic	(3)	(3)			(2)	(2)				
Florida	1	1								
North Carolina	1	1			1	1				
South Carolina	1	1								
Virginia					1	1				
East North Central	(42)	(26)	(2)	(2)	(5)	(1)	(39)	(30)	(5)	(1)
Illinois										
Chicago	17	1	1	1	5	1	6	1	5	1
Rest of State	4	4	1	1			11	11		
Indiana	6	6					2	2		
Michigan	8	8					8	7		
Ohio	2	2					1	1		
Wisconsin	5	5					11	8		

EXHIBIT 7: SPIEGEL continued

West North Central	(6)	(5)			(1)	(1)	(18)	(11)		
Iowa	1	1					8	7		
Minnesota	1	1								
Missouri	4	3			1	1	6	2		
Nebraska							4	2		
East South Central	(1)	(1)								
Mississippi	1	1								
West South Central	(13)	(11)			(1)	(1)				
Arkansas	3	2								
Louisiana	1	1								
Oklahoma	1	1			1	1				
Texas	8	7								
Mountain					(1)	(1)			(1)	(1)
Arizona					1	1			1	1
Nevada									1	1
Pacific									(19)	(15)
California									19	15
Total	67	48	2	2	11	7	57	41	25	17

a Children's departments were included in ten of the Fashion stores.
b The company operated four bargain outlet stores and a service station in Chicago. The units in California and Nevada were Federal stores.

SOURCE: Company records.

EXHIBIT 8: SPIEGEL

Retail Sales and Profits by Divisions
1944–1954

1. Sales *(In Millions)*

Year	Fashion Chain	Farm Auto, Hardware Chain	Stores for the Home Chicago	Stores for the Home Out-of-Town	Federal Store Chain	All[a] Other	Total Sales
1944	$ 12.2					$ 2.4	$ 14.6
1945	17.0		$ 2.6		$ 5.6	4.7	29.9
1946	17.1		4.8		5.9	21.1	48.9
1947	17.4	$ 9.2	4.1	$11.3	6.1	7.9	56.1
1948	20.6	9.2	3.7	9.9	6.5	4.6	54.4
1949	18.4	8.2	3.2	7.5	6.1	2.9	46.2
1950	17.0	8.6	4.3	8.8	6.1	3.3	48.0
1951	17.4	8.3	3.6	8.5	6.3	2.4	46.4
1952	17.5	8.0	4.0	8.8	6.4	2.8	47.5
1953	16.0	7.2	4.3	8.0	5.6	0.1	41.2
1954	14.9	6.5	2.0	7.6	4.8		35.7
Total	$185.4	$65.2	$36.4	$70.4	$59.3	$52.2	$468.9

II. Profits: before taxes and liquidation losses *(In Thousands)*

Year	Fashion Chain	Farm Auto, Hardware Chain	Stores for the Home Chicago	Stores for the Home Out-of-Town	Federal Store Chain	All Other	Total
1944	$ 685						$ 685
1945	1,291		$(294)		$935		1,932
1946	(83)		(5)		907		819
1947	161	$898	(424)	$219	680		1,534
1948	641	433	(830)	(296)	544		(1,492)
1949	(97)	(400)	(586)	(468)	283		(1,268)
1950	(5)	(18)	(203)	123	321		218
1951	(423)	(211)	(534)	(15)	381		802
1952	75	108	(177)	10	411		427
1953	(216)	(53)			64		251
1954	(374)	(145)	(218)	(159)	(588)		(1,484)
Total	$1,655	$612	$(3,271)	$(586)	$3,938		$2,302

a The volumes recorded under *all other* comprise actual retail sales from several chains in 1946; thereafter these sales include those made from the company's manufacturing sources as well as sales from the bargain outlet stores in Chicago.
SOURCE: Company records.

EXHIBIT 9: SPIEGEL

Corporate Sales by Distribution Channel
1945–1954 *(In Millions)*

Year	Mail Order Direct Mail	Direct Contact	Retail Stores	Total	After-tax Net income
1945	$39.2	$ 1.5	$29.9	$ 70.6	$1.2
1946	57.8	3.9	48.9	110.6	2.8
1947	64.6	4.5	56.1	125.2	2.2
1948	74.0	6.2	54.4	134.6	4.4
1949	77.1	9.5	46.2	132.8	2.0
1950	79.9	15.7	48.0	143.5	3.3
1951	81.3	18.6	46.4	146.3	2.3
1952	77.2	21.3	47.5	146.1	1.7
1953	69.5	23.3	41.2	134.1	1.2
1954	70.3	23.2	35.7	129.2	(2.3)

SOURCE: Company records.

EXHIBIT 10: SPIEGEL

Percent Credit to Cash Sales
1960–1964 *(In Thousands)*

Year	Cash Sales	Credit Sales	Percent Credit to Total Sales
1960	$43,067	$225,767	84.0
1961	42,203	235,076	84.8
1962	43,768	231,791	84.1
1963	45,461	254,880	84.9
1964	39,760	258,910	86.7

SOURCE: Beneficial Finance Company—Spiegel, Inc., Proxy Statement.

EXHIBIT 11: SPIEGEL

Growth of Credit Accounts and Average Balance
1960–1964

Year	Aggregate Customer Accounts Receivable*	Number of Accounts*	Average Balance
1960	$246,361	1,752	$141
1961	291,758	1,981	147
1962	310,686	2,032	153
1963	341,994	2,068	165
1964	375,142	2,086	180

* In thousands.
SOURCE: Beneficial Finance Company–Spiegel, Inc., Proxy Statement.

EXHIBIT 12: SPIEGEL

Merchandise Lines as a Percentage of Total Sales
1962–1964

Year	Apparel	Household Furnishings	Other
1962	56.5	14.7	28.8
1963	55.7	14.5	29.8
1964	53.2	14.7	32.1

SOURCE: Beneficial Finance Company–Spiegel, Inc., Proxy Statement.

EXHIBIT 13: SPIEGEL

Net Sales* and Net Income
1954–1964 *(In Thousands)*

Year	Sales	Net Income
1954	$129,202	$ 2,290†
1955	130,434	4,322
1956	129,947	3,849
1957	128,265	3,539
1958	134,842	4,988
1959	216,669	10,937
1960	268,834	11,753
1961	277,279	6,963
1962	275,559	7,174
1963	300,341	8,195
1964	304,670	9,042

* Includes time-price differential on credit sales.
† Does not include loss from sale of retail outlets.
SOURCE: Spiegel, Inc., *Annual Report*, 1954–64.

309

Notes

Unless otherwise indicated, all the papers
and records of Spiegel and its affiliates
are in the archives of Spiegel, Incorporated.

1 THE ROOTS OF AN ENTERPRISE

1. Rufus Learsi, *Israel: A History of the Jewish People* (Cleveland: World Publishing Co., 1949), p. 440.

2. From the geneology of the Greenebaum family, M. J. Spiegel, Jr. papers. Also, Sara Hart, *The Pleasure is Mine* (Chicago: Valentine-Newman, 1947), p. 25.

3. Learsi, *Israel*, pp. 440–41; A. J. P. Taylor, *The Course of German History: A Survey of the Development of Germany Since 1815* (London: Harnish Hamilton, 1945), pp. 70–71; Janet P. Trevelyan, *A Short History of the Italian People*, 4th ed. (London: George Allen & Unwin, Ltd., 1956), p. 346.

4. Learsi, *Israel*, p. 441.

5. Gordon A. Craig, *The Politics of the Prussian Army: Sixteen Forty–Nineteen Forty-Five* (Oxford: The Clarendon Press, 1956), p. 82.

6. Taylor, *The Course of German History*, p. 88.

7. Learsi, *Israel*, pp. 485–86.

8. *The Cleveland Plain Dealer*, November 21, 1861; *The Holmes County Farmer*, November 21, 1861.

9. U.S. Census Reports, 1840, 1850, by counties and townships. Records in the Historical Society and State Library, Columbus, Ohio. Also, the Hamlin family papers, the collection of Mrs. Abraham Freyler, Glencoe, Illinois.

10. Journal of Lizzie Barbe and the undated letters of Marcus Spiegel to Caroline Spiegel in the Freyler collection.

11. Marcus Spiegel to Caroline Spiegel, undated, in the Freyler collection.

12. Certified copy of Officers List, June 18, 1860, the Ohio Convention of the Independent Order of Odd Fellows, in the Freyler collection.

13. *Holmes County Farmer*, September 5, 1861.

14. A. N. Marquis, ed., *The Book of Chicagoans: A Biographical Dictionary of Leading Men and Women of the City of Chicago* (Chicago: A. N. Marquis & Co., 1911), p. 637.

15. *Holmes County Farmer*, November 21, 1861.

16. Commission dated November 13, 1861, signed by David Tod, Governor of Ohio, in the Freyler collection.

17. *Cleveland Plain Dealer*, November 21, 1861.

18. *The Official Roster of the Soldiers of the State of Ohio in the War of the Rebellion, 1861–1866*, the Ohio Roster Commission (Akron, Ohio: Warner Printing Company, 1887), 5:578 (hereafter cited as the *Ohio Official Roster*).

19. Franklin Sawyer, *A Military History of the Eighth Regiment, Ohio Volunteer Infantry* (Cleveland: Fairbanks and Co., 1881), p. 28.

20. *Ohio Official Roster*, 5: 789–95.

21. Special Orders, No. 101, Hq., VII Corps, Fortress Monroe, Virginia, September 15, 1862, in the Freyler collection.

22. Governor David Tod to Captain M. M. Spiegel, September 22, 1862, in the Freyler collection.

23. Hq., 67th Ohio Volunteer Infantry Regiment, Suffolk, Virginia, September 20, 1862 to Office of the Adjutant General, State of Ohio, in the Freyler collection.

24. The War Department, *War of the Rebellion: A Compilation of the Official Records of the Union and Confederate Armies*, 3rd ser., pt. 1, vol. 5 (Washington, D.C.: U.S. Government Printing Office, 1902) p. 807 (hereafter cited as *Official Records*).

25. Ibid., pp. 939–40.

26. Ludwell H. Johnson, *The Red River Campaign: Politics and Cotton in the Civil War* (Baltimore: Johns Hopkins Press, 1958), p. 47.

27. *Official Records*, 34th ser., p. 475.

28. Hart, *Pleasure is Mine*, pp. 6–7.

29. *Chicago City Directory* (Chicago: Richard Edwards, 1869), listed the business as "H. Liebenstein & Co. (Henry Liebenstein and Joseph Spiegel), 167–169 Randolph Street."

30. A. T. Andreas, *A History of Chicago from the Earliest Period to the Present Time*, 2 vols. (Chicago: A. T. Andreas, 1884), 2: 446–47.

31. Ibid., p. 657.

32. Hart, *Pleasure is Mine*, p. 6.

33. *Chicago City Directory* for 1874 provided no listing for either firm.

34. Ibid., 1885–86.

35. Examples of these advertisements appeared in the following issue of the *Chicago Tribune*: July 13, July 18, 1886; October 16, November 6, November 30, December 4, December 7, and December 18, 1887.

36. G. P. Greene Electrical Company to Spiegel & Company, July 28, 1891.

37. *Chicago Tribune*, November 11, November 18, 1888.

38. Ibid., March 10, 1889.

39. *Oriel Cabinet Company* vs. *Joseph Spiegel, et al., September 24, 1892. Brief and Charges of Plaintiff, Superior Court of Cook County, Illinois, September Term. General Number 142 505, Term Number 3819 (Chancery).* Archives of the Superior Court of Cook County, Illinois.

40. Notes assembled from the brief of Isaac H. Mayer, filed May 5, 1899 in the Superior Court of Cook County, Illinois. Archives of the Superior Court of Cook County, Illinois.

41. Joseph Spiegel to Oriel Cabinet Company, September 16, 1892.

42. Ibid., September 23, 1892.

43. Copy of petition of George H. Plummer and the *Brief and Charges of Plaintiff, Oriel Cabinet Company vs. Joseph Spiegel, et al.* Archives of the Superior Court of Cook County, Illinois.

44. Ibid.

45. *Suggestion of Damages of Certain Defendants, Oriel Cabinet Company vs. Joseph Spiegel, et al., October 11, 1892.* Archives of the Superior Court of Cook County, Illinois.

46. Affidavits taken from defendants in the matter of the injunction hearings and filed with the records of *Oriel Cabinet Company vs. Joseph Spiegel, et al.*

47. *In the Matter of Oriel Cabinet Company vs. Joseph Spiegel, et al., Order Number G 142 505, Term 647, January 4, 1897.*

48. Appellate Court, First District of Illinois, March Term. Filed August 10, 1897, reversing the decision and remanding to the Superior Court of Cook County, Illinois.

2 THE SPIEGEL HOUSE FURNISHINGS COMPANY, 1893-1903

1. Lloyd Lewis and Henry J. Smith, *Chicago, A History of Its Reputation* (New York: Harcourt, Brace and Co., 1929), p. 194.

2. U.S. Bureau of the Census, *Historical Statistics of the United States, Colonial Times to 1957,* D589–602 (Washington, D.C.: U.S. Government Printing Office, 1960), p. 91.

3. Spiegel House Furnishings Company, application for charter to the Department of State, State of Illinois, January 7, 1893.

4. Spiegel House Furnishings Company, *Minutes of the Board of Directors,* January 21, 1893.

5. Ibid., February 1, 1893.

6. Interview with Jay Seadler former Spiegel House Furnishings salesman, August 12, 1957. Also, Jay Seadler memorandum, January 9, 1951.

7. Seadler interview and memorandum.

8. Seadler interview, also interview with George Meinig, August 10, 1960.

9. Seadler interview.

10. Frederick W. Spiegel memorandum, November 1950.

11. Interview with Frederick W. Spiegel, October 12, 1957; also, the records of Municipal and Cook County Courts, 1893–1930.

12. Survey of metropolitan Chicago newspapers, 1865–1955.

13. Seadler interview; also Frederick W. Spiegel memorandum, November 20, 1950.

14. Russell Lynes, *The Tastemakers* (New York: Harper & Brothers, 1949), p. 186. Also, a sampling of advertisements from Chicago daily and Sunday newspapers, 1893–1930.

15. Spiegel House Furnishings Company, *Minutes of the Stockholders Meeting*, January 22, 1894.

16. Ibid., January 22, 1895.

17. Ibid., January 23, 1897.

18. Ibid., January meetings, 1898–1904.

4 SPIEGEL, MAY, STERN AND COMPANY MERCHANDISING ACTIVITIES, 1907-1921

1. Spiegel, May, Stern and Company, *Minutes of the Board of Directors*, January 3, 1907 (hereafter cited as SMS, *Directors' Minutes*).

2. Ibid., January 3, 1907; January 8, 1908; January 12, 1909; and January 17, 1910.

3. Interview with Frederick W. Spiegel, October 12, 1956.

4. Interview with Thornton L. Adams, March 6, 1957.

5. For example, see Federal Reserve System, Board of Governors, *Consumer Instalment Credit, Conference on Regulation*, pt. 2 (New York: National Bureau of Economic Research and U.S. Government Printing Office, 1957), 1:76 (hereafter cited as *Consumer Instalment Credit*).

6. Ibid.

7. Ibid.

8. SMS, *Directors' Minutes*, January 8, 1908.

9. The Clement Company, *Minutes of the Meeting of Stockholders*, May 30, 1908 (hereafter cited as Clement).

10. Spiegel, May, Stern Company and Clement, Memorandum of Agreement, January 5, 1909, in the Mayer, Meyer, Austrian, and Platt archives, Chicago).

11. SMS, *Directors' Minutes*, January 11, 1911; balance sheets, 1912, 1917; copy of contract of purchase of Clement, October, 1923; *Directors' Minutes*, January 9, 1910.

12. Contract Agreement, October 1, 1923, Clement and Spiegel, May, Stern.

13. Spiegel, May, Stern, spring and fall catalogs, 1916–22; Clement catalogs the same years.

14. SMS, *Directors' Minutes*, January 11, 1911.

15. Ibid., January 10, 1912.

16. Ibid., January 8, 1913.

17. J. A. Campbell to Hal C. Bangs, Mayer, Meyer, Austrian and Platt, Chicago, April 28, 1913.

18. Martha Lane Adams Company, *Minutes of the Stockholder's Meeting*, January 19, 1914 (hereafter cited as MLA).

19. MLA, *Stock Register Book*, September 30, 1914; SMS, *Directors' Minutes*, January 13, 1915.

20. SMS, *Directors' Minutes*, November 1, 1917; MLA, *Directors' Minutes*, November 1, 1917.

21. MLA, *Directors' Minutes*, July 16, 1918; January 29, July 30, 1919; January 5, September 10, 1920; and February 3, 1921.

22. MLA, *Directors' Minutes*, July 17, 1917, also interviews with M. J. Spiegel, Jr., Jay Seadler, Frederick L. Innis, and Mrs. Mae Spiegel.

23. SMS, *Directors' Minutes*, July 12, 1909.

24. Interviews with Frederick L. Innis, J. Spiegel, Jr., and Charles Folger, October 1956.

25. Boris Emmet and John E. Jeuck, *Catalogues and Counters: A History of Sears, Roebuck & Company* (Chicago: University of Chicago Press, 1950), chap. 7 (hereafter cited as *Catalogues and Counters*).

26. Spiegel, May, Stern, *Refrigerator Catalog*, 1907, 1911.

27. *Catalogues and Counters*, p. 105.

28. M. J. Spiegel, Jr., memorandum, July 23, 1936.

29. Spiegel, May, Stern, *"Back to School" Sale Book*, September 1920.

30. *Consumer Instalment Credit*, pt. 2, 1:179.

31. Letters from Arthur H. Spiegel to Messrs. Ladenburg, Thalman & Co., and to A. G. Becker & Co., November 18, 1913.

32. Interview with H. George Meinig, July 7, 1959.

33. *Catalogues and Counters*, pp. 268–70.

34. Interview with Reuben Don, March 16, 1957.

35. *Gramophone Catalog*, June 1909; *Beckman Piano Catalog*, June 1909; *Sewing Machine Mailer*, May 1909.

36. *Catalogues and Counters*, illustration opposite page 67.

37. Ibid., p. 77.

38. Spiegel, May, Stern, *Christmas Sale Book*, 1913.

39. M. J. Spiegel, Jr., memorandum, July 23, 1936.

40. Spiegel, May, Stern, *"Back to School" Sale Book*, September 1920.

41. Interview with H. George Meinig, July 7, 1959.

42. *Catalogues and Counters*, pp. 268–70.

43. Spiegel, May, Stern, *Consolidated Fall Catalog*, 1907.

44. Spiegel, May, Stern, *Spring Catalog*, 1909.

45. Spiegel, May, Stern, the *Spring Furniture Catalog* follow-up letter, 1913.

46. Spiegel, May, Stern, *Spring Sale Book*, 1909.

47. Ibid., 1911.

48. Spiegel, May, Stern, *Spring Furniture Catalog*, 1911.

49. *Catalogues and Counters*, pp. 233, 246, 256–61.

50. Ibid., pp. 92–95.

51. Ibid., pp. 189–90.

52. Ibid.

5 OPERATIONS, FINANCING, AND REORGANIZATION, 1907-1921

1. Spiegel, May, Stern, Corporate Records (hereafter cited as SMS).
2. Ibid.
3. Interview with Frederick L. Innis, October 1956.
4. Interview with M. J. Spiegel, Jr., April 1957.
5. Boris Emmet and John E. Jeuck, *Catalogues and Counters: A History of Sears, Roebuck & Company* (Chicago: University of Chicago Press, 1950, p. 287 (hereafter cited as *Catalogues and Counters*).
6. Harold Barger, *Distribution's Place in American Economy Since 1869* (Princeton, N.J.: Princeton University Press, 1955), p. 148.
7. SMS, Corporate Records.
8. Ibid.
9. Spiegel, May, Stern and Company, *Minutes of the Board of Directors*, December 8, 1909 (hereafter cited as SMS, *Directors' Minutes*).
10. Ibid., January 9, 1913.
11. Ibid., January 11, 1914.
12. Ibid., January 8, 1917.
13. Ibid., January 6, 1919; January 12, 1920; January 8, 1921; January 7, 1922.
14. SMS, Corporate Records.
15. SMS, *Directors' Minutes*, October 17, 1922.
16. *Catalogues and Counters*, pp. 196–215.

6 THE FAT AND LEAN YEARS IN MAIL ORDER, 1922-1932

1. U.S. Bureau of the Census, *Historical Statistics of the United States, Colonial Times to 1957*, D589–602 (Washington, D.C.: U.S. Government Printing Office, 1960), p. 73 (hereafter cited as *H.S. of U.S.*).
2. Frederick Lewis Allen, *Only Yesterday* (New York: Harper & Brothers, 1931), p. 116.
3. *H.S. of U.S.*, p. 417.
4. Ibid., p. 379.
5. Allen, *Only Yesterday*, pp. 115–16.
6. *H.S. of U.S.*, p. 139.
7. Interview with M. J. Spiegel, Jr., April 23, 1957.
8. Spiegel, May, Stern and Company, *Minutes of the Board of Directors*, January 23, 1923; January 21, 1926 (hereafter cited as SMS, *Directors' Minutes*).
9. Corporate Charter, M-S Company and May-O Company, March 4, 1927. Also, memoranda for each company, in the Mayer, Meyer, Austrian, and Platt archives, Chicago.
10. SMS, *Directors' Minutes*, March 17, 1927.
11. Ibid., May 11, 1928.
12. All data on the public underwriting are from the corporate records of Spiegel, May, Stern.

13. Harold Barger, *Distribution's Place in American Economy Since 1869* (Princeton, N.J.: Princeton University Press, 1955) pp. 148–49.

14. Boris Emmet and John E. Jeuck, *Catalogues and Counters: A History of Sears, Roebuck & Company* (Chicago: University of Chicago Press, 1950), pp. 272–74.

15. Ibid., p. 204.

16. Barger, *Distribution's Place in the American Economy Since 1869*, p. 81. Also, Martha Lane Adams, trial balance ledger.

17. Martha Lane Adams, *Directors' Minutes* (Special), May 26, 1927.

18. *Saturday Evening Post*, January 13, 1923, p. 53.

19. Edward L. Swikard, "Spiegel Seminar" (transcript), August 1941, p. 83.

20. SMS, *Directors' Minutes*, June 12, 1928.

21. Ibid., February 7, 1929, September 26, 1929.

7 RETAILING AND INITIAL RESPONSES TO THE DEPRESSION, 1922-1932

1. Spiegel, May, Stern and Company, *Minutes of the Board of Directors,* January 12, 1926 (hereafter cited as SMS, *Directors' Minutes*).

2. Spiegel, May, Stern, various financial records for 1926 and 1927.

3. Interview with M. J. Spiegel, Jr., May 17, 1959.

4. SMS, *Directors' Minutes*, February 6, 1929.

5. Ibid., April 9, 1929.

6. Ibid., July 17, 1929.

7. Ibid., June 2, 1930.

8. Ibid., July 1, 1930.

9. Ibid., April 6, 1931.

10. Ibid., June 22, 1931.

11. Ibid., March 17, 1932.

12. Spiegel, May, Stern, various financial records for 1931–33.

13. SMS, *Directors' Minutes*, July 17, 1929.

14. Interview with H. George Meinig, October 17, 1955.

8 NO CHARGE FOR CREDIT, 1933-1937

1. Letters from Frederick L. Innis to M. J. Spiegel, Jr., January 14, 1933 and Frederick L. Innis to Edward L. Swikard, June 15, 1933.

2. Spiegel, May, Stern and Company, *Minutes of the Board of Directors,* October 5, 1933, December 7, 1933 (hereafter cited as SMS, *Directors' Minutes*).

3. Spiegel, May, Stern, *Stockholders' Minutes*, February 15, 1934; April 7, 1936; April 6, 1937.

4. SMS, *Directors' Minutes*, February 15, 1934.

5. Ibid., April 6, 1937.

6. Boris Emmet and John E. Jeuck, *Catalogues and Counters: A*

History of Sears, Roebuck & Company (Chicago: University of Chicago Press, 1950), p. 653.

7. Dean Langmuir Report, February 20, 1935, based on this financial analyst's conversation with executives of Sears and Ward.

8. Spiegel, May, Stern, *Annual Report*, 1937.

9. Dean Langmuir Report, p. 6.

10. Spiegel, May, Stern, "Budget Notes for Spring Campaign, 1937," January 19, 1937.

11. Memorandum from William H. Garvey, Jr., to Board of Credit Control, November 29, 1939.

12. Dean Langmuir Report, p. 1.

13. Spiegel acquired Goodman in October 1933 and resold it two years later for the original purchase price. *Annual Report*, 1933; 1935.

14. Interview with Thornton Adams, March 6, 1957.

15. Dean Langmuir Report, p. 6.

16. Memorandum from M. J. Spiegel, Jr., to Frederick W. Spiegel, April 26, 1940.

17. *Business Week*, April 5, 1941, pp. 38–41.

18. Dean Langmuir Report, p. 3.

19. *Business Week*, January 29, 1938, p. 22.

20. Interview with H. George Meinig, July 7, 1959.

21. Spiegel, Inc., *Annual Report*, 1937; also, interview with M. J. Spiegel, Jr., April 23, 1957.

9 MODI OPERANDI AND THE QUALITY CONCEPT, 1938-1943

1. Harry J. Carman, Harold C. Syrett, and Bernard W. Wishy, *A History of the American People*, 2nd ed. rev. (New York: Alfred A. Knopf, 1961), 2:707.

2. *The Five Year Plan*, January 16, 1939.

3. Interview with M. J. Spiegel, Jr., January 5, 1955.

4. Memorandum from M. J. Spiegel, Jr., to Frederick W. Spiegel, April 26, 1940.

5. Federal Trade Commission, Complaint no. 4863, November 4, 1942.

6. U.S. Federal Trade Commission, *Federal Trade Commission Decisions* (Washington, D.C.: U.S. Government Printing Office, 1944), 36:736–37; 37:22–33.

7. Commerce Clearing House, *Trade Regulation Reporter*, 9th ed., *Federal Trade Commission Proceedings, New Orders and Complaints* (Chicago: Commerce Clearing House, 1948), 3:11, 470.

8. Unless otherwise noted, all of the following quotations are from *The Five Year Plan* (the Complete Store).

9. The original of this letter is in the files of the Spiegel public relations department and has been personally verified.

10. Interview with Mrs. Hazlehurst, Robert E. Engleman, and M. J. Spiegel, Jr., March 8, 1955.

11. Interview with William H. Garvey, Jr., H. George Meinig, and M. J. Spiegel, Jr., March 8, 1955.

12. Spiegel, Inc., *Annual Report*, 1940.

13. Various examples drawn from "Survey of Spiegel Suppliers," 1940, conducted by Elmo Roper Organization.

14. Spiegel, Inc., *Directors' Minutes*, April 4, 1939.

15. Spiegel, Inc., *Finance Committee Minutes*, May 3, 1939, May 17, 1939.

16. Interview with M. J. Spiegel, Jr., June 17, 1955.

17. "Spiegel Seminar, 1941." The outside members were Louis J. Cowan, radio producer and public relations counsel; E. T. Gundlach, mail-order advertising executive; Homer J. Buckley, Buckley Dement Company, direct mail advertising; Dean Langmuir, investment counselor; Harold Lachman, John Plain Company, mail order; Frank Folsom, executive head of Goldblatts' Department Stores, Chicago; H. G. Wellington, Wellington and Company, investment bankers. Spiegel personnel included M. J. and F. W. Spiegel; Elmo Roper, director; Earl Weil; E. L. Swikard; H. G. Meinig; W. A. Gatzert; T. S. Adams; W. H. Garvey, Jr.; W. E. Rose; H. R. MacKenzie.

18. Ibid., pp. 2–5.

19. Ibid., pp. 161–62.

20. Ibid., p. 25.

21. Ibid., pp. 11–12.

22. *New York Times*, July 22, 1941, quoted in Boris Emmet and John E. Jeuck, *Catalogues and Counters: A History of Sears, Roebuck & Company* (Chicago: University of Chicago Press, 1950), p. 429.

23. *Business Week*, October 25, 1941, pp. 44–45.

24. Ibid., September 27, 1941, pp. 56–57; October 25, 1941, pp. 44–45.

25. "Reorganization Memorandum, M. J. Spiegel to Executives of Spiegel," February 11, 1943, p. 1.

26. Ibid., p. 3.

27. Spiegel, Inc., *Directors' Minutes*, April 6, 1943.

28. Spiegel, Inc., *The Postwar Merchandising Conception*, 1934.

29. Spiegel, Inc., *Minutes of the Defense Bond Committee*, January 30, 1942; February 6, 1943.

30. Spiegel, Inc., *Minutes of the Finance Council*, January 9, 1942.

10 FRUSTRATION DECADE

1. William H. Whyte, Jr., *The Organization Man* (New York: Simon & Schuster, 1956).

2. James S. Deusenberry, *Income, Savings and the Theory of Consumer Behavior* (Cambridge: Harvard University Press, 1949), pp. 21–22.

3. George Katona, *The Powerful Consumer* (New York: McGraw-Hill Book Co., 1960), p. 27.

4. C. Wright Mills, *White Collar* (New York: Oxford University Press, 1956).

5. Memorandum of Agreement, Arnold and Seymour Askin and Spiegel, Inc., December 30, 1944. Also, Spiegel *Directors' Minutes,* December 27, 1944.

6. Booz, Allen & Hamilton, "Report of the General Survey of Spiegel Inc.," New York, August 1946, p. 14.

7. Ibid.; also *Spiegel Annual Report,* 1945.

8. Booz, Allen & Hamilton, p. 14. Also, "Spiegel: History and Performance," December 11, 1950 (from M. J. Spiegel's private file); Spiegel *Directors' Minutes,* April 3, 1945; Memorandum of Agreement, Dorris Heyman and Spiegel, Inc., July 17, 1945; Memorandum of Agreement, W. W. Morrison and Spiegel, Inc., October 20, 1945.

9. C. D. Ryan, *W. H. Whitney & Company: "The Whitney Store,"* 1947. Brochure.

10. C. D. Ryan to M. J. Spiegel, Jr., March 26, 1947. Also, *Time,* October 6, 1952, p. 89; May 23, 1949, p. 86.

11. Transcript of a seminar held by Spiegel at the Blackstone Hotel, Chicago, June 26, 1945, p. 93.

12. Memorandum of Agreement, Sydnor & Hundley, April 10, 1946.

13. Memorandum of Agreement, Robert Keith and Spiegel, Inc., July 1, 1946. Also, M. J. Spiegel, Jr. to James Kemper, Edward Keith, and Robert Caldwell, Kansas City, June 18, 1946.

14. Spiegel, Inc., *Directors' Minutes,* October 9, 1946.

15. Ibid., April 25, 1946.

16. *Executive Committee Minutes,* Spiegel, Inc., May 23, 1946; *Directors' Minutes,* July 25, 1946; Walter A. Gatzert to Robert Stecker, December 30, 1947.

17. M. J. Spiegel, Jr. to Thornton S. Adams, January 25, 1949.

18. U.S. Bureau of the Census, *Historical Statistics of the United States, Colonial Times to 1957,* D589–602 (Washington, D.C.: U.S. Government Printing Office, 1960), p. 519.

19. W. E. Cowan interview; R. A. Engelman interview (undated).

11 THE END OF AN ERA

1. Carl Rieser, "The Monster Spiegel Keeps, Keeps Spiegel," *Fortune* 63 (June 1961):152.

2. This brief review of Spiegel's operations between 1955 and 1965 is, unlike the earlier material, based exclusively on secondary sources. Much of this research was conducted by Richard M. Reese, a doctoral candidate at the University of Texas.

3. Rieser, "The Monster Spiegel Keeps, Keeps Spiegel," p. 203.

4. Ibid., p. 151.

5. Ibid., p. 210.

6. Beneficial Finance Company, Spiegel, Inc., Proxy Statement, September 20, 1965, p. 35 (hereafter cited as Proxy).

7. "Aggressive Approach to Credit Sales Pays Off in Bigger Net for Spiegel," *Barrons* 41 (January 2, 1961):20.

8. Rieser, "The Monster Spiegel Keeps, Keeps Spiegel," p. 214.

9. Calculated from the increases in net properties after reserves, as stated in Spiegel, Inc., *Annual Reports*, 1958–61.

10. "Mail Order House Spends $3 Million to Save Money [Spiegel Automates]," *Business Week*, January 27, 1962, p. 56.

11. "Mixed Results for Mail Orders with Data on Leading Company," *Financial World* 110 (September 10, 1958):6.

12. "Mail Order House Spends $3 Million to Save Money," p. 57.

13. Spiegel, Inc., *Annual Report*, 1961, 14.

14. Ibid.

15. Spiegel, Inc., *Annual Report*, 1951, 10.

16. Proxy, p. 33.

17. Ibid.

18. The Fairfax Family Friend (personal loans) was incorporated in 1962 and produced a "modest income" in 1963 and 1964. The German company Medallion Mode GmbH was acquired in 1963 and sold four years later for a profit of just over $1 million.

19. Spiegel, Inc., *Annual Report*, 1963.

20. *Financial World* 122 (September 2, 1964):35.

Index

Adams, Thornton, 186, 208–9,
227–28, 251
Add-on. *See* Credit
Advertising: 29, 37, 66–68, 70,
77, 97–102, 140, 150,
156, 162, 175, 189–90, 227,
241, 244, 279, 291; in newspapers, 16–17, 35–36, 43–45,
176; in magazines, 89, 104,
114, 161, 203
A. G. Becker and Company, 28n,
29, 124, 130
Al Kolbert Technical Institute,
282
American Correspondence School,
60
Annual Report, 1951, 288
Anti-Semitism, 223, 238
Apparel: 64–67, 71–72, 76–77,
80, 82–83, 113, 129, 137,
151–53, 168, 203, 206, 209–
10, 214, 256–57, 259–60,
262, 264, 273, 280, 283, 288–
89; first expansion into, 63;
abandonment and reintro-
duction, 149, 155–56; Saindon Models, 216
Askin-Beverly Stores, 261–62, 278
Assets, 19, 52, 56, 122–23, 130–
31, 177, 179, 248, 263, 286
Automobile: effect on mail-order
industry, 81, 110, 133–35,
137, 260
Avery, Sewell L., 195, 214, 217,
235–36, 252, 264
A. W. Shaw Company, 60

Bankers, 18–19, 29, 39, 61, 74,
83–85, 123–26, 128, 131,
145–48, 150, 168, 181–83,
196–98, 217

Barger, Harold, 149
Baum, Albert S., 54, 139, 143,
174–75
Becker, A. G., 18, 21, 28n, 131
Becker, Nathan, 28n
Beckman Piano Company, 73
Beneficial Finance Company,
284, 292, 295
Bergman, Alexander, 19
Bernard Mayer and Company,
65–66, 68, 71, 111
Biefeld, Joseph, 28n–29n
Billing. *See* Customer
Board of Budget Control, 228
Board of Collection Control, 228
Board of Credit Control, 228
Board of Merchandise Review,
228
Bolshevism, 133
Bonaparte, Napoleon, 1
Borax. *See* Merchandise quality
Boston Store, 25
Branch plants, 265, 272–76, 290
Brand names: 69, 234, 253; Air
Castle, 215; Argyle, 215; Big
Chief, 215; Columbia, 215;
Gateway, 215; National
Brands Campaign, 215
Brownstein, Abraham, 261
Budget Power Plan, 284–86
Burd, Jim, 282
Burley Company, 178–79, 180,
191
Burroughs, 118–19
Businessman's Publishing Com-
pany, 60
Business Week, 247
Buying. *See* Merchandising
Buying and Selling Division, 250–
51
Buying Power. *See* Credit

321